MAKE THEM GO AWAY

MAKE THEM GO AWAY

Clint Eastwood, Christopher Reeve & The Case Against Disability Rights

Mary Johnson

The Advocado Press

Make Them Go Away: Clint Eastwood, Christopher Reeve & The Case Against Disability Rights.

Published by The Advocado Press, Inc., P.O. Box 145, Louisville, KY 40201
www.advocadopress.org

FIRST EDITION

Photo of Clint Eastwood Copyright 2000 by Tom Olin.
Photo of Christopher Reeve Copyright 2000 by Michael Reynolds.

Library of Congress Cataloging-in-Publication Data

Johnson, Mary, 1948-
Make them go away : Clint Fastwood, Christopher Reeve and the case against disability rights / by Mary Johnson.-- 1st ed.
p. cm.
ISBN 0-9721189-0-X
1. People with disabilities--Legal status, laws, etc.--United States. 2. People with disabilities--Government policy--United States. I. Title.

KF480 .J64 2003
342.73'087--dc21
2002014675

CONTENTS

ACKNOWLEDGEMENTS

This book could never have been written had I not had the fortune of being an observer and reporter of the disability rights movement that grew and spread across the United States during the 1980s, and whose activists pushed through the unlikely bill that would become the Americans with Disabilities Act in 1990. These advocates taught me about disability rights as I reported about it in the pages of *The Disability Rag*; they made me understand the disability rights vision and they showed me the countless ways in which our society acts on its prejudice against people it has labeled "disabled" or "handicapped," even as it insists that "no one is against the handicapped." Thanks to them for their continuing good humor and persistence in the struggle, and for believing that eventually things will turn for the better for everyone, for continuing to insist that disability rights has the power to transform society.

Among my first and truest teachers was Cass Irvin, without whose ongoing support I would not likely have stuck with reporting on disability rights. Thanks go to her for reminding me why we do what we do when we write about disability rights.

I hope that most of those who shared their stories and insights with me will find that I learned from them and got those insights at least mostly right as I wrote this book. Lucy Gwin, irrepressible editor of *Mouth* magazine, says more true things than almost anybody I know; I hope I learned some of what I put into this book from her. Tom Olin's photos always remind me of the vitality of the disability rights movement, I am more than thankful he was at the Senate hearing to get the photo of Clint Eastwood on the cover of this book. Cyndi Jones and Bill Stothers, the longtime publisher-and-editor team of *Mainstream* magazine, for the past few years have been engaged, along with me, in trying to get disability issues onto the radar screen of our nation's media; they have helped me see more clearly the Sisyphean task this is.

Julie Shaw Cole and Barrett Shaw of The Advocado Press stuck with me through rough drafts of the book and made all kinds of suggestions, more of which I should have taken. Cal Montgomery pushed me to refine my thinking on the hard subjects associated with disability rights, of which there is no dearth. I should have taken more of her suggestions, too.

Finally I want to thank my husband, Robin Garr, without whose encouragement this book would still be on little scraps of paper piled all over the house. His editorial perceptiveness and suggestions made this a more focused, readable book.

Louisville, Kentucky
September, 2002

*A law cannot guarantee
what a culture will not give.*

Introduction

"And now I sign legislation which takes a sledgehammer to another wall, one which has, for too many generations, separated Americans with disabilities from the freedom they could glimpse, but not grasp."

Arthur Campbell sat sweltering in his suit and tie as he listened to President George Herbert Walker Bush's words floating out over the crowd on the White House lawn. Many were disability rights advocates in wheelchairs, like he was, or on crutches, with guide dogs. Others were using American Sign Language.

Most places had been off-limits to Campbell all his life. Steps barred his entrance to stores, to restaurants, to public buildings. He couldn't use city buses — there were no wheelchair lifts on them. He'd had no formal education; growing up, kids like he was, with cerebral palsy, rarely went to school. Companies would never hire a man whose speech they couldn't understand. Campbell had created his own job: He worked as a disability rights organizer.

Over the past few years, a loose coalition of advocates like Campbell had accomplished a goal many would have thought impossible. They had pushed through Congress a civil rights law barring discrimination against people with disabilities in jobs, in public services and public accommodations. It had passed almost unanimously, and with President Bush's support.

"We rejoice as this barrier falls," Bush was saying. "We will not accept, we will not excuse, we will not tolerate discrimination in America!"

The President picked up one of the many ceremonial pens he would use in the next few minutes, as cameras clicked in the summer sun. "Let the shameful wall of exclusion finally come tumbling down!" he called out, and it was done: The Americans with Disabilities Act was law. It was July 26, 1990.

Less than two years later, on the campaign trail, Bush told listeners that, were he re-elected, his administration would see to it that all the "able-bodied worked."

What had become of Bush's sledgehammer? The Americans with Disabilities Act said disabled people had a right to work, should be allowed to work, that not letting a disabled person work amounted to illegal discrimination. But neither George Bush nor his campaign ad directors had thought twice about that remark. Seeing to it that the "able-bodied worked" was simply what one said. It was what everybody believed — that only the "able-bodied" could, after all, work.

The Americans with Disabilities Act was the law of the land. But its major philosophical underpinnings had never really entered the national consciousness. When it passed in 1990, it received little public discussion; a decade later, enough federal courts had actually declared parts of the law unconstitutional that the Supreme Court agreed to look into the matter: Was the ADA unconstitutional? Congress likely had no right passing it in the first place, said its opponents.

In the years following 1990, the case against disability rights continued to build. Why was there so little rebuttal? The disability rights movement was very good at getting laws passed — better, it seemed, than gays or women's groups — but the movement shied away from public discourse. It seemed afraid to open up the issue of disability rights to public debate lest it lose the debate. It did not seem to want to acknowledge that the other side of the debate was going on full bore without it.

Why was there so little support for disability rights?

It was true that the organized disability rights movement avoided the media. Its leaders felt they had good reason. Most stories about disability were inspirational features about disabled people who had overcome personal affliction with a smile and a bundle of courage, and disability rights advocates said this was not the story they wanted to convey. They seemed to believe, perhaps with justification, that they could not convince reporters or editors of any other approach.

While they were silent, others were not — particularly those who disliked the idea of granting rights to yet another group. The case against disability rights had the same "you can't make me!" free-market histrionics one always got from social conservatives when it came to civil rights issues; the difference was that in this case, almost no liberal groups spoke out in support of disability rights.

Why was that? Most liberals and progressives believed that the problems racial minorities, women and gays faced were the result of *animus*, the work of a discriminatory society. When it came to disabled people, though, liberals' views were similar to those of the anti's. They believed disabled people faced essentially private, medical problems rather than problems of discrimination. What a disabled person needed, they felt, was medical intervention — a cure. Lacking that, they should be given help, through private charity or government benefits programs.

Almost everyone instinctively felt that rights was simply the wrong lens through which to view the disability situation. "The first object of a wise but concerned policy cannot be to make people with serious disabilities move as if they did not have them," wrote *The New York Times*.

Christopher Reeve, who had become disabled five years after the ADA had become law and was now the most famous disabled person since Roosevelt, was not that concerned about access or rights himself. "I'm not that interested in lower sidewalks," he told a reporter. Reeve's goal was simply to walk again; he took his quest for cure before millions on ABC's *20/20* and *Larry King Live*. He spoke to millions more from the pages of *Time* magazine. His view of what disabled people needed — a way to consider their disabilities "as a temporary setback rather than a way of life" — resonated with most people. Most of us believed that no one held any *animus* against disabled people or intentionally kept them out of buildings. If you were disabled you had something wrong with you — the word itself meant "incapable," everybody knew — but you weren't part of an oppressed minority like African-Americans. You were just disabled.

The nation provided for its disabled primarily through special — segregated — approaches: special housing, special transportation, special education. Disability rights was simply unnecessary, went this argument. And many well-meaning people believed it.

The ADA is based on a sociopolitical concept of disability that people don't understand, as one law professor put it. Although it was conceived as a civil rights law, people did not understand it as one. Judges said the ADA was poorly crafted. Almost all legislation for the disabled was benefits legislation. Judges felt the ADA wasn't well-constructed as a benefits law. That was true, because it wasn't one. But few seemed to understand that — or wanted to understand the law for what it was designed to be. Legal forays against the law during the 1990s focused mainly on finding ways to use it to determine whether someone deserved to avail themselves of its protections. Were they "disabled" as the ADA defined it?

Intended to protect anyone against discrimination based on disability, just as the Civil Rights Act of 1964 protected anyone against discrimination based on race, religion or gender, the ADA was interpreted increasingly as a benefits law by the courts throughout the decade.

Drafted during a decade in which public good had come to be measured in economic, not moral, terms, the law as passed by Congress contained something the nation's lawmakers had not permitted in its other civil rights law — an economic loophole: Rights didn't have to be allowed if they cost too much. This ensured that most of the public discourse against disability rights would focus on cost. Much of what was said about the cost of providing accommodation and access was inflammatory and ill-reasoned. Much of it was simply wrong.

Twelve years later, most people still do not understand the nature of disability discrimination. And there is still very little public discussion about it.

Not long after Ella Williams took a job at the Toyota plant in Georgetown, Kentucky, moving her family all the way across the state because she was so happy to have landed a job alongside other assembly line workers whose average annual pay was $62,000, she "got lumps the size of a hen's egg in my wrists, and my hands and fingers got curled up like animal claws." Repetitive-stress injuries — RSI — accounted for more than a third of the 1.7 million workplace injuries reported in 1999, according to the Bureau of Labor Statistics, and Williams was one of those statistics. "I used pneumatic tools that really vibrated, and I was always having to reach above my head," she explained.

She pressed Toyota for accommodation. She got some; but later she was put back on another assembly-line job that hurt her wrists again. After a number of legal skirmishes, Toyota eventually dismissed her. "When you get RSI, they show you the door," she said.

Ella Williams's fight against Toyota went all the way to the Supreme Court. Williams was not "disabled" under the ADA, the Court said in 2002. The ADA was supposed to focus on the "wheelchair bound," not "carpal tunnel syndrome or bad backs!" Justice Sandra Day O'Connor had snapped from the bench the previous fall.

In a series of decisions the spring this book was being finalized, the Supreme Court, interpreting the ADA as a kind of law it never was, succeeded in imposing the benefits reading on it firmly enough so that much of its broad-ranging vision is now hamstrung. A crabbed medical proof of "true" disability will now be required of any employee who seeks redress against a company that has discriminated against them on the basis of disability. Whether or not any disability discrimination has actually occurred seems even less of interest to the Court than it ever was.

The ADA presents a set of new ideas for people, and most people — including judges — do not know yet what to do with those ideas. The real purpose of protection from disability discrimination is actually to provide equal opportunities for all of us — not to identify a particular group of individuals who are entitled to some kind of special treatment.

People called "disabled" by society are just people — not different in any critical way from other people, except in that they often encounter a form of discrimination that the rest of us seem mostly unaware of. To understand the reason disability rights advocates call the disabled "a discrete and insular minority," we must first recognize the all-pervasive, albeit sugar-coated, nature of this disability discrimination. To understand the promise of disability rights, we first have to "come to grips with the underlying realities of human abilities and disabilities," as the law's original architect puts it.

Disability is simply a natural part of human lives, he said. Sooner or later, it will touch most of us. "The goal is not to fixate on, over-react to or engage in stereotypes about such differences," he says, "but to take them into account and allow for reasonable accommodation for individual abilities and impairments that will permit equal participation."

Is dismissing a worker who can't lift her hands above her head, rather than modifying the equipment so that she can reach it, reasonable? Is it a form of discrimination based on disability? Is running a non-ergonomic factory a kind of disability discrimination? Is it reasonable that a company tell a worker he can't take a break but every three hours, when the worker needs to lie down for a few minutes every hour or so and can show that the brief rest period does not decrease his work output? These are the kinds of disability rights questions we should be discussing publicly. Instead, we find a McDonald's menu on the wall overhead, unable to be read by anyone with low vision — and no alternative. A too-harried counter worker who refuses to read it to the low-vision customer. A subway system serving 14 million people with entrances down steep flights of steps. A library with its entrance up a flight of steps, effectively excluding a portion of its would-be patrons.

"Why would San Francisco set up its visitors' center in a plaza that has absolutely no access to people with disabilities?" Disability Rights Advocates' Larry Paradis asked.

Is it not discriminatory that a public lecture have no way for someone who doesn't hear well to also enjoy it, that a multi-million member e-mail service be upgraded in such a way that blind people can no longer use it?

Hotels, groceries, home-and-garden discount centers all come with automatic doors. Yet a business will balk when asked to provide an automatic door for people who cannot open doors manually.

Public discussion has still not gotten around to the new ideas that underpin the disability rights vision. Reasonable accommodation, demedicalization, universal design, customization and integration are simple enough concepts to understand, but hard to implement when the society you live in continues to see people with disabilities as having something wrong with them, needing cure or charitable help, or as sly malcontents trying to get some special rights they don't deserve, creating nothing but problems and extra costs for the rest of us.

PART 1
The Case Against Disability Rights

ONE

Clint Eastwood and Christopher Reeve

In the spring of 2000, actor Clint Eastwood took on the 10-year-old Americans with Disabilities Act. His Mission Ranch hotel in Carmel, California, had been sued for access violations under the law, and he'd been slapped with a lawsuit he'd never seen coming, he said.

"Dirty Harry wants revenge, Washington style," said *The Wall Street Journal.*

This time, it is a gang of trial lawyers staring down Clint Eastwood, asking themselves about taking him on: "Do I feel lucky?" These "sleazebag lawyers," the veteran actor says, his voice constricting, messed with the wrong guy when they "frivolously" sued him and hundreds of other small-business owners for failing to comply quickly enough with the Americans with Disabilities Act. Mr. Eastwood...is striking back with a Washington lobbying campaign for new legislation to modify the law. "I figure I won't back down because of all these people...who can't defend themselves."

Florida Republican Congressman Mark Foley's proposed ADA Notification Act would ease the pain for businessmen like Eastwood charged with access violations. The Act would require that a disabled person who wished to file suit under the ADA give 90 days' notice first.

With Eastwood noisily involved and the media looking on, Foley's proposal moved onto the fast track. Rep. Charles Canady, chair of the House Judiciary Committee's Subcommittee on the Constitution, extracted it from the legislative mire where so many bills languish and scheduled it for a hearing in just a few weeks.

Foley sent out an announcement over *PR Newswire*:

Since the Americans with Disabilities Act was enacted in 1990, public accommodations are more accessible to everyone. That progress, however, is threatened by a growing number of trial lawyers who generate huge legal fees for pointing out often simple fixes that would bring properties into compliance with the ADA's accessibility standards. This variety of litigation abuse stems from the lack of any notification provision in the ADA. Currently there is no notification provision in the Americans with Disabilities Act. Consequently, businesses who may fail to comply with ADA accessibility standards are givecompliance prior to the initiation of costly litigation.

"What happens is these lawyers, they come along and they end up driving off in a big Mercedes," Eastwood told reporters, "and the disabled person ends up driving off in a wheelchair."

In the days leading up to the hearing, Eastwood appeared on the talk shows *Hardball* and *Crossfire*; he was covered in a *Fox News Special*. The *National Journal* quoted him. Columnists covered his comments. *Newsweek* used the "Mercedes" quote on its "Perspectives" page.

The seasoned Hollywood actor had his script and he stuck to it: He wasn't against disabled people. He wanted to help disabled people, who were being preyed on by moneygrubbing lawyers. The law was the problem; had been all along. The law needed to be fixed.

"Did you really keep disabled people out of your hotel?" *Crossfire's* Robert Novak asked Eastwood.

"No chance," Eastwood replied. "The first thing I did was put in handicapped bathrooms, even before the ADA."

The day before, on CNBC's *Hardball*, host Chris Matthews had said, "Well, everybody I think watching this show of *Hardball* right now can understand this situation. A lot of places have been changed radically in the last 20 years. You can actually take a wheelchair up a ramp. You get into a bathroom, you see one of the stalls has good arm rests. You can get through doors with a wheelchair. Those are all good things, right?"

Things were getting better for the handicapped. And yet still, it seemed, it wasn't enough; still they whined for more things to be done and more changes to be made.

"Are the organized groups coming after you, the organized disabled groups?" Matthews asked. Yes, Foley answered. "They think we're trying to harm the law." That wasn't true, though, he said.

"We want people that are disabled to know this is not about hurting or harming them," Foley added. "That's important," he stressed to Matthews. He didn't want anybody thinking that he or Eastwood were "against disabled people." They wouldn't be changing the law, just amending it, he stressed — for fairness to business.

Eastwood was a celebrity sniper in a shouting war against the ADA that had been going on for a long time. In the spring of 2000 the media had Eastwood; a few months earlier they'd had ABC's John Stossel, as relentless a critic of disability rights as you'd be likely to find. Stossel could himself be considered disabled. He stutters. But he did not see himself as disabled. He did not see himself as anyone who would use a law and claim "victim status," as he put it, just because of a physical condition he had.

On his March 3 "Give Me A Break!" feature on ABC's *20/20*, he'd paraded the story of "well-paid lawyers suing small businesses who violate parts of the Americans with Disabilities Act." It was no coincidence that Stossel's theme would become Eastwood's. It was a tune that had been being sung for years by the critics of disability rights: that lawsuits under the ADA — an "endless string of lawsuits," Stossel claimed — had overwhelmed society.

"When President Bush signed this well-intentioned bill, he acknowledged that some people were worried about" lawsuits, said Stossel, reporting that a southern California man had filed 200 lawsuits and that the man's attorney "admits to filing 700" for disabled plaintiffs. Opportunistic attorneys had even sued a disabled Florida couple, business owners, for failing to install "handicapped parking" signs. It was a "shakedown," Stossel told viewers, in which many businesses simply settle, paying thousands of dollars, rather than bearing the expenses of litigation. "As with most things Congress does, we get stuck picking up the tab."

"Best of intentions, absolutely," he agreed. "But it's by no means clear it's accomplishing what they thought." It was making lawyers richer, but "a lower percentage of the disabled are getting jobs since the law was passed. It's a lot of bureaucracy and no clear gain."

Stossel had been harping on the ADA for years. In 1994, in an *ABC Special Report*, he fingered the ADA as the problem behind people refusing to take responsibility for their own lives. "The Blame Game," which first aired in October, 1994, was such a vitriolic attack on the law that it would be specifically cited by the U. S. Commission on Civil Rights several years later as having almost single-handedly turned American public opinion against the law. Indeed, the principles articulated in Stossel's piece would find their way into the U.S. Supreme Court's reasoning five years later, as they ruled on a series of cases drastically restricting who could use the law for protection against discrimination.

Several years before all this, even before the law's access requirement had gone into effect, the conservative Cato Institute was calling for amendments to rein in a law it called "objectionable on moral as well as economic grounds." In early 1995, it produced "Handicapping Freedom: The Americans with Disabilities Act," as clear an exposition of the case against disability rights as there had ever been. No pro-access organization spoke up to contradict it.

When *Crossfire's* Bill Press asked the actor why it had taken him so long to fully comply with the 10-year-old law, Eastwood replied that "Even when President Bush signed it into law, he anticipated that there would be problems and mentioned that he thought there may be abuses."

If the "Bush had warned there'd be problems" line sounded a lot like something Stossel had said on *20/20,* one could be forgiven for wondering if the case against disability rights were not just a bit more orchestrated than it might at first appear.

"If a black person is not allowed to enter a business because of his race, he's not required to send a letter. If a woman is not allowed to, she's not required to send a letter. Why should disabled persons be the only class of persons required to send letters?" That was a point the attorney pressing the case against Eastwood had made; now Press asked Eastwood the question.

"Well, in the first place, you're not going to reconform a whole building based upon the entrance of a black person or a woman coming in," the actor responded. "I can't think of a parallel situation."

He would not "back down," he'd told *Wall Street Journal* reporter Jim Vandehei, "because of all these people...who can't defend themselves."

The National Association of Protection and Advocacy Systems, a group of federally funded disability rights public law offices, released a statement from its director, Curt Decker: "Mr. Eastwood would not be facing any lawyer's fees or fines had he complied with the ADA, a law that was passed nearly 10 years ago in 1990." Only the *National Journal* noticed it, quoting Decker saying that "Despite a decade of legal requirements nationally, [businesses] are basically being given a free ride for not complying with the law" — and Eastwood saying, "I totally support the ADA laws."

The National Federation of Independent Business, the U.S. Chamber of Commerce, the National Restaurant Association and the International Council of Shopping Centers had joined Eastwood's campaign, said *The Wall Street Journal.*

"Mr. Foley understands the sensitivity of modifying the ADA, regardless of how meritorious he thinks his bill may be," wrote Vandehei. Because of this, he wrote, the two "want to recruit a well-known politician who helped write the original law or a high-profile disabled person to work with them. Mr. Foley has approached Democratic Sen. Max Cleland, of Georgia, a triple amputee, who is reviewing the bill. Bob Dole, the former GOP Senate majority leader who helped write the ADA, and disabled actor Christopher Reeve will be approached soon, he says."

On June 5, 1995, Christopher Reeve lay in a recovery room in the ultra-modern University of Virginia Medical Center. The 42-year-old actor and amateur equestrian had arrived at the hospital by helicopter on May 27, just hours after he had been thrown from his mount at a Culpeper, Va., horse show. He had fractured the first two vertebrae in his neck.

Reeve was known as something of an activist for progressive

causes. He had helped found the Creative Coalition, whose members included Susan Sarandon and Glenn Close and whose concerns ran from homelessness to the environment. He had helped Vice President Al Gore clean up a New Jersey beach two years earlier. In 1987, he had traveled to Chile on behalf of writers jailed for their political beliefs. Just a few months before his accident, he had come to Washington to testify before a Senate committee, arguing against a Republican proposal to eliminate funding for the National Endowment for the Arts.

Reeve had never attained the Hollywood status of Clint Eastwood. Yet he had been Superman. To see Reeve's "larger-than-life form diminished, to see a man of prodigious strength reduced to a helpless person" rattled our own sense of safety, as novelist Merrill Joan Gerber wrote to the *San Francisco Chronicle*. If the Man of Steel could be felled in seconds by an earthbound accident, then where did that leave the rest of us mere mortals? *Indianapolis Star* movie critic Bonnie Britton wondered. We were all "pretty damn vulnerable."

In the days since Reeve's arrival, the area around the University of Virginia Medical Center had taken on the trappings of a full-blown media circus. More than 145 news organizations from around the globe had contacted the hospital's news office about Reeve. Reporters from as far away as South Africa and Australia had arrived. CNN had broadcast a bilingual Reeve special from Charlottesville to all of South America. There were so many reporters and cameras that the hospital had to have guards keep them out of the lobby.

Reporters and cameramen loitered on the sidewalk outside the UVA Medical Center that hot day in June as Reeve lay on the operating table. Hospital receptionist Wendy Ingalls was standing on the sidewalk as well, silently staring at the building, when caught by a reporter. "I'm hoping somehow, some way, he recovers," Ingalls told him, her voice almost breaking. "I'm really sad about this. It's a terrible thing to be paralyzed."

Washington Post medical reporter Don Colburn described spinal cord injury for his readers. Reeve's fall had injured the top two cervical vertebrae, making him unable to breathe on his own. There was no more devastating injury, wrote Colburn. "Not only are you fully damaged but you remain aware of it, an otherwise normal person trapped inside a useless body."

Nearly a quarter of a million people in the U.S. had spinal cord injuries. Pulitzer Prize-winning syndicated columnist Charles Krauthammer had been paralyzed at age 22 in a diving accident. Singer Teddy Pendergrass had been a quadriplegic since a 1984 car accident. Jockey and Triple Crown winner Ron Turcotte had become a paraplegic in a fall at Belmont Park in 1978. Former star football players Dennis Byrd of the New York Jets, Mike Utley of the Detroit Lions and Darryl Stingley of the New England Patriots had all sustained spinal cord injuries. Because of his spinal cord injury, journalist John Hockenberry used a wheelchair.

Since Reeve's arrival at the hospital, employees and volunteers had worked overtime to cope with press inquiries and frantic fans. It was rumored that some of the British tabloid guys had stolen some hospital scrubs and were sneaking around inside.

New York Daily News celeb gossiper A.J. Benza had gotten hold of a nurse on Reeve's floor, who told him doctors were privately saying that Reeve wouldn't walk again. "He has been told that he may well never move again." Sharron Churcher of *Penthouse* magazine's "USA Confidential" was having a hard time with her emotions. "Can you imagine this? Just being trapped — a mind in a body?" It had to take incredible bravery, she thought. She knew it was a cliché, she said, the Superman Falls image. "But I don't know how the rest of us would cope."

Nearly half a million letters would find their way to Reeve and his family. "The men on San Quentin's death row are pulling for you," wrote Chris, Doug and Mickey. "We are praying for your full recovery." "We know your return to health will not be easy, but we believe that you are the man who can succeed where others might fail," Clyde Willis, editor of the real Metropolis, Illinois *Planet*, wrote to Reeve. "You *can* do it," Reeve's third-grade teacher wrote "You learned way back in third grade."

As Reeve lay on the operating table, on the other coast the *San*

Diego Union-Tribune was running an editorial against the ADA. Because the law so broadly defined a disability, said the paper, quoting the definition of disability as "a physical or mental impairment that substantially limits a major life activity," it had "multiplied the numbers of Americans who may be considered disabled." Twenty percent of complaints filed had come from people with back problems; 12 percent, said the paper, were from people experiencing emotional troubles. "We suspect that most San Diegans would not consider such people disabled," said the paper.

It was a lot like John Stossel's theme in "The Blame Game" special eight months earlier, but that wasn't surprising. In the months since the show had aired, media outlets from national television to radio talk shows to trade publications to local daily newspapers and opinion magazines had run stories or opinion pieces making similar points. Stossel and others were getting their information from conservative groups like the free-market libertarian Cato Institute and *Reason* magazine.

The ADA's mandates were "costly to public, private sectors," ran the *Union-Tribune's* headline.

The day neurosurgeon John Jane was talking to a reporter about Christopher Reeve's cure, *The Wall Street Journal* was talking about the Americans with Disabilities Act's "parade of absurdities." On June 22, the editorial page of *The Wall Street Journal* carried an opinion piece by right-wing pundit James Bovard. "The Disabilities Act's Parade of Absurdities" was a shorter version of his "The Lame Game" in the then-current issue of *The American Spectator*.

The Act was producing "absurd results," wrote Bovard: a 410-pound Bronx subway cleaner suing the city for refusing to be given a promotion to a train operator (Bovard said the man claimed he couldn't climb under trains to make adjustments as the job description required); a motorist suing when he'd been ticketed for not wearing a seatbelt, even though he claimed his disability, claustrophobia, gave him a legal excuse; a man with a history of blacking out suing for being denied a job as a bus driver.

Citing an Equal Employment Opportunity Commission ruling

"expanding the definition of disability to include an inability to perform functions such as 'thinking, concentrating, and interacting with other people,'" Bovard told readers that the ADA "parade of absurdities practically promised to get worse....With its 'accommodate almost everything' mandate," the ADA could "pose threats to nondisabled workers," wrote Bovard, citing suits by people with "manic depression or narcolepsy," people whose presence, said Bovard, was actually a danger to their coworkers.

A deaf woman had sued Burger King for its drive-through window service that offered no way for her to place an order. Quoting a judge who called an ADA suit "a blatant attempt to extort money," Bovard argued the lawsuit was the fault of the law itself; if the law hadn't existed, there'd be no lawsuit. The "blatant attempt to extort money" theme was one that Clint Eastwood would use a lot, too.

In those cases in which Bovard chose to mention an outcome, only the suit by the deaf woman had resulted in change: Burger King settled "by agreeing to install visual electronic ordering devices at ten restaurants." Another case was thrown out, yet another lost. On the rest he was wisely silent.

There were two conversations about disability going on in America the summer Reeve became disabled. Most people would never have thought to think of disability rights in connection with Christopher Reeve, and, indeed, only one man seemed to have thought to join the two. Art Blaser, like Christopher Reeve, was a quadriplegic. An associate professor of political science at Orange County's Chapman University, Blaser wrote that Reeve would be able to take advantage of disability laws. *The Orange County Register* carried Blaser's article a month or so after Reeve's injury. It was the only article, out of the hundreds written about the law and the thousands written about Reeve's injury, to make any connection whatsoever between Reeve and disability rights.

"Thanks to the [Americans with Disabilities] Act" and other laws, Blaser wrote, Reeve would find accessible buildings. "But Reeve will also have to face our country's attitudes, which are not

T W O

Passing the Americans with Disabilities Act

In 1990, the Americans with Disabilities Act passed both houses of Congress by huge majorities. Although news coverage in the days surrounding its passage called it a "civil rights law," it had certainly not been preceded by the kind of national uproar and soul searching that had led to the passage of the Civil Rights Act in 1964. Indeed, most Americans were unaware of it, before and after its passage.

The law came with a "but": rights would be extended, yes — but not if providing the access (the "accommodation," the law called it) would inconvenience others too much. A civil rights act with an economic loophole built in, the ADA said if rights cost too much, they didn't have to be granted.

The terms in the law were "undue hardship" and "reasonable accommodation": If it was too hard for a business, it didn't have to be done; if the accommodation wasn't "reasonable," it didn't have to be provided. The product of an era in which the public language of discourse was economics, not the moral imperatives of the civil rights era, the bill offered nondiscrimination protections to "persons with disabilities" — and included a three-part definition to explain just who those were.

The economic loophole was considered reasonable because people believed disability rights were different than other civil rights. The way the argument went was this: with women and minorities, removing the discrimination was a relatively painless act of simply no longer telling people they couldn't come in your store, couldn't hold that job, and so on. With disabled people, something else had to be done, generally something physical: A ramp had to be installed. A sign language interpreter had to be hired for a meeting. A meeting agenda had to be printed in a large-print format. Seats had to be removed. Physical things — costly things, said businesses.

The ADA had no federal enforcement mechanism. To get it enforced required a lawsuit. The Department of Justice could file a suit; or suits could be filed by aggrieved disabled people. When the bill was in Congress in 1989, disability advisors had told President George Bush, privately, that most individual disabled people would be quite unlikely to sue.

"Let the shameful wall of exclusion come tumbling down," said President Bush, his words floating out over the throng of disability advocates gathered on the White House lawn for the bill's July 26 signing. "For the first time, Americans with disabilities will enjoy full civil rights protection."

"The bill seemed to come out of nowhere," *The New York Times*'s Steve Holmes remarked not too long after it had become law. Even this reporter assigned to Congress hadn't seen it coming, although it had been the central agenda item of the organized disability rights movement for a number of years. They had been trying unsuccessfully to get the 1964 Civil Rights Act extended to cover disability discrimination.

Many people, reporters, editors and pundits included, didn't see disabled people, who they knew were barred from much of society by barriers in buildings, as having as moral a claim to redress as had blacks, who people knew had been barred from society due to what lawyers called "*animus*," or pure ill will. Yet in a move exactly counter to that employed by organizers who'd planned Mississippi Freedom Summer in a bid to draw national attention to the situation of Southern blacks, in a move counter to that undertaken by the Campaign for Military Service to draw national attention to the Pentagon policy of dismissing gays in the armed forces, in a move counter to the efforts put forth by the women's movement to draw national attention to pay inequities, to sexual harassment, to rape as a crime of violence, the organized disabled who labored in Washington to craft what would be come the only major piece of civil rights legislation to pass in nearly a quarter century eschewed trying to educate the public about the moral wrongness of disability discrimination.

It was a conscious strategy: there would be no effort made to explain the sweeping anti-discrimination legislation to the press. "We would have been forced to spend half our time trying to teach reporters what's wrong with their stereotypes of people with disabilities," one explained.

"The best way to describe news coverage of the Americans with Disabilities Act was that there was very little of it," said journalist Joe Shapiro, who was writing a book about the disability rights movement. There was some. *The New York Times* ran what Shapiro described as "an alarmist lead story" on its Aug. 14, 1989 front page. Headlined "Bill Barring Bias Against Disabled Holds Wide Impact," the story by Congressional reporter Susan Rasky left the unmistakable impression that the wide impact would be mostly in the form of "a wave of lawsuits"; the piece almost exclusively reflected business fears about the burdens of the bill. A follow-up editorial on Sept. 6, 1989 asked whether Congress wasn't writing "a blank check for the disabled."

The bill that eventually passed was a much-compromised piece of legislation.

In 1988, a draft bill referred to only half-jokingly as the "scorched earth" version had been introduced — a bill which called for virtually all public and commercial buildings to be retrofitted for access for disabled people within several years. It prohibited discrimination, which, said the bill's drafters, included "outright intentional exclusion," "the discriminatory effects of architectural, transportation, and communication barriers," "overprotective rules and policies," "failure to make modifications to existing facilities and practices," "exclusionary qualification standards and criteria," "segregation" and "relegation to lesser services, programs, activities, benefits, jobs, or other opportunities." Introduced as HR 4498 by Rep. Tony Coehlo and S 2345 by Sen. Lowell Weicker, the bill applied to anyone who could show they were being treated in a discriminatory manner "because of a physical or mental impairment, perceived impairment or record of impairment." Anyone who faced such discrimination gained the law's protection. The definition of "impairment" was a broad one, too.

A nondiscrimination provision added to a rehabilitation bill in 1973 had first raised the idea of protecting people from discrimination based on disability. But that provision — Title V of the Rehabilitation Act — covered only programs and contractors getting federal money. The new law would cover society at large. Its lobbyists would argue it was merely an extension of protections already afforded under the 1973 law; that law, they argued, had caused no one any trouble. What they did not say was that it had rarely been enforced.

The 1988 version made little headway in Congress. But savvy disability lobbyists saw that with President George Bush's election, they could get a disability rights act through Congress during even a decidedly anti-rights era if they revised the bill in certain ways. Bush, no friend to liberal causes, nonetheless had ties that disability rights insiders knew could be used to their advantage.

Worried that a law prohibiting discrimination based on disability would still be seen as a novel idea, that judges might think that nondiscrimination "meant treating the individual simply as if he or she did not have a disability, and we'd end up having blind people suing to be allowed to be bus drivers," they added an explanatory caveat: Onto the term "individual with a disability" they attached the word "qualified."

The revised bill mandated accommodation and access only when it would not inconvenience business too much. Unlike the Civil Rights Act of 1964, which prohibited employers from using cost (or any other rationale) to justify disparate treatment of employees on the basis of race, it was a civil rights act with a dispensation: if rights caused business "undue hardship," they didn't have to be granted.

The original bill had covered all commercial entities. Sen. Lowell Weicker, who had introduced it, had said that "simple justice argues strongly for requiring the removal of barriers that exclude or limit participation." Modeled on provisions in the Fair Housing Act, the original 1988 bill provided for both compensatory and punitive damages, payments which would compensate the disabled person for having met with discrimination and punish the offending business which had refused access.

But Bush's attorney general, Richard Thornburgh, did not think those remedies should be used for this law. And Sen. Bob Dole, the major Republican sponsor, insisted the "damages" section be dropped. Wanting a bill that would have bipartisan support, Democratic Sen. Tom Harkin, chief sponsor of the re-introduced 1989 bill, eventually capitulated.

In the bill that passed, "places of public accommodation" had replaced "commercial entities" — a smaller group altogether. "Private parties" — meaning the individuals who had sued — could obtain only "injunctive relief" — a legal term meaning the business has only to make the access modification or provide the accommodation the disabled person sued for. The damages section was gone. (It had been "excluded in order to head off predatory lawsuits," the Cato Institute would explain five years later.)

Under the Americans with Disabilities Act that passed, a disabled person who sued could get no monetary award of any kind.

"Given the highly publicized struggle to pass the Civil Rights Act of 1964 — and the fact that the ADA was the most extensive civil rights bill since then — the relatively little scrutiny the ADA received" was startling, Shapiro noted. Maybe it wouldn't matter that lobbyists had sold the need for rights protections for disabled people directly to Congress without going through their public.

Yet the tone of coverage found in *The New York Times* became the belief about the ADA for much of the nation and almost all of the press. "No one wishes to stint on helping the disabled," *The Times* editorialized when the bill that would become the ADA passed the Senate in the fall of 1989, by a vote of 76 to 8. "It takes little legislative skill, however, to write blank checks for worthy causes with other people's money."

The Orange County Register, as conservative as *The Times* was liberal, took much the same tack: The ADA, if passed, would be a "bad law" — it would actually debase those it purportedly helped. Under the headline, "Hampering the disabled," the paper wrote,

"Some companies doubtless will be bullied into treating them better. But many other companies, though now favorably disposed toward them, may look on hiring the disabled as an invitation to lawsuits." The ADA actually hurt the disabled, it said, by making it less likely that businesses would hire them, fearing lawsuits.

Frank R. wrote to his representative in Congress, Bob Stump, a Republican, asking that he support the bill. Stump wrote back that he wasn't sure he could. The bill might "create more problems than it is designed to address," he said. The definition of disability was so broad that it might be interpreted to cover even people with AIDS; and it would "require small businesses to modify structures and programs for dozens of disabilities, even if a person has not asked for assistance.

"As written, the bill makes no distinction between intentional and unintentional discrimination," Stump went on, parroting a key message of the forces fighting the bill. "It is not so much an advancement of the civil liberties of the disabled community as it is a retreat from a logical approach to the protection of the disabled."

Frank R. thought Stump failed to recognize the importance of a law like this for his son, who was disabled. Our progress as a nation should be able to be measured, he thought, by how enthusiastically it embraced, or at least accommodated, people who had traditionally been excluded. He wasn't surprised at Stump's attitude; what he was surprised at was that Stump would so openly express ideas which in Frank R.'s opinion were extremely bigoted.

Views like Stump's were expressed whenever discussion of the ADA appeared in the press — which wasn't often. Frank R.'s views, on the other hand, received no coverage as the bill made its way through Congress. There'd been no national public discussion about "disability rights" as understood by Frank R. and other advocates; no national public discussion as to even what the concept meant.

But then, there'd been no national public discussion about wheelchair activists' push for lifts on public buses, either, which had been fought in the streets of dozens of our nation's largest cities during the 1980s, with mass arrests and jailings. No national public discussion — certainly no debate — over why the nation's transit systems had balked at installing wheelchair lifts, or about what it meant to not be even allowed to get onto a bus in light of the fact that another civil rights movement had erupted simply because one had to sit on the back of a bus. There was no national thumbsucking from the chattering classes about the special "paratransit" that public transit companies wanted to offer instead — what it was, what it meant, how worked (whether or not it *did* work); whether it was segregation. There'd never been any real national discussion over the issue of segregating disabled people into special programs, special classrooms, special institutions, either.

There had been stories on all these topics, of course. Small stories, sometimes even large ones; sometimes even on the front pages of local newspapers; sometimes, if the activist group ADAPT were in town creating a ruckus with buses and getting arrested, even front-page stories for several days. There were stories about special education, and about people being kept in institutions.

But no disability rights issue had ever truly become a national, public issue. None had ever garnered the attention of national commentators. None had been seen as part of our national debate. None had been viewed by the national media as trends. And the bill that was to become the ADA was proving no exception.

Thornburgh had told the bill's backers that requiring all commercial entities to become accessible was too difficult for businesses. How would businesses know what kinds of changes they needed to make to avoid being sued? Small businesses must not be harmed, he insisted. So, although the scope of businesses covered by the law remained broad (the final law specifically outlines 12 types of "public accommodations" that must be accessible, including laundromats, shopping centers, restaurants, movie theaters and golf courses), the term "readily achievable," which had been in the law as a way to ease the burden on business, became more specific: the size and financial resources of the business were added as factors explicitly to be considered when determining whether an accommodation was "readily achievable," to make clear that the burden on small businesses would be minimal.

Newly constructed or altered buildings of less than three stories would not be required to have elevators unless they were shopping malls, or, given that disabled people were thought to need doctors a lot, offices of health care providers. To this day, over-the-road buses like Greyhound are not required to have bathrooms on board that a wheelchair can enter.

Even today, if one finds a building inaccessible, in violation of the Act, little can be done, for not just anyone can take the lawbreaker to court. One must be a "qualified person with a disability." The lack of access itself, though illegal, brings no fines, no punishment. There is no federal enforcement mechanism for the Americans with Disabilities Act other than lawsuits.

Given that business didn't have to do anything "unreasonable" to accommodate people, a bill passed easily in the spring of 1990. Reporting on the backroom Congressional maneuvering that had brought about the compromised bill was scant. The *Boston Globe's* Michael Kranish noted that the newly-passed law allowed "most existing buildings to remain inaccessible" and permitted "a company to avoid compliance if complying poses 'undue hardship'"; business groups, he wrote, "still opposed the measure as too costly."

"Today we reach a major milestone in our nation's history," said liberal bastion Sen. Ted Kennedy, a major sponsor, getting up to speechify on the bill's passage. "We begin a new era of opportunity for the 43 million disabled Americans who have been denied full and fair participation in our society." Harkin, whose brother was deaf, said the newly passed law sent "the world a clear and unequivocal message that people with disabilities are entitled to be judged on the basis of their abilities — and not on the basis of ignorance, fear and prejudice." "This is a great day in the history of our country because, for the first time, Americans with disabilities will enjoy full civil rights protection," said Pres. George Bush.

When, in a series of campaign ads 20 months later, Bush told listeners that, were he re-elected, his administration would see to it that all the "able-bodied worked," it simply showed that the law had done little to change his understanding.

While the disability movement was congratulating itself on its legislative success, the campaign against disability rights began in earnest. Groups ranging from the National Retail Federation and the American Banking Association to the Baptist Joint Committee, the American Bus Association and the YMCA had already weighed in opposing the idea that barriers would have to be removed from buildings. Even those who pushed other progressive agendas seemed to think access was too much of a change to ask. The Leadership Conference on Civil Rights, a major player in the ADA lobbying effort in Congress, had not made its offices wheelchair accessible. Neither had Manhattan's Project Vote.

When Dot Nary of Nichols, N.Y. attended a Congressional hearing on Rural Health Care issues in Olean, N.Y. well over a year after the ADA had become law, she found the meeting location had no restroom she could get into. Nary wasn't surprised, but she was irritated.

"I doubt very much that a hearing would have been held in a setting that lacked restroom facilities for the non-disabled," she wrote to New York Congressman Amo Houghton. "In fact, it would be absurd to consider it." Why, then, she asked, was it considered appropriate to have a hearing somewhere that had no restrooms people with mobility problems could use? Nary knew Houghton had voted for the ADA. But she also remembered attending meetings where his response to questions from disabled constituents had been "to pat them on the head."

The nursing home industry raised a stink over proposed rules that 50 percent of a nursing home's rooms be wheelchair accessible. That was "overly restrictive," they complained. It "would add significant square footage and cost" to new nursing homes, said the Alabama Nursing Home Association. Health Facilities Management Corporation's Ann C. Mitchell insisted in a bizarrely erroneous statement that "the handicapped population of long-term care facilities is not greater than that of the general public, and thus only five percent of the rooms need to be accessible." Gail R. Clarkson of MediLodge, in Romeo, Mich., insisted nursing home residents were content with their inaccessible rooms: "In my 17 years in long-term care, I have never received a complaint regarding difficulty in this area." The American Association of Homes for the Aging didn't see any sense in nursing home entrances being accessible either, for much the same reason.

"We are not able to admit residents who have wheelchair needs because our bathrooms were constructed for ambulatory seniors," Marla Turner, facility administrator the Taylor Living Center for Seniors in Taylor, Mich. wrote to those developing the regulations for the new law. "Our building structure would be destroyed if the bathrooms would need to be expanded"; it would be "cost prohibitive and unnecessary." "Homes for the aged," she wrote, should be exempt from having to comply with the access requirements of the new Americans with Disabilities Act.

Stirred up by groups like the National Federation of Independent Business, business owners began to worry. "Potentially anyone can sue, for any alleged reason," Roy Hunt, president of Hunt Tractor, Inc., told the Louisville *Courier-Journal*. Attorney Jeff Fort warned Toledo government officials that the new law "armed fully 17 percent of the American population with the federal cause for action against any company that discriminates. This means that someone in a wheelchair may sue if they can't reach a book on top of a library shelf." Everyone who had looked at the law, said Fort, knew it would "mean a lot of litigation"; it would be "a real battleground."

Such comments in the months following passage of the ADA served to create a climate of hostility, which encouraged businesses to dig in their heels and refuse accommodations, forcing disabled people to use the only recourse the new law gave them — filing lawsuits. Business owners' recalcitrance on access created a self-fulfilling prophecy, in which the only way access got achieved was to file a suit. Then the organized disabled were blamed — for doing nothing but filing lawsuits.

A few days after the ADA had been signed, journalist John Hockenberry was having a conversation with the man who owned the local bike shop where he bought tires for his wheelchair.

"'I see there where your President signed that law for you guys!'" Hockenberry is imitating the Bike Shop Man.

"'You mean the Americans with Disabilities Act?' I say.

"'Yeah!' he says. 'Things are going to be great for you guys!'

"So I say, 'Well, it probably means you're going to have to ramp that front step of yours.' I'm even being friendly about it, kidding around. Because I actually thought he was interested in discussing it.

"I was absolutely wrong. Because, without a pause, the man says, 'Oh, no! No no no! See, it's for new stuff. Not me. Just for new stuff.'"

The Bike Shop Man, with his erroneous understanding of the new law, was, Hockenberry said, "equipped with an entire mentality that opted him out of thinking he had to do anything whatsoever — except under extreme coercion — to change. Yet he got all the benefits of thinking that, 'hey, it's great! Everything's gonna be perfect for you people.'"

THREE

The complaint against disability rights

Anger against disability rights focused on the Americans with Disabilities Act, but in truth it extended to all disability rights laws. And there was a staggering array of them. The disability rights movement — the organized disabled, as *Hardball's* Chris Matthews called them — seemed astonishingly good at getting laws passed. Pundits used the ADA as their whipping boy, but disability nondiscrimination was also written into the Fair Housing Act, the Air Carrier Access Act, the Telecommunications Act and many others. Virtually all states had access laws; and although some had special disability nondiscrimination laws that mimicked the ADA, in a number of states disability rights advocates had gotten "disability" added to state laws that protected against discrimination on the basis of race, sex, age, national origin (which was what national disability activists had wanted to do with the Civil Rights Act). California had one of the strongest antidiscrimination laws in the nation; it covered disability as well as age, ancestry, color, national origin, race, religion and sex. California had one of the best state building codes, too, when it came to disability access requirements.

The laws were routinely ignored. Although it seemed disingenuous to disability activists, in fact it was quite conceivable that Clint Eastwood and his renovation crew had simply forgotten, or never known about, requirements for wheelchair access at Mission Ranch. Even though he had been mayor. Even if he knew about the access requirement, he could publicly say that he didn't — and people would believe him in a way that no one would have believed him had he said he didn't know there was a Civil Rights Act, or a Clean Air Act. People would likely sympathize with him, because it would seem reasonable that he wouldn't know about such a law. People didn't know very much about disability rights.

Other laws have their detractors. Battles against affirmative action and women's rights are well known. But that's just it: they are battles; there are sides. While there have been articles in both scholarly journals and national tabloids deconstructing affirmative action's "horrors," there have been competing articles, of as much if not more vigor, in competing media, articles written by well-respected supporters of rights in a liberal society. There has been, in a word, debate.

The years following the passage of disability laws, the decades of the 1980s and 1990s, were inimical to all sorts of rights. But people at least heard the debate — both sides. In the news, they heard civil rights organizations — the N.A.A.C.P., the Urban League — and their spokespersons. They heard from Jesse Jackson. They saw Ms. magazine's Gloria Steinem quoted, the National Organization of Women's Eleanor Smeal and Patricia Ireland interviewed on national television.

There was a disability rights movement. But it was hard to find it, even when one searched national news stories for clues to its existence. Unlike Jackson or Steinem, there was no "name" anyone knew associated with disability rights; no NOW; no N.A.A.C.P.

Disability rights seemed to have but one sensible side: the "against" side. The only thing that might clue a persistent searcher to the fact that there was another side, sensible or not, was the vitriol of the attacks: who was it they were attacking, if not another side? But that other side was, for the most part, invisible.

"Things are going to be great for you guys!" said Hockenberry's Bike Shop Man.

"A lot of places have been changed radically in the last 20 years," NBC *Hardball's* Chris Matthews had said, talking to Clint Eastwood. You could actually take a wheelchair up a ramp; places usually had a ramp; you saw them. Bathrooms had a stall with "good arm rests" to let you "adjust yourself into the seat." You could be self-reliant. You could get through doors with a wheelchair.

"Those are all good things, right?"

"Sure. You bet."

"And you have all those things in your hotel."

"We have — we have those. But see this is — these are professional litigants, so it doesn't matter whether you have it or not."

Because it's never enough. He didn't use those words, but that was the subtext.

"Things are getting better, but still they whine!"

"Things are getting better — haven't we done enough for them?"

"Nobody disabled comes in here anyway."

In the case against disability rights, this is the complaint one hears over and over. It has several aspects that we should look at, because they explain the basis for the case against disability rights:

1. "No one is against the handicapped. What they want, though, goes against common sense."

2. "We'll give them their special toilet, bus, courtroom, classroom, housing complex — just don't ask that we change the regular world for them.

3. "They are hurting us — make them go away!" ("We wouldn't have to do it if it weren't for them.")

Disability rights run counter to common sense

New York's J. M. Kaplan Fund had offered to pay for a few high-tech streetside toilets, which, if they worked and weren't vandalized, would then sprout on street corners all over Manhattan, courtesy of JCDecaux of Paris.

"We'd like to have them all accessible," said Doug Lasdon of New York City's Legal Action Center for the Homeless. "But Decaux isn't offering that."

The JCDecaux proposal had come about in response to a lawsuit by the Center charging that the city had no public toilets that anyone, homeless or otherwise, could use. The ones the city did have, mostly in subway stations, were kept locked, which was unfair, the lawsuit said. Decaux's proposal had been met with other charges — these from New York City's disability community, who said the high-tech toilet kiosks would have to be accessible to wheelchair users. New York City had a law requiring wheelchair access to new structures. The ADA had been the law of the land for several years as well.

That was too bad, said *The New York Times.* "Unfortunately, federal law requires newly constructed public facilities to be accessible to the handicapped," the newspaper wrote in an editorial. "That means street toilets large enough to accommodate wheelchairs."

Decaux was not offering accessible units, so "the issue most likely to doom the plan is access for the handicapped," wrote *The New York Times*'s Celia Dugger.

"Washington officials might be willing to bend the rules if local officials and disabled groups can get together," *The Times* continued. "One possibility is to provide a fixed percentage of wheelchair accessible toilets that would be kept locked; the disabled would enter with special cards." That was what Decaux had said he would offer, as a compromise. Yet, wrote *The Times,* "representatives of the disabled...oppose that idea as discriminatory." Their response, *The Times* lectured, was unrealistic. "Groups representing the disabled need to see the folly of clinging to unrealistic hopes that obstruct public needs."

The complaints that make up the case against disability rights can be illustrated pretty well by the brouhaha over New York's streetside toilets. It wasn't that anyone was against handicapped — "We'd like to have them all accessible," Lasdon avowed — but what they wanted was simply unrealistic. The complaint that what disability rights advocates want runs counter to common sense, that it is unrealistic, is heard repeatedly in the case against disability rights.

"The issue most likely to doom the plan is access for the handicapped," said *The New York Times.* This could as easily have been framed the opposite way: that the nondisabled world was preventing people in wheelchairs from access to public toilets. But that was an interpretation only the organized disabled would make. One of the recurring themes in the complaint against disability rights was that they, the disabled, were hurting us, the regular people: During the civil rights era, newspapers like *The New York Times* took the side of the oppressed and called society to change. But when it came to disability rights, *The New York Times* saw disability rights advocates' insistence upon access as simply unreasonable.

When charges of denial of access arose, the solution offered to the disabled is either "help" — charity — or segregation, which is always called "special." In this case, it was the latter: "a fixed percentage of wheelchair accessible toilets that would be kept locked; the disabled would enter with special cards."

Manhattan attorney Philip K. Howard's 15 minutes of fame arrived in 1994 with the publication of his slim volume, *The Death of Common Sense: How Law is Suffocating America*, which quickly climbed the bestseller lists. Howard's Exhibit A of those things that ran counter to common sense were disability rights laws, more specifically, access laws — most specifically, the ADA and New York City's own access laws. He used the streetside toilet controversy to illustrate his point: "Rights cede control to those least likely to use them wisely, usually partisans like disabled activists who have devoted their lives to remedying their own injustices." His snippy phrasing was simply the complaint sung to the tune of "things are getting better but still they whine."

The disabled have no real right to whine, say those arguing the case against disability rights — no real right, because we have given them enough already. Howard accurately quoted New York disability official Anne Emerman as calling the separate toilet proposal "discrimination in its purest form," but he did so with a sneer: "When someone had the nerve, at a public forum, to ask how many wheelchair users there might be compared with other citizens who might benefit, including blind and deaf citizens, the questioner was hooted down for asking a politically incorrect question," he wrote. "At stake, at least for the disabled, were their 'rights.' When you have a right to something, it doesn't matter what anyone thinks or whether you are, in fact, reasonable."

What is behind the statement that disability rights go counter to common sense? What is behind it is the conviction that a "disabled" person's claim to "rights" is simply not a valid one; it is bogus. Disabled people are not like racial minorities, are not in fact a minority at all, say those who make this complaint. Their problems, unlike those of racial and ethnic minorities, do not stem from *animus*, ill-will. Their problems stem simply from the fact that their bodies don't work correctly. Medical research was seeking cures constantly; that's how society was helping the disabled. Beyond that, they were given special help and assistance. But it was wrong for the organized disabled to blame society for their problems.

A *New York Times* editorial the previous decade, questioning the reasonableness of disabled people having a right to ride on the public's buses and subways, had put it like this: "Going to incredible expense to remodel trains and buses would be justifiable only if the handicapped, as some insist, have a fundamental legal, even constitutional right, to use public facilities without difficulty."

"The first object of a wise but concerned policy cannot be to make people with serious disabilities move as if they did not have them," wrote *The Times*. The problems disabled people experience are the result of their bodies' inabilities to do "normal" things, *The Times* was saying; and that was not something public policy had any way to remedy. This belief forms the cornerstone of the case against disability rights.

That a person's disability is a personal, medical problem, requiring but an individualized medical solution; that people who have disabilities face no "group" problem caused by society or that social policy should be used to ameliorate: This is what disability rights activists call "the medical model" of disability. Despite the proliferation of disability rights laws, our nation has never really accepted any other way of thinking about its disability problem.

A significant segment of the public now believes that the problems besetting racial minorities, women and gays stem from irrational discrimination — discrimination caused by society, by those of us in society who are not part of the oppressed group; that it is the society itself that is causing the problems besetting these minorities.

But people's disability problems continue to be seen by almost everyone as being caused by their own bodies' failures. And what they need, it seems clear, is a way to fix these failures — to get cured. If they are incurable, they need help — from us, who don't have disabilities ourselves.

A paralyzed person seems dependent on someone else to feed him, bathe him, help him use the toilet — in short, to keep him alive. To a walking, hearing, sighted person, it seems logical to assume that a blind person would have to depend on sighted people to guide her through the world; a deaf person depend on someone who can hear to tell him what others are saying; a person who cannot walk depend on someone who can help her up steps and over curbs. This fact seems clear and incontrovertible, and most people simply do not stop to consider that this dependency might be the outcome of a social — or cultural — decision on the part of anyone. It seems that it's just how things are. It seems common sense.

Thus, although it would be regarded as patronizing to racial minorities, women or gays, it seems reasonable to most of us to openly feel sorry for disabled people. Only truly disabled people are allowed by public policy to not work — that was the point of President Bush's contention that he'd "see to it that all the able-bodied worked." Though in reality this often translates into being kept from working, even when one wanted to, the sentiment seems laudable to most people.

Such sentiments, though, are only extended to the *truly* disabled. Only a tiny portion of those who called themselves "disabled" are considered to be truly disabled — they are the ones who are "all messed up"; who "can't help it." They're the only ones who are even grudgingly considered to have a possible claim on public largesse.

Only "the deaf, the blind and the wheelchair bound" make up the truly disabled in the minds of those against disability rights. All others laying claim to the "disabled" label are, in the final analysis, fakers.

The truly disabled are the only remaining "deserving poor" of the welfare state. No public outcry against helping them is sustained for long: this is the source of the "nobody wants to stint on helping the handicapped." Yet even this has begun to feel onerous to a society fed for the last three decades on the me-firstism of the free-market conservatives who push the case against disability rights, and has started to breed resentment.

The discussion of who is "truly disabled" — thus deserving of some special consideration — in truth has made up most of the public pronouncements against disability rights in the 1990s. We will look at this discussion, and what it means, in the next chapter. The determination of who is "disabled" has had a profound impact on the outcome of the case against disability rights. And, as we will see, it is based on the medical model, and is totally at odds with disability rights.

When Clint Eastwood insisted that he should have been given a letter notifying him of changes that needed to be made at his resort, rather than being simply sued for having violated a 10-year-old law, attorney Paul Rein, who had taken the case for wheelchair user Diane zumBrunnen, had argued that neither black people nor women barred from facilities would be required to send a letter to the organization in advance of suing them. Why, he'd asked, "should disabled persons be the only class of persons required to send letters?"

Eastwood's response to *Crossfire*'s Bill Press, who had brought up Rein's comment, shows why people think disability rights are beyond the bounds of common sense: "You're not going to reconform a whole building based upon the entrance of a black person or a woman coming in," Eastwood had said.

Disability rights seemed to be asking that society actually change physically "just for them," as those opposed to disability rights put it. No other oppressed group had asked for such physical changes.

To make matters even more ludicrous, the disabled weren't even a real minority (a "suspect class," in legal terms) but simply individuals, whose bodies didn't work properly. And despite the propaganda of the organized disabled, they were really a tiny group — the deaf, the blind and the wheelchair bound constituted fewer than a million people, said those who pressed the case against disability rights.

When the organized disabled first tried to acquire protection from discrimination by getting the 1964 Civil Rights Act extended to protect people from discrimination on the basis of disability, traditional civil rights groups said it would dilute the effectiveness of the law. Privately, many found it absurd to suggest people with disabilities were mistreated as blacks had been. People with disabilities did have problems, but they stemmed from the fact that they were "naturally deficient....naturally limited rather than as being artificially limited by arbitrary and prejudiced social practice."

According to a number of legal scholars, there was irrational discrimination, like that against racial minorities, and there was rational discrimination, which meant that the person was treated differently, but there was a sound, rational reason for the disparate treatment.

Anti-discrimination laws "started as a way to defend the people who had been made victims by segregation, discrimination and oppression," said Roger Conner of the American Alliance for Rights and Responsibilities on John Stossel's "The Blame Game." "Then other groups began to see the benefits of elevating your interest to the status of civil right. And the temptation now is for people who have problems that they can cope with with great effort being convinced to give in and wallow in their fate as a victim."

The understanding that some people did face real discrimination and were therefore deserving of protection from it — racial minorities, for example — and others had simply glommed onto the discrimination model but did not in fact face real discrimination — irrational discrimination, that is — was a main tenet of anti-rights agendas of the 1990s, and it was applied to gays as well as people with disabilities. In the case against disability rights, the way this was most often expressed was that disability rights was beyond the bounds of common sense; that disability rights laws, though well-intentioned, had had unintended consequences, the subtext being that those who had created the laws didn't really know what they were doing; that they applied an erroneous understanding to the disability situation. And the result was that disability rights would cost society an exorbitant amount of money if something weren't done to rein in the laws.

We'll give them their special toilet, bus, courtroom, classroom, housing complex — just don't ask that we change the regular world for them.

In a test run, the Decaux toilet kiosks for the general public, open to anyone at the drop of a coin, averaged over three thousand flushes a month, but "the larger units reserved for the disabled were basically unused," said Howard. He did not mention that, to use one, it was necessary first to go find a key from a nearby store (if one could find the store owner who had the key), and that they were not conveniently located, but in odd locations off the beaten track.

"Just the other day I was over at St. Paul's Chapel, over at Columbia," said wheelchair user Frieda Zames at the height of the streetside toilet controversy. "I had to go, but the only accessible toilet was locked. And the person who had the key had gone.

"I had to go look around for an accessible one. The one I found was a few blocks away" (not a Decaux kiosk, but a restroom in a building). "But then, I know the city. And I can stand up and walk a little, too. If I hadn't been able to do that, I don't know what I would have done."

While JCDecaux's regular units opened at the drop of a coin, the Kaplan Fund's Suzanne Davis had insisted that the larger, segregated units be kept locked so they'd be safe for the disabled.

Philip Howard, like *The New York Times*, railed against New

York City's disability advocates for not politely acquiescing to the special solution of segregated public toilets. He was angry that they pushed to assert legal rights they'd been granted. They should have, instead, been grateful to accept what nondisabled society deigned to give them — something special. When Howard's book made the bestseller lists, *Time* magazine's Richard Lacayo took Howard to task for inaccurate reporting. But with his argument against disability rights no one raised any public quarrel at all.

The time-honored way of providing for the disabled has been to give them something special, that is to say, segregated. "Special" has been our country's sanctioned way of dealing with disabled people, and a large part of the complaints of those against disability rights is that disability rights advocates are no longer content with special, no longer willing to accept it, even when it is best for them. This refusal to accept what has been deemed the appropriate way to deal with disabled peoples' problems with access is bitterly criticized — it is as if disability advocates no longer know their place.

It is important to understand the role of special programs in propping up the case against disability rights. It wasn't that society had ignored disabled people or given them nothing, said those who opposed disability rights; no, far from it; society had given disabled people special help, through special things, like the special toilets Decaux offered.

It is because there are so many special programs for the handicapped, and so much money poured into them (at truly exorbitant costs) that the case against disability rights becomes particularly heated when the organized disabled press for integration and rebel at special. People opposed to disability rights are often the strongest supporters of "special." Whether this is because they see it as a way to keep the disabled separated from regular society, or whether it's because they honestly believe people with disabilities have such different needs that they cannot possibly be met in an integrated setting does not so much matter; what matters is they are infuriated by calls for integration. Decaux was happy to give disabled people special toilets; it was only when they demanded access to the same toilets nondisabled people used that they were called "unreasonable."

They are hurting us

Those who advance the case against disability rights base another of their complaints on the fact that, despite what the organized disabled insist, the truly disabled are a minuscule group. "ADA proponents claimed that 43 million of the 260 million American citizens, 16.5 percent of the population, were disabled. In fact, those numbers are highly inflated," wrote Robert P. O'Quinn in a paper for The Cato Institute a year after the ADA had become law. It was really only "the blind, the deaf, and wheelchair users" that the public saw as "groups of disabled individuals who deserve some form of special assistance," he said. "About 400,000 Americans are blind, 1.7 million are deaf, and 720,000 use wheelchairs — for a total of 2.82 million." The fewer of them there were, the less one could rationally argue that the majority should change to accommodate them.

Because they were such a small number, and because their problem was mainly that their own bodies did not work properly, their wanting society — regular society — to change its normal way of doing things, to retrofit society itself, to be accessible to them, was therefore highly unreasonable. No other group had ever asked such a thing. This was the source of Howard's contention that disabled activists had "devoted their lives to remedying their own injustices." He meant that they wanted everything to work as easily for them as it did for us — to, as The New York Times put it, "use public facilities without difficulty." Even kindhearted public policy couldn't be expected to help with that; it couldn't make people with serious disabilities move as though they didn't have those disabilities, was how The Times put it.

The segregated toilet kiosk solution proposed by Decaux and championed by The New York Times voiced the "there aren't but a few disabled people" complaint, but it was really an Us vs. Them issue: access, because it was for "the disabled" and not regular New

Yorkers, simply wasn't that important.

"What we question is why it has to be 100 percent," Real Estate
Board president Steven Spinola said in the early 1990s, complaining about the New York City law that required that when renovations were made in apartments, they be done in such a way as to
ensure that they could be used by people in wheelchairs. "We said,
if the disabled community is 10 percent," (which was probably
high, he added in an aside, "because not all of them are in wheelchairs"), "then what's wrong with having 10 percent or even 20
percent?" He answered his own question: "They believe that, if
they want, they should be able to pick and choose from any apartment." "When the law was passed," said New York City architect
Bob Marino, "it said every single square inch should be adaptable
[for later access] — it wasn't good enough if one bathroom was
accessible."

Why, he asked, did all bathrooms have to be accessible?

The "there are just a few disabled people, so not everything
should be accessible" complaint is kin to "they want too much."

Nearly a decade earlier, pundit Andy Rooney had whined at his
employer, CBS News, about much the same thing:

There is a men's room and a women's room on each floor. The
men's room has three sinks, one designed for a handicapped person. It has two urinals and two toilets, one of which is specially
designed to accommodate a person in a wheelchair. A usually well-
informed source tells me there is one handicapped toilet in each
ladies room, too. (I still call them ladies rooms even if the company doesn't.)

There are nine floors and two bathrooms on each floor. That
means there are 18 toilets for handicapped people.

What's wrong with 18 toilets for handicapped employees?
What's wrong is that there are no handicapped employees working
in the building. It would be better for the handicapped if they had
nine handicapped employees and a toilet for them on every other
floor.

Nobody but the organized disabled seemed to believe in complete and full physical access to everything for disabled people at all
times. They'd had to fight to get Madison Square Garden renova-

tors to make the bathrooms in the luxury sky boxes accessible, and didn't win but part of the battle; larger bathrooms in these high rollers' gamewatching rooms would cramp partying space. What they didn't say: nobody in a wheelchair's gonna be up here anyway. Getouttahere!

The cost issue

Nobody seems ashamed to say full access is going too far — like they might if the issue were race or gender — because with access, money has to be expended. Access costs too much. The complaint about cost is not about cost as much as it is about the fact that the cost is being expended for *them*, a tiny group of complainers. If they'd just go away, we wouldn't need to do anything.

"You can accomplish 90 percent of access for reasonable cost," said Marino. "But for 100 percent access, he said, "the cost is unreasonable. The disability community wants everything completely accessible," he said, but builders "simply can't give it to them because it costs too much money."

Mother Teresa's Missionary Order of Charity wanted a waiver from the New York City access law. Two Bronx buildings were to be gutted for a homeless shelter, but access to homeless people in wheelchairs did not figure in the group's renovation plans.

The story of Mother Teresa and the elevator led Howard's book. The elevator "would add upward of $100,000 to the cost," he wrote. The Order did not believe in elevators, wrote *New York Times* metro columnist Sam Roberts. The city law requiring the elevator in buildings open to the public — like homeless shelters — "offended common sense," Howard wrote. "There are probably 1 million buildings in New York without elevators," Howard wrote in the opening pages of his book. "Homeless people would love to live in almost any one of them. Walking up a flight of stairs is not, after all, the greatest problem in their lives."

In stating his reasoning like this, Howard was suggesting that access is a bogus issue cooked up by disability rights advocates; that nobody really needs the modification — at least nobody worth worrying about. Howard's sentence, "Walking up a flight of stairs is not, after all, the greatest problem in their lives" — says that sensible people don't worry about access, that nobody worth worrying about needs access; that access is not for us but for "them," the other, the tiny few, who, after all, don't have to go out and about in society because they can be helped by others. What homeless people with wheelchairs were supposed to do when all that was available to them were inaccessible shelters was never discussed. Were they supposed to continue to live on the street? Most did; they could find neither housing nor homeless shelters they could get into in their wheelchairs. If they were really bad off, they'd go to the emergency room, and from there to a nursing home, where they were kept — the nursing home operator getting upwards of $100,000 a year in public money for keeping them there.

In stories about bond issues for renovations, for schools, libraries and other public facilities, the specific item that almost always got singled out as a reason for expenses was not the need for new air conditioning and heating, the need for new paint and flooring, the need for new windows, but "the handicapped" — the "disabilities act." "We wouldn't need to do it if it weren't for them," is the subtext; it's the reason why this particular cost is singled out for comment. A 2001 *Chicago Tribune* story about a Joliet, Ill. 10-year, $73.9-million bond issue to improve the district's aging schools listed among the specifics only the ADA. "Addressing deficiencies, such as meeting the standards of the Americans with Disabilities Act, in 20 schools and six other buildings, some of which are leased to community groups, would cost $29.7 million," readers were told.

The Warwick, R. I. public school district provided *The New York Times* with a list of what they said it had cost to make one school accessible to resolve a complaint. "Outfitting a school to make it accessible to disabled people, in compliance with Federal laws, can cost up to $200,000," ran the headline. The actual list totaled a great deal less — a little under $52,000 — and included "fitting 260 interior doors with new levers and handles" ($10,400); "Modifying restrooms to meet the minimum requirements for use by a disabled person" ($10,000); "300 raised-letter signs for the blind" ($7,500); "accessible lab tables, language-lab booths and machine-shop equipment" ($3,000); and "lowering fire alarm boxes" ($2,000). No matter the cost, the article seemed to say, it was too much.

In 1993, the health department in Burlington, Vt. moved into a new building, paid for with $12 million in state money. It had a beautiful long ramp, 36 inches wide as required by the state building code's access provisions. But it wasn't all according to code: the builders hadn't bothered to make the turning spots on the ramp the required 60 inches; they cut it to 50 inches — to save money.

The first wheelchair user to try to get into the building discovered he couldn't. One simply couldn't make the switchback turns on the ramp; there wasn't enough room. The only way they could be negotiated was to have someone along to manually lift up the back of the wheelchair and pivot it around the corner.

Critics of access laws seemed to think that dimensions set out in the codes were simply silly; that they were nitpicky; that it was just the organized disabled wanting more. When *The Burlington Free Press* reported the ramp had to be altered, and that fix would cost "up to $6,000," even though the cost was borne not by the taxpayer but by the architectural firm that had committed the gaffe, the story was heard as a cautionary tale: access was expensive, disabled people never satisfied.

New buildings continued to be erected by architects who paid little attention to the access standards specified in building codes. But when a building owner got caught, as happened in Burlington, and the building had to be redone for access, then the ADA, or the state law — and access in general — was blamed for escalating costs.

The cost of access vs. the cost of compliance

Some architects used stories like that of the Burlington ramp as proof the ADA was simply costly and caused trouble. In new buildings where access had been added on afterward, because somebody didn't obey a law, wheelchair users often found them-

selves having to go in via an out-of-the-way door in the back and
travel a circuitous and much-longer path to avoid the changes in
level that were popular in places like large hotels and restaurants.
Access, "added on" rather than made an integral part of the original design, often simply didn't work as well. The patched-up
building was then touted as "what it meant to comply with the
ADA," even though it "looked like hell."

Four years after the ADA had become law, although the Los
Angeles City Council had found money to restore City Hall's
faded murals, people in wheelchairs could not get in to see them
— the building was inaccessible. Branch city halls in Van Nuys and
West Los Angeles were equally inaccessible. After a $6.1 million
remodeling of offices in the Kenneth J. Hahn Hall of
Administration — ironically named in honor of a man who used a
wheelchair — the building still had no toilets people in wheelchairs
could use.

After a $9 million expenditure for security devices, none of Los
Angeles County's 43 court facilities met access requirements under
the ADA, either. The law's Title II, which pertained to services and
buildings of state and local governments, was ignored as much as
its Title III requiring private businesses to become accessible.

The mayor's office was not accessible. The county's
Handicapped Access Appeals Board could not meet at the Public
Works Building in Alhambra; it was inaccessible to wheelchairs.
Los Angeles' Criminal Courts Building had no accessible toilets.
The Commission on the Future of the Courts, which invited dis-
ability leaders in Los Angeles to attend a hearing to "address access
problems in the legal system," had selected an inaccessible site for
the hearings.

Los Angeles County in 1994 was no different from any city in
the U.S. Across the nation, most city and state buildings were inaccessible to people in wheelchairs. Public phones had no TDD
access for deaf people. Blind people could not get public documents on tape or in large print — certainly not in Braille! No sign
language interpreters appeared at public meetings.

Yet laws had been passed, again and again, requiring access —

full access. New York City and New York state, and California, had some of the strictest access laws in the nation. But often such laws were seen as "feel good" measures. "Disability policy, I've never known any partisan debate on it," Sen. Tom Harkin would say later. Legislators knew their laws would be honored only in the breach, and so it was fine to have them — it showed no one was against the handicapped.

The problem came when people tried to get access laws enforced.

Sen. Harkin had seen his dream of a strong law that would make America's buildings accessible evaporate under the compromises insisted upon by Sen. Dole and the Bush Administration. Thornburgh "predicted there would be sufficient voluntary compliance," but because the ADA allowed no damages to be paid to disabled people who brought suit against places that were inaccessible, Harkin believed that disabled people would bring few lawsuits; that the law would be "underenforced."

Those who pushed the case against disability rights complained incessantly of the ADA's vast spawning of "frivolous lawsuits" (according to them, all lawsuits were frivolous) and trotted out the same few cases — Philadelphia's Melrose Diner was a favorite, as was Denver's Barolo restaurant. Yet eight years into the law, Harkin was being proved right. There had been astonishingly few lawsuits for access. Of all the ADA cases that had been heard by U.S. courts of appeal, only five percent concerned access. There had been only 16 published verdicts in the entire nation concerning access under the ADA; decisions had been handed down by the U.S. courts of appeal in only 25 cases.

Some states' civil rights acts included disability, and in those cases disabled people could usually get damages if they won an access lawsuit. A Santa Clara County, Calif. jury awarded plaintiffs $74,097 in economic damages (and $160,000 in noneconomic ones) when it found that Sunnyvale Town Center, a mall, had failed to provide crosswalks and parking for people with disabilities. But the money was never awarded; the case was settled for $145,000, including costs.

The problem wasn't that the ADA cost businesses too much but that failing to obey it cost them so little. Firms had no financial incentive to obey the ADA's access requirements. It seemed far more sensible — far cheaper, that is — to ignore it.

Not too long after President Bush signed the Americans with Disabilities Act, Philadelphia's Disabled In Action tried to get an International House of Pancakes to ramp the 5-inch step into its restaurant.

Members spoke to management several times during the year following the law's signing, asking them to ramp the single step that barred people in wheelchairs from entering the restaurant. It was a simple modification, one that clearly fell under the "readily achievable" standard of the law. The group asked repeatedly in 1991 for the renovation. But nothing happened.

On the day after the regulations on public accommodations took effect, early in 1992, a small group from DIA picketed in front of the restaurant. The picketing accomplished little. A few weeks later, the group's president wrote a letter to the management once again.

"Your restaurant does not require an extensive overhaul in order to become accessible to people with disabilities," he wrote. The one-step entrance could easily, inexpensively, be converted into an accessible entrance "with a permanent, concrete ramp."

This letter got a response — from an attorney at IHOP corporate headquarters in Glendale, Calif. The attorney was not writing to say they would install a ramp, however. Things were "not always as simple, easy or inexpensive as they may appear," she wrote. Installing a ramp for the one-step entrance was infeasible; it would encroach on a city sidewalk.

"We have considered the use of a portable ramp which could be stored on the premises and put in place as needed, with a doorbell that could be used by the disabled individual to call for the ramp to be put into place," the attorney continued. But IHOP had "concerns that in order to ensure that no one would have to wait for access...we might need to hire an employee specifically to be available to put the ramp in place and remove it." That would clearly be too costly; to do this would mean the access no longer fell under the law's "readily achievable" standard. Thus IHOP wouldn't have to do it at all, since only access that was "readily achievable" and did not create an "undue burden" was required under the ADA.

Discrimination in places of public accommodation was prohibited under the law — but access was to be provided only if it didn't hurt a business too much. It wasn't "discrimination" if the business could "demonstrate that making such modifications would fundamentally alter the nature of such goods, services, facilities, privileges, advantages, or accommodations"; or that it would "result in an undue burden" — or if the change wasn't "readily achievable" — which the law defined as "easily accomplishable and able to be carried out without much difficulty or expense."

The one-step entrance might in fact "actually be a structural slab that constitutes the ceiling of the garage below the restaurant as well as the floor of the restaurant." If this were the case, she wrote, installing a ramp — or a lift — would likely entail having "to construct some additional structural support for the garage. As you can readily envision, this alternative may quickly become a major architectural and engineering project. We have asked our architect to investigate the question," she wrote. The architect, of course, would cost the firm additional money.

IHOP's response was an example of the ways businesses tried to convince disability groups who complained about access that it was far too costly to allow: They would insist the project was not the simple one the disability group imagined; they would drag in architects and engineers that, if nothing else, succeeded in jacking up the cost for the project in fees they were charging to investigate the problem.

"We hope this letter gives you both assurance that IHOP is concerned about addressing the situation and some further insight into the magnitude of a simple-appearing problem," the letter ended. IHOP got the benefit of letting Disabled in Action know they were concerned ("no one is against the handicapped") yet doing nothing.

A letter such as the one DIA got from IHOP's attorney would have scared many groups into backing off. This has been the case for a decade now when small local groups of disabled people have tried to push for access, only to be told, firmly, by the business, that it would simply "cost too much" or be "infeasible." They go meekly away, accepting their defeat.

But DIA had worked two years on the case, believing, hoping that a simple appeal to the business to obey the law would have the result Sen. Harkin had hoped for. They had not planned to bring in an attorney or move to legal action at all. But nothing would happen, they saw, unless they sued. So attorney Steve Gold filed a lawsuit against the International House of Pancakes some months later, charging the restaurant with violating the Americans with Disabilities Act.

Several months after that, IHOP's legal counsel responded in a letter to Gold. As it turned out, the restaurant could, after all, install a ramp. The engineer had assured the firm that no structural problem would ensue from doing it. Since they were cutting a piece out of the step in order to form the ramp, rather than creating an extension, there would be no need to get permission to extend onto the city sidewalk, either.

One no longer finds "Whites Only" signs on the doors of restaurants; people know that kind of discrimination is wrong. A Denny's Restaurant in Maryland which had failed to serve six African-American Secret Service agents while groups of white secret service agents were repeatedly served was the target of two class action lawsuits in the mid-'90s; the suits were filed under federal and state civil rights law. The reported settlement, two years later, was $46 million, "and the discharge of more than a hundred employees for discriminatory behavior."

"Denny's relatively prompt attempt to settle this lawsuit reflects the changing moral climate that has occurred since 1964," said Ohio State University law professor Ruth Colker. "It is no longer good business for a restaurant chain to have the image of excluding African American customers."

Yet the moral climate, when it comes to disability, remains pretty much where it always has been.

The nation has heard the arguments and learned the ideology of rights as applied to blacks, to women, to gays. Perhaps we agreed with those arguments, perhaps not — but we did hear them.

The nation heard, and eventually believed, that slavery was wrong. It heard and learned to believe that Jim Crow segregation was wrong; that treating people different simply because of their race was morally wrong. That was really what the Denny's $46 million was about.

Yet the nation passed disability laws with almost with no public discussion of the moral issues that led people who themselves had disabilities to push for those laws. There are indeed moral issues at the basis of disability rights. But they are almost never articulated.

There has never been any "disability question" as there was a "Negro question" a century ago. There was never any real question in peoples' minds as to the proper way to handle the nation's truly disabled: Their problems were their nonfunctioning bodies; the solution, cure. If a cure were not yet available, then rehabilitation was needed, to make them as normal as possible, rehabilitation and help, in the form of private charity or government subsidies for those who could not pull their own weight. And special programs.

The reason people pay so little attention to the claims of disability rights is that for most of us it doesn't answer any need. The nation feels it doesn't need the disability rights solution; it has a time-honored solution already: "help the handicapped."

"No one is against the handicapped"

People had been violently hateful of "Negroes." People hated the Irish, the Italians. People are violently, angrily, religiously against gays and lesbians and gay rights. But people had never been against the handicapped. Whenever people complained about disability rights, they preceded their complaint with this: "No one is against the handicapped."

"No one is against the handicapped" is why disability rights has had so little hearing in this country. The phrase says that there is no *animus* against disabled people — even though they are segregated and kept from full access to society, even though the special programs society affords them make for a much circumscribed life — far more circumscribed than what any nondisabled citizen would settle for (we will see this in Chapter 13). The purpose of the phrase is to stifle dissent, although it is doubtful those who use the phrase so unthinkingly are fully aware of what they are doing.

Clint Eastwood was not against the handicapped, he explained to reporters; far from it. His effort to change the ADA, as he explained over and over, was only to help.

"No one wishes to stint on helping the disabled," *The New York Times* had editorialized when the ADA passed the Senate, nevertheless going on to add that access "cost too much."

The Orange County Register, which, at the other end of the ideological spectrum, had simply called it a bad law, wasn't against the handicapped either, its editorial writer hastened to add — nor was hardly any "decent" person. "All decent people sympathize with the disabled and try to help them when necessary. The charity of Americans is renowned worldwide. And most Americans go out of their way to treat fairly, in the workplace and elsewhere, those whom Providence has disabled."

That, said the writer, was the precise reason the ADA wasn't needed. While it was true that there was some discrimination; "and the disabled sometimes suffer unnecessarily at the hands of others," the fact was that "not all injustice can be eliminated in this world." This was a parroting of the Right's views about "the handicapped," based firmly on the medical model of disability.

FOUR

Whiners, victims and the truly disabled

> *We all have sympathy for those unfortunate
> individuals who have genuine physical or
> mental disabilities.*
>
> — R. Richardson King

Five years before Clint Eastwood took on the ADA, while
Christopher Reeve was still in rehab, R. Richardson King wrote to
the New Orleans *Times-Picayune*. Prefacing his remarks with the
usual not-against-the handicapped "We all have sympathy for those
unfortunate individuals who have genuine physical or mental disabilities," King repeated for readers some cases James Bovard's
Wall Street Journal article had highlighted: the "410-pound Bronx
subway cleaner who was refused promotion to train operator
because his 60-inch girth precluded him from climbing under a
stalled train to make adjustments" and sued; the woman whose
suit claimed that Burger King's drive-through windows discriminated against deaf people; the telephone operator who sued when
her employer refused to provide reasonable accommodation for
her narcolepsy. The cases showed what happened when the ADA's
"absurd mandates" were not reined in, he said.

Like the alligator in the sewers of New York City, like the worms
in the Big Mac, these tales — of the high school guidance coun-
selor who sued the school that had fired him, claiming his cocaine
addiction a disability, the man who claimed his mental disability
required he carry a gun in the office; the driver with epilepsy
who'd won $5.5 million from Ryder under the ADA when all
Ryder had been trying to do was keep the roadways safe — were
not questioned as to their accuracy. They served a different purpose: examples of people trying to gain protection from a law they
had no right to use, they were a warning to others not to try the
same thing.

On July 26, 1995, the fifth anniversary of the signing of the ADA, *The Wall Street Journal* published a rebuttal to Bovard from U. S. Attorney General Janet Reno and former Attorney General Dick Thornburgh. They wrote that the ADA had "opened doors" for the disabled. But not much changed in the drumbeat of irritation.

Richardson, like the San Diego *Union-Tribune's* editorial page writer a few weeks earlier, was parroting the conservative think tanks' party line: that the law's "absurdities" would get worse unless Congress intervened and amended the ADA. The immediate source of their ire was the rule the Equal Employment Opportunity Commission had issued earlier that year "expanding the definition of mental disability."

Of all the complaints against disability rights, none was heard more frequently than the complaint about who was entitled to use disability rights laws — specifically the ADA. This complaint focused on the definition of disability, and before we can truly understand why there is so little counterpoint to the case against disability rights, we need to first understand what this complaint is about.

Like pornography, disability continues to elude efforts to define it. One doctor will declare "disabled" a woman whom another says is not. A man told by doctors that he is disabled is not viewed by his co-workers as anything but a lazy complainer. Subjective always, "disabled" is in the final analysis either a political act or a moral judgment, based not on anything about the individual in question so much as on the viewer's own perception and attitudes about the way society should function.

When one says that "no one is against the handicapped," what that really means is that no one is against the "truly handicapped" — the people who "can't help it," who are "all messed up." It seems self-evident to most of us that this encompasses relatively few people — people like Arthur Campbell and Christopher Reeve.

The throngs of others who "claim disability" are trying to get something — the ADA's protection — that they don't really deserve.

The harshest judgment is that they are faking. The charitable judgment concedes that these people do sincerely believe they're disabled, but that they are in fact simply lazy or unmotivated, perhaps due to poor upbringing or the general laxness of society; people who think they should be given something — rights, special rights — for nothing, like Toyota worker Ella Williams.

These people were the focus of John Stossel's *ABC News Special Report,* "The Blame Game."

Defining 'disability': a moral judgment

"The Blame Game" was John Stossel's manifesto against people who didn't fit his personal definition of "disabled" but who nonetheless tried to use the Americans with Disabilities Act.

"The Blame Game" divided disabled people into two groups — those who didn't whine about rights (and who, not incidentally, didn't use the ADA, either), and those who did use it: whiners, complainers, people looking around for someone to blame for their own troubles, people who wanted others to solve problem they just didn't want to cope with themselves. In Stossel's word, "victims."

"If we're victims, we're not responsible for what we do," Stossel told viewers. Things "once considered just bad habit or lack of self control are now called diseases," he said. "And since diseases aren't really your fault, you're entitled...."

"Everybody has rights. Nobody has responsibilities."

But Stossel distinguished his victims: the "truly disabled" were "real victims," as opposed to the fakers, who Stossel dubbed "so-called victims." Roger Conner called fakers the "quote, unquote, disabled."

Stossel often turned over the microphone to Roger Conner. The name of Conner's group, the American Alliance for Rights and Responsibilities, pretty much says it all.

Stossel's example of a "responsible" disabled person was a man the transcript identifies as "Marc Simitian, Blind but Gainfully Employed," the description itself quite revealing. One goal of the

ADA was to "help people like Marc," says Stossel. "It's not easy for Marc to get to work," Stossel tells viewers as we watch Simitian's progress via the public transit system. "First he has to take the train. Then he walks two blocks maneuvering down broken sidewalks to find the right bus."

"Mark was just a toddler when he started losing his sight and now he's completely blind. But he doesn't consider himself a victim," Stossel tells us. "Mark's commute from New York City to the suburbs takes more than an hour, but he doesn't mind."

> Now Mark says it's by no means clear that the ADA got him this job. He's had jobs before. Still, the ADA may have helped. Who knows if Northwest Airlines would have spent the extra $4,000 to install this equipment and give Mark special training? The investment paid off, though. In just two months, Mark's become one of the office's top ticket sellers.

The problem was that people filed lawsuits. "Word of these lawsuits spills out into society, enters into the national conversation," said Conner. "And people start thinking that this is the appropriate way to live."

"Every month, as more people hear about the new law, more sue," added Stossel. "In just two years, 33,000 claims have been filed. The biggest category? Back problems. Of course, the courts are already jammed with all kinds of employment discrimination cases involving not just disability but sex, race and age. After all, the ADA is just the newest of five civil rights laws establishing special protections against discrimination for lots of other groups. And suing under all of these laws is now more lucrative than ever."

The ADA was vague, to boot. "Vague laws," says Stossel, "invite so-called victims to be inventive."

"The Americans with Disabilities Act started as real help for real victims," says Conner. "Now you've got latism, upism, downism, people that are afraid of moving trains, people that are afraid of slow trains, all of them claiming victim status and all of them claiming the right for somebody to come in and take care of them or give them an award for — in some way because they're, quote, unquote, disabled." There was debate in the medical community about whether multiple chemical sensitivity even existed, said Stossel.

He continued,

> I've met many workers who seem to feel entitled to victim's benefits even when they cheat. Like this guy, who said he couldn't work because of injuries to his wrist, back, head, shoulder and knee.
>
> And this guy who said he was disabled by a bad ankle.
>
> And this man who said he couldn't work because he was disabled by anxiety....
>
> The employment lawyer says victims of discrimination need more protection. And it turns out, I'm eligible. My being a stutterer qualifies me as disabled under the ADA.

If Stossel had an ideological comrade-in-arms, it was *U.S. News and World Report's* John Leo. Leo didn't like the fact that "drug addicts and alcoholics are protected under disability laws." There was a whole lot more he didn't like:

> Hypersensitivity to tobacco smoke is a "handicap" under the Rehabilitation Act of 1973, infertility has qualified as a disability, and multiple chemical sensitivity, about which everything is known except whether it really exists, is sometimes recognized as a disability by the Social Security Administration. As one doctor said about MCS cases: "Too many people are walking around thinking they have a medical problem when they just have life...."
>
> Objecting to a character flaw is dicey because almost all bad behavior can be construed as the result or expression of a disability. Rude behavior, for instance, might be the result of missed social cues or boorishness, known as dyssemia....[A]lmost any punishment of objectionable behavior can be a violation of disability law.

If in fact the ADA were only for people like Christopher Reeve, then, on the very few conceivable occasions that such a person might actually meet up with discrimination, it would of course be good to have a law like the ADA to protect them, said the critics.

Of course, said those critics, most problems people like Reeve faced were not due to any ill will on the part of others. Most places where people have problems with steps, or a problem reading a menu, the problem isn't due to the owner's meanness. Business owners hold no ill-will toward the truly disabled; they simply haven't been educated.

Someone who had a condition for which bright fluorescent lights brought on nausea and even seizures should simply know better than to go to places where there was fluorescent lighting. If this meant that she had to mostly stay in her own home, or outside, if it meant she could never hold a job in an office, well, that was too bad — but it was to be expected with her medical condition. Businesses could not be expected to accommodate someone like that. People whose bodies do not function normally, *The New York Times* had reminded its readers, simply cannot expect to do everything normal people do.

The problem with the organized disabled, said critics, was that they seemed to forget this. They put the "discrimination" label on things that aren't discrimination at all; that are just the way society is designed. People read using print; people listen to speeches, people live in houses designed with steps. That's just how society is designed. There's no ill-will in any of that. Laws like the ADA simply create false expectations in people; telling them they have a "right" to have what people have whose bodies work normally have. This is nonsense, says the case against disability rights.

With its vague definition of "disability," the ADA was allowing too many people to think they have a right to its entitlements. Thus went the argument against the ADA.

Stossel was airing the most common criticism of the ADA: that it encouraged vast numbers of people to call themselves "disabled" merely as a way to claim entitlement to the ADA's protections — people who, in an odd turn of phrase often heard, "might have something wrong with them but aren't truly disabled." They wanted to get something that they didn't deserve: rights. Special rights.

This criticism signaled both that the ADA's "rights" were something extra that most people didn't "deserve" (only the truly disabled deserved them) — and that these people might "have something wrong with them" but weren't "truly disabled."

The first suggests something about the nature of the rights that the ADA is thought to confer. The second speaks to how we really understand (or don't understand) "disability" as a political concept.

In fact, we might concede that everyone who sought the ADA's protection (to quote Stossel: the man "who said he couldn't work because of injuries to his wrist, back, head, shoulder and knee," the "guy who said he was disabled by a bad ankle," the "man who said he couldn't work because he was disabled by anxiety") did indeed "have something wrong with them." But if it was something that we thought they could snap out of if they'd just shape up, then they weren't "truly disabled." We felt such people didn't deserve to get the benefits we thought the law conferred.

Vague and shifting, depending on circumstances, this was above all a judgment of a moral nature. It explained why the case against disability rights repeatedly singled out people who had what we called "emotional disabilities" and criticized their right to the ADA's protection. Or why people with "bad backs" came in for such a tarring: in critics' minds, these people could work if only they'd grit their teeth and get on with it. They might be suffering a little, but not enough to get the special rights that the ADA doled out to people. A year after "The Blame Game," *Simpsons* creator Matt Groenig would air "King Sized Homer," with Homer Simpson trying a work-from-home scam due to his size (the "Am I Disabled" book he consults lists "hyper-obesity" and "lumber lung"); *King of the Hill* would air an episode in which Hank is forced to hire a man on drugs because of the ADA.

At the other end of the spectrum were the "truly disabled," people like Christopher Reeve and Marc Simitian. What sanctioned them as truly disabled was the severity of their disabilities: totally paralyzed, totally blind. It is not by happenstance that in order to receive Social Security disability benefits one has to be "totally disabled." The phrase "totally" signals that the person cannot possibly pull themselves up by their bootstraps at all anymore — so, in effect, they deserve our help. A synonym for "the truly disabled" is "the deserving disabled." When George Bush said that he wanted to "make the able-bodied work," his sentiments sprang from this belief.

Note that this is not about rights. It is about help. That is a key to understanding why critics so oppose the ADA: because it is couched in "rights" language. Pundits and politicians who denounce the ADA oppose the changes that our nation's rights agenda of the last half of the 20th century have put in motion, and so for them the case against disability rights can be understood as part of this larger anti-rights agenda.

But it would be wrong to think that this explained the opposition fully. With disability rights, there is more: this nation truly does not understand dealing with its disabled through the prism of rights; does not believe it is the correct way to understand the situation. The correct way to understand the situation can be seen in how we view Christopher Reeve's situation: as a medical tragedy, whose solution is cure. The way the U.S. understands dealing with its disabled who have not been cured is through private charity or public benefits, which are seen as a form of charity, even though, with veterans' disability benefits, Social Security disability benefits and private disability insurance benefits, they have been "earned" — through actual payments or through military service. Medical help, too, of course — to cure those who can be cured. And with special programs for those who are eligible.

"Instead of perceiving the range of individual abilities, society categorizes people as either blind or sighted, either epileptic or not epileptic, either handicapped or normal," wrote attorney Robert L. Burgdorf, Jr. in 1983 in a report for the U.S. Civil Rights Commission, where he worked. *Accommodating the Spectrum of Individual Abilities* was the shot fired across the bow by activists intent on amending the nation's Civil Rights Act. That law already protected U.S. citizens from discrimination based on race, color, religion, national origin or sex. Anyone — black, white, brown, yellow, red — could use it if they had faced discrimination on the basis of race or national origin; men as well as women could use its Title VII to fight sex-based discrimination on the job. Anyone could use it — if they had faced the particular kind of discrimination it forbade.

Burgdorf and others wanted the law amended to include protection from discrimination based on disability as well. But efforts to do this, which had been going on since the 1970s, had met with little success. Civil rights groups did not want more groups added to the law; they thought it would dilute its force. And they simply didn't see the problems disabled people faced as being of the same nature as racial or sexual discrimination.

As with most things related to disability, the problems the advocates wanted addressed were seen by civil rights groups as being more accurately problems of a medical nature than actual denials of rights. Plus, there was a long history of dealing with disabled people's problems with special, separate programs — disabled people were put in special "homes," were sent to special "schools" (if schooled at all). If a law were needed to protect them, it would be best it if were a special law for their special circumstances.

To get protection from disability discrimination, activists saw that they would have to get Congress to pass a special law.

The organized disabled had been pretty good at getting laws passed. A law first enacted in the postwar years to provide nationwide vocational rehabilitation programs had undergone a drastic overhaul; because the overhaul occurred during an era of civil rights fervor, the 1973 Rehabilitation Act included at its end a provision, Title V, that barred discrimination against people with handicaps by programs that received federal funds. Like most laws concerning disability, the Rehab Act was a law concerning not rights, but benefits — "entitlements," as they were called. To get the benefits (in this case vocational rehabilitation services), you had to qualify as a "disabled person." A doctor's OK was involved.

As noted earlier, the initial bill that disability activists crafted and got introduced into Congress in 1988, the one modeled on the 1964 Civil Rights Act, requiring barrier removal and forbidding discrimination in virtually all commercial establishments, never had a chance for passage. But the disability lobbyists who rallied to get a compromise bill through the 101st Congress believed lawmakers could be convinced to pass a bill that didn't seem "strange" to them; so they stressed that the ADA was much like the

Rehabilitation Act's Title V. The Rehabilitation Act, which offered a national program of vocational rehabilitation — a benefits program — defined who was eligible for it. It included a definition of "person with a handicap." That definition (today changed to the politically correct "individual with a disability") was moved almost unchanged into the bill that would become the ADA: an "individual with a disability" would be defined as someone who "(i) has a physical or mental impairment which substantially limits one or more of such person's major life activities, (ii) has a record of such an impairment, or (iii) is regarded as having such an impairment."

The bill now read less like a true civil rights law than a strange hybrid based on the understanding our national legislators and their staffs had about disability law, which in general was benefits-based legislation that gave something to a group of people, like Social Security disability benefits or rehabilitation services — services that you only got if you qualified as disabled.

In the fifteen years since the Rehab Act, disability rights advocates' own language had changed. "Handicapped" had been replaced by "disabled" at advocates' insistence.

"Handicapped," they said, was a term they'd been saddled with by professionals. In a misguided exercise of self-determination, these activists insisted that no, it was society that handicapped them; in themselves they did not have handicaps but "disabilities" — the term they used to signal their condition: paralysis, cerebral palsy, epilepsy. Thus, they chose "disability" for their moniker: "I am a person with a disability, not a handicapped person. It's society that handicaps me."

This exercise of linguistic empowerment had a serious flaw. As with most things in disability rights, the rationale never permeated beyond advocates. Most of us hearing the words "disabled" or "disability" still take the word to mean what it has always meant to society: "unable," "incapable." "People with disabilities" means, simply, people who lack ability, who are incapable.

No wonder it seems absurd for such people to insist they are qualified for the same jobs as people who have no "disabilities"!

Because prohibiting discrimination based on disability was a novel idea, those drafting the law worried that judges would think that nondiscrimination "meant treating the individual as if he or she did not have a disability" — and that if this were the case, "we'd end up having blind people suing to be allowed to be bus drivers," Burgdorf would say later.

It should have been a groundless worry. Even though, unlike race, disability did sometimes have an impact on performance, the fact was that disqualifying a person from a bus-driving job for inability to drive would not be an act of disability discrimination. It would be "an evenhanded application of a job-related qualification standard," as Burgdorf put it. Disqualifying a person with no legs from a typing job, on the other hand, would be an act of discrimination, because having legs had no bearing on any rational job-related qualification standard for typing.

There was therefore no need for any of this in an antidiscrimination law. The Civil Rights Act did not define "race." The presence of these definitions, said some, would suggest to the unsophisticated legal practitioner eligibility issues not appropriate in a law prohibiting discrimination — and baseless issues in any case, because the law's employment antidiscrimination protections only applied to someone who could meet job-related standards anyway. A "qualified individual with a disability" was defined as "an individual with a disability who, with or without reasonable accommodation, can perform the essential functions of the employment...." And it was right in the front of the law. Some warned that this would come back to haunt them later. But they were overruled.

It was against this understanding of disability — as a medical problem making you incapable of working, and, with a doctor's OK, thus entitled to benefits — that the ADA was enacted. Disability rights activists had conceived it as a civil rights law, but almost nobody else understood what "civil rights" could possibly mean when it came to disabled people. It's safe to say that many of the Senators and Representatives who voted for the law saw it only as an extension of the kinds of special benefits and programs that blind and disabled people had been given in the years after World War II. And if this got it passed, went the thinking, that was OK.

In truth what the Rehab Act's drafters had been trying to accomplish when they'd grafted a civil rights title onto the end of that social welfare law about rehabilitation benefits was to create a definition that would in effect encompass everyone, and function as the kind of protection the Civil Rights Act afforded people. That was the intent, and they did it by what at the time seemed an ingenious idea — a three-part definition of "handicapped individual" that would encompass virtually everyone: not only people who had an impairment that affected a major life activity (these were the people everyone thought of as "the truly handicapped") — that was just the first part of the definition — but also people who "had a history" of disability: in this instance they were thinking of people who met up with discrimination when employers knew they'd had cancer. Finally, the definition's third prong would encompass anyone — *anyone* — who had been "regarded as" disabled, and discriminated against because they were regarded as disabled by whoever was doing the discriminating.

It was this "regarded as" part of the definition that was to be the workhorse that would carry the law's protections to virtually all Americans. For, the reasoning went, if one were being "regarded as disabled," whether or not one really had a disability, and one were being discriminated against because one was thought to be disabled, then one would also be able to afford oneself of the law's protections. It seemed a clever solution to the problem of making a benefits law, which had to define who was eligible to use it, into a civil rights law. It just didn't work out that way.

Because there was in the law a definition of a "qualified" "individual with a disability" — unlike the other, "real" U.S. civil rights law, which had no definition regarding "race" or "national origin" — the ADA came to be regarded by attorneys as requiring first of all a "threshold determination" that an individual was a "qualified" "person with a disability" before they could even use the law — discrimination or no discrimination. Its drafters had intended no such thing; but it was how things turned out.

Is it disability status — or discriminatory treatment by others — that the ADA is about? Most judges and many attorneys still don't seem to know.

And a series of decisions the summer before Clint Eastwood began his campaign seemed to say that most members of the Supreme Court didn't know either, as we will see in Chapter 6.

Because we already understood what disabled people's real problems were — their bodies were all messed up — we did not look for or accept any newer understandings. We already had the explanation we believed in. We already had a sanctioned and beloved way of dealing with our disabled: by giving deserved help and searching for cures. As a nation we had no real interest in switching over to a new understanding predicated on rights. We simply thought it was wrongheaded, and wrong.

Because it is called a civil rights law, people who invoke the law's protections say they have been discriminated against and thus make the point that it is a law about discrimination, about rights. Because of this, people on some level compare it to the other civil rights law everybody knows about: The 1964 Civil Rights Act. Indeed, that was exactly what the ADA's crafters wanted.

But the problem is that when most ordinary folks make this mental comparison, rather than it making them see that someone with a disability does indeed face discrimination (just as racial and ethnic minorities have), generally just the opposite happens. It doesn't make sense to them. It doesn't fit the reality they know. They say, "Joe (or Edna or Chuck) isn't like a black person who's discriminated against — Joe's just got a bad back. That's his problem. He's not part of a 'minority'. He's just a regular person — but with a medical problem — a disability."

People who drool, who shake, who repel us, about whom we think, "My God! Isn't it awful to be that way?" are the "truly disabled." If they are in wheelchairs, they're said to be "wheelchair bound" or "confined to a wheelchair." Expressions most disability activists loathe (they insist the phrases are inaccurate, that wheel-

chairs are really tools of movement and liberation — and they got
the *Associated Press Stylebook* to say the phrases were no-nos), they
continue to be used by reporters and editors because they express
a psychological reality people cling to: that if you really can't get
out of the wheelchair, if you're "bound" to it or "confined" to it,
it's a useful indicator — you are one of the truly disabled, not a
faker. Other people are likely fakers.

That's what Andy Rooney figured when he took on the "special
right" that angered almost everyone: "handicapped parking": "Are
too many parking spaces being set aside for the handicapped, and
is it really the handicapped who are using them?"

Rooney, cameraman in tow, visited a New York airport. He
watched as a car pulled into marked spot "and this man walked off
towards the terminal. We couldn't detect much of a limp. Maybe
his handicap was mental," Rooney joked.

> In hours of shooting in half a dozen locations, we saw thou-
> sands of handicapped parking places, and lots of license plates with
> wheelchairs on them. We saw only one wheelchair.
>
> At a mall we watched for more than an hour as people pulled
> in and out of handicapped parking places. If some of them were
> handicapped, it must have been with a bad cold.
>
> We didn't see many legitimately handicapped people who real-
> ly needed a parking space near the door. Some of these people may
> have disabilities that don't show, of course, heart problems, maybe.
> It's one of those maddening things. We do something that's right
> by providing handicapped parking spaces, and then people ruin it
> for everyone.
>
> We saw one man park his pickup at a mall before we had our
> camera set up, so we waited until he came out. We thought maybe
> he'd gone in to buy a wheelchair. We just couldn't tell what this
> man's disability was.
>
> Maybe it was that he didn't know right from wrong. This
> seems wrong. If no one but truly handicapped people put their cars
> in handicapped parking spaces, there'd be a lot more parking for
> everyone.

Rooney didn't need any legal definition to tell him whether
someone was disabled or not. Like pornography, he knew it when
he saw it. The people he saw weren't all messed up. So they
weren't truly disabled — that is, they didn't deserve the special,

better, parking spots.

The real clue as to whether someone is truly disabled is if we feel sorry for them being that way; if we secretly are horrified at the prospect of being like that ourselves. That horror, that emotion, is the measure. Nothing else, in fact, is as fail-safe a measure: The yardstick we use to determine who's a deserving disabled person is an emotional one.

While it's generally safe to assume that those whose situation makes us feel awful for them ("I'd rather die than be like that") are the truly disabled, the deserving disabled, something messes even this system up: the droolers, people confined to wheelchairs, totally blind people who have jobs.

Marc Simitian works. Christopher Reeve directs films. Stephen Hawking works. So does John Hockenberry. When confronted with situations like these — the situation also arises when we read about someone "confined to a wheelchair" who has a job, like Congressman Jim Langevin — we simply label them Exceptions to The Rule. Our emotional measure of what it means to be "disabled" does not, in fact, change, because public discourse does not require that it change. We simply consider disabled people who work exceptions to the rule and don't think any more about it.

The line between someone who is truly disabled and someone who isn't shifts constantly, though. We make exceptions all the time. We believe "disabled" means "unable to work," yet we cheer Christopher Reeve's debut as a film director. Still, we consider him one of the truly disabled, even though it's clear that he works.

But if the line is redrawn by each individual, how can there be any socially agreed-upon demarcation, on the one side of which are those everyone considers the disabled, on the other side those who aren't? Every attempt to draw such a line has failed, and we are left with a growing realization that this is not how one can measure disability.

As with homosexuality, the moral overtones of defining someone as truly disabled spring from the belief that the condition is in some respects voluntary, at least for most of the vast numbers who are considered by public policy measures "disabled" — the folks

on the Social Security benefits rolls, for example. A person could
shape up, could change their condition, if they only put some
effort into it.

Hardly any of us will blame another for a situation that is
thought to be truly immutable, truly something which the individual can do virtually nothing to change. Although people no
longer seem to really believe that people born disabled or
deformed are the result of some transgression on the part of parents — this was a medieval notion — there are plenty of us who,
if one digs a little beneath the surface, will be found to believe that
most people with disabilities are either malingerers — or saints. For
that is the flip side of the coin, and from it comes the notion that
a disabled person like Christopher Reeve is "an inspiration" —
"brave" and "courageous." The adjectives might fit, or they might
not. But they are used with no real effort to discern whether they
fit or not: they are simply applied to "good" disabled people — the
ones who aren't malingerers, the ones who don't cause trouble,
who accept their lot, who don't expect others to do for them, who
certainly don't invoke the Americans with Disabilities Act.

When Minn. Governor and former pro wrestler Jesse Ventura,
whose daughter has both seizures and a learning disorder, told
Business Week that

> A person who is disabled should be disabled by no act of their
> own. If you become disabled because of alcoholism, drugs, or
> things of that nature, I do not think those conditions qualify
> someone to be called disabled. I think those conditions result
> from personal decisions.

he was showing just how much the definition of disability is in
reality a moral judgment. Parroting the right-wing free-market
economist view of the ADA, Ventura told *Business Week* the ADA
had good intentions but it was too vague — and it let too many
people claim disability status.

We can tell that society sees disability as a moral problem
because the way society responds to the problem is by issuing
behavioral injunctions to disabled people to shape up: That is what
the articles by Bovard and the special reports by Stossel are really
doing: they are issuing injunctions to malingerers. This way of con-

sidering the disability state is in truth Victorian more than anything else; a holdover from the 19th century. And the Victorians' approach to dealing with disability — Charles Dickens's Scrooge is perhaps its most famous adherent — gets its marching papers from the same source as Puritanism, the belief that one must do one's own work, and that those who do not earn their own daily bread, who don't pull their weight in society, are simply laggards.

Yet what is apparent in the case against disability rights is that what we believe is immutable, and what we believe is within the individual's own power (and obligation) to change, varies along with our ideological stripe. In the disability rights view of things, conservatives are those who believe that the problem is within the power of the individual to change — or they believe that the problem is one that resides in the individual, rather than in society.

The medical model positing the problem in the individual and the right-wing anti-welfare ideology positing the problem in the individual seem to coincide here, although they come from different traditions. But the reason the case against disability rights has such power over most people is because most people tend to see things as conservatives do in this instance: most people really believe that disability is an individual rather than a group problem. They see it as a medical problem besetting an individual, or a moral problem inherent in someone who fakes and whines. Sometimes they see it as both. In either case, they do not see it as a problem of discrimination — not, that is, a problem of society's making or society's responsibility to remedy. Whether intentional or not, whether brought on by one's bad habits or laziness or attitudes, or a "genuine" medical problem, disability is a problem of the individual's own doing.

Because the medical-model positing of the problem in the individual is so like the right-wing anti-welfarers' penchant for locating the problem in the individual, the conservative reading of the issue seems to most people to be common sense, while the disability rights take seems to most people simply inaccurate.

People like John Stossel merely speak aloud what most people seem to really believe on an emotional level: that "people who have problems that they can cope with with great effort [are] being convinced to give in and wallow in their fate as a victim." No one has ever answered the cry he raises in equally emotional terms, showing us just how morally bereft his analysis is. No one, in truth, has given us anything new to put in its place.

Defining 'disability': a political act

"We never thought of the President as handicapped," a Roosevelt family friend told historian Hugh Gallagher. "We never thought of it at all." He was seen by most as not being disabled, writes Gallagher.

When we signal that someone is one of us, is a regular guy, is part of our group, we say, "We never considered him disabled." Because the disabled are always They, The Other. Not us.

Making this distinction is in essence a political act.

People who have disabilities are actually neither "us" nor "them." Or, more accurately, they are both — either — depending on who's doing the looking, and the judging, and the relationship that person bears to us who are doing the judging. The concept of disability is fluid, and it shifts constantly. The same person who is "regarded as disabled" in one circumstance is seen as no other than our dear, dotty Uncle Mark in another circumstance — none of us consider him "disabled!"

So the same person can be both disabled and not disabled, depending on circumstance. Nobody in the family may consider Uncle Mark "truly disabled," but in fact Uncle Mark is on "total disability" because he was in an industrial accident that caused brain damage, and he got to "retire on disability." I recall an uncle from childhood who fascinated me by the way he made telephone calls: He would call the operator and ask that the operator dial the number for him because he was legally blind. He was a disabled vet; he never held a job. He couldn't drive, either; he and my aunt always took cabs. Yet none of us growing up ever considered Uncle Bob disabled. We knew he didn't hold a job; everyone knew he had been injured in the war and that's why he didn't work. But he could see a little, and he was just a regular uncle in our minds.

Haven't you heard someone say, "Oh, I don't consider myself disabled"? How many times have you said it yourself about someone? It's meant as a compliment. What does that mean? That to say someone is disabled is in a way an insult — saying something bad about them. It can't be otherwise.

Disability advocates have known this, at least on an instinctive level, for a long time; it's the real reason behind the push toward what they call "people first" language — and it's why the Americans with Disabilities Act is called that, rather than, for example, the Disabled Americans Act. (Great Britain's similar law, passed in 1995, is more appropriately called The Disability Discrimination Act.) It's the reason behind the increasingly silly constructions of "people with" that get mocked so regularly: "people with vision impairments," "people with autism," "people with cerebral palsy," "people with spinal cord injuries." Advocates of "people first" constructions say it is important to realize that the person is not "disabled" but rather that they "have" a disability.

This and a lot of other psychological and linguistic gyrations can't hide the fact that to be disabled is to be considered something bad. When John Stossel tells us admiringly that Marc Simitian "doesn't consider himself a victim," he's making the same point.

"Don't call me disabled," Nick Ackerman told reporters. The Iowa college senior, who had used prosthetic legs since an accident in early childhood, who won the NCAA Division 3 wrestling championship, told a reporter that "I don't have a disability, I have ability and I'm going to use it" and that "I always thought I was normal."

An admiring *New York Times* obituary reported that Celeste Tate Harrington, "a quadriplegic street musician whose buoyant personality and unremitting chutzpah brought astounded smiles to everyone who watched her play the keyboard with her lips and tongue on Atlantic City's Boardwalk," "didn't consider herself disabled." Nana Graham was born with "undeveloped legs and feet that curved inward and upside down." Her legs were amputated when she was 13. But her daughter told a reporter Graham was "not handicapped." Hearing-impaired actress Vanessa Vaughan insisted she was not disabled and refused to be interviewed by the *Toronto Star* for an article about disabled performers. Wheelchair tennis star Dan Bennett, "born with spina bifida, leaving him without use of his legs," did not consider himself disabled. "The more we play, the more words like 'handicapped' and 'disabled' can begin to disappear," wheelchair tennis player Joe Babakanian told a reporter.

Although the ADA had been used successfully in California to win cases in which fat people faced employment discrimination, activists for overweight people considered the cases bad because it put fat people in a "disabled category." "Most fat people do not consider themselves disabled," Laura Eljaiek, head of the National Association to Advance Fat Acceptance, told a reporter.

The obituary for Bob L. Thomas, chief justice of the 10th Circuit Court of Appeals in Waco, Tex., noted that he had achieved "success in law and politics despite total paralysis in all but his left hand," having "contracted polio at the age of 15." He used a wheelchair until his death, yet a colleague remarked that he didn't consider himself disabled. "He had an absolute determination to overcome his disabilities," said another.

When Louisvillian Dan Massie died, a story noting his role as a 1970s disability activist reported that although his wife pushed him everywhere in his chair, he "didn't act as if he was disabled." "He didn't take a penny of Social Security disability money," a friend told a reporter. "He sold jewelry on street corners and at festivals, and earned all his money."

If my grandmother has arthritis, but she isn't "really disabled," what we are saying is that she does not have the attributes we believe those poor schmucks "the disabled" have. Or, if we think she does have those attributes, it's a signal she's left the "us" and moved to the "them" category, and we no longer see her as being like us but as being like "the disabled."

Even people who don't have any real luxury of shifting in or out of the "disabled" category — people like Christopher Reeve and John Hockenberry who everyone can tell are clearly disabled —

are brought into the "us" camp by the statement that they don't "act disabled." Congresswoman Barbara Jordan, who had multiple sclerosis, did not discuss her disability openly.

People do not want to identify as disabled and will do almost anything to avoid it. If we act normal and don't get involved in that disability rights stuff, then we're not really disabled, we think. If we keep on trying to recover, then, we think, we're not truly disabled. President Roosevelt, even though he could not walk unaided, nevertheless called himself a "cured cripple." It was his way of doing the same thing.

"'Disability' is an ideological term," says political scientist David Pfeiffer. "To name a person as 'disabled' is to give them an inferior position in society."

Everyone who is disabled is "them"; anyone who "happens to have a disability" but doesn't "consider themselves disabled" is "us": what we have done is carve off from "us" certain individuals whom we label as "disabled" in an act of assigning them a lesser status in society. More than with racial minorities, more than with sexual minorities, more than with women, what we do as a society by this act is to say that people with disabilities are The Other — by definition not us. Or, more accurately, "they" are the group beyond the pale — outside the wall — the scapegoats. Of course we don't want them to have the same rights as us. We have made them "them," not us, because we want to distinguish them *from* us. If they are equal to us, then we've lost the entire reason we're labeling them as "disabled" in the first place. In truth, we want to make them go away and stop bothering us.

Sociologist Erving Goffman in the 1960s got at this in a way that no one has managed to do better: He said in his classic book, *Stigma: Notes on the Management of Spoiled Identity,* that disabled people were considered "failed normals" — people whose identities have been spoiled. They've failed — and we want them to know it in no uncertain terms. The label "disabled" is in this sense really a punitive term. The disability rights movement's "new paradigm" that sees disability as simply one of many characteristics, has not permeated society. Goffman's view is right on the money. It certainly explains John Stossel's not considering himself disabled, even though he has a stutter. It explains Chief Justice Sandra Day O'Connor's not considering herself disabled either, although she has had breast cancer. Both have removed themselves from "the disabled," ensuring that they are regarded as "us," not "them."

People don't buy the disability rights movement's argument that people who have various disabilities form a minority group, either, even though it says so, right in the ADA's first section, the Findings. The bill's drafters used the phrase "discrete and insular minority" in hopes that this phrasing would ensure the same understanding we held about blacks.

In 1985, in a case involving a permit for a group home for mentally retarded people, the Supreme Court had ruled that people with mental retardation were not a true minority. The legalese involved the terms "suspect" class (people who were true minorities, like blacks) and "quasi-suspect" class: Justice Byron R. White wrote,

"[I]f the large and amorphous class of the mentally retarded were deemed quasi-suspect for the reasons given by the Court of Appeals, it would be difficult to find a principled way to distinguish a variety of other groups who have perhaps immutable disabilities setting them off from others, who cannot themselves mandate the desired legislative responses, and who can claim some degree of prejudice from at least part of the public at large. One need mention in this respect only the aging, the disabled, the mentally ill, and the infirm. We are reluctant to set out on that course, and we decline to do so.

Framers of the ADA made sure that the phrase "discrete and insular minority" was right there in the law itself. But that doesn't mean people believe it.

If your solution is a hammer, all your problems look like nails. If your solution is a civil rights law, then your problems will look like discrimination; so it makes sense that the organized disabled would see things that way, say critics. But to most people, the problem appears to be the body — it doesn't work right — and the solution is cure, or, lacking that, some sort of help, assistance, charity.

"Anybody can become disabled." "Everybody will become disabled sooner or later." "We're all just TABs — Temporarily Able-Bodied." Although most of us snicker when we hear a person say something like this, considering it the ultimate in political correctness, it also happens to be true. Disability is the one condition we all encounter. And we move in and out of it.

Of course normal people have problems with things like cancer, or stuttering, or back pain, or arthritis, or a broken knee from a skiing accident, or a depressive episode, we say. But, we add, they aren't "really disabled."

When we say that, we are intuitively using Goffman's definition of a disabled person as being a "failed normal." If we don't see them failing at being a regular Joe, then they're not disabled. They're only disabled if they've failed in some way. Thinking this way means viewing disability in moral and political terms.

It is only in these terms that the case against disability rights can truly be understood. And it is only by understanding this can we come to understand the true nature of disability discrimination. We will look at this in Chapter 13.

"Most reasonable people with glasses — like me — wouldn't consider themselves disabled," wrote Jacqueline Rolfs, whose article in the *Minneapolis Star Tribune* blasted the ADA. "But that issue went all the way to the Supreme Court," she wrote, "before reason finally prevailed."

FIVE

The Right's stuff

Underpinnings of the case against disability rights came from a group of law professors, mostly connected to the University of Chicago, who worked feverishly in the immediate post-Reagan era to concoct theory to prove that government must be reined in, allowing the market economy unfettered growth, if the nation were to achieve a prosperous society. Libertarian think tanks used this "law-and-economics" output to press Congress to ban environmental and safety rules as unfair to business. Welfare and affirmative action were attacked as programs that wrongly seek to regulate the market by helping those with fewer resources. (The market regulates itself, goes the law and economics line; anyone who can't succeed deserves to fail; government should not interfere.) Nothing that hurt business should be allowed.

Conservative policy — "market theology," as one political scientist called it — had moved to the center of the nation's political conversation when the bill that would become the Americans with Disabilities Act was being fashioned. It's little wonder the law carried the caveat that it mustn't hurt business.

Think tanks like the Heritage Foundation, the American Enterprise Institute, the Cato Institute; magazines like *Reason* and *The American Spectator* pushed efforts to limit government, freeing markets from regulation, and worked to harness public opinion to achieve these ends. As the ADA was taking effect in 1992, a dozen leading conservative philanthropic foundations were putting over $200 million into the anti-government, unregulated markets agenda. Tens of millions of dollars were invested in the law-and-economics movement alone. Over $40 million went into "educating the media"; in 1995, a single think tank generated over a thousand op-ed articles and provided "backgrounders" to hundreds of newspapers who had signed up for policy briefings. It was these groups who supplied the philosophical underpinnings of the case against disability rights.

In the Cato Institute's glossy magazine *Regulation* in the spring of 1995 (just a few weeks before Christopher Reeve became disabled), its director of regulatory studies took on the ADA in a full-court press.

"Few would disagree that, unlike able-bodied citizens, Americans with real physical disabilities face special challenges as they attempt to earn their livings and enjoy their lives," Edward L. Hudgins wrote. "It is also understandable that policymakers would want to ease the burdens that disabled Americans face," he added, preceding his complaint with the curious "no one is against the handicapped" disclaimer that almost always prefaced any exposition of the case against disability rights. But although "President Bush and his supporters in Congress promoted the ADA as a civil rights law," the 1964 Civil Rights Act had merely restrained business from doing evil and required no further action of them ("A business that hires the best job applicant regardless of race is following a wise and profitable practice, and certainly does not incur any additional direct costs," he wrote), whereas the ADA "requires local governments and private enterprises to pay the costs of accommodation out of their own pockets."

It was the fifth anniversary of the ADA's passage, and if the organized disabled were not providing the media any analysis of how the law was working, the opposition was not going to waste the opportunity. They knew editors would be assigning at least a few stories about the law's effectiveness at its five-year benchmark. They could shape the discussion.

Much of the case against disability rights was nothing more than boilerplate law-and-economics free-market rhetoric. At its core its message was the old complaint: "They are hurting us." Hudgins called the ADA "one of the worst cases of the Bush-era reregulation of the economy," grousing that it "added to the costs for enterprises to do business" with "few if any offsetting benefits." A few years later he would call it "a horrendous, atrocious, repressive government apparatus." Its "requirements that state and local governments provide special facilities, many of which go under- or unutilized" were "unfunded mandates." It devalued property — by telling owners they had to make changes but didn't pay them any "compensation." This last, a concept cooked up by libertarians out of the "Takings" clause of the Fifth Amendment, claimed that if a government rule caused an owner to lose potential future earning on property it constituted an "illegal taking" for which the government must reimburse the owner. Zealots pushing use of the Takings Clause have mostly yelled about environmental rules; the Supreme Court once ordered South Carolina to pay a landowner for future income he claimed he lost when an environmental law kept him from building houses on fragile beachfront land. Hudgins said that due to the ADA, "the owner has the value of his property reduced through government restrictions....parking garage owners must set aside handicapped spaces and leave them empty for disabled drivers' use, even if the garage is full and nondisabled customers are turned away"; thus it "deprives owners of the use of and profit from their property."

And, said Hudgins, the ADA "harms the very group it means to help: disabled Americans."

Any effort to impose restrictions on free markets by telling businesses they could not discriminate against certain kinds of workers, that they must accommodate a worker's job-related needs, would merely end up backfiring, hurting those very people it was intended to help, said the theorists. Employers, fearing lawsuits, would simply avoid hiring such people altogether.

It was transparent selfishness — business wanted no restrictions and this was a kind of "you can't make me!" bullying — but since the Reagan era it had become widely accepted. Its chief apologist was libertarian free-market legal economist Richard A. Epstein of the University of Chicago Law School.

Epstein explained how the ADA was bad for business in his 1992 book *Forbidden Grounds: the Case Against Employment Discrimination Laws.* "Administrative costs of state coercion" — by which he meant laws like the ADA — "are always high," "and promise to be especially so under the ADA."

"Insisting that disabled individuals be accorded job opportunities that cost more than they are worth means that the mutual gain condition of voluntary contracts is no longer satisfied." By this he means simply that the business is doing something it doesn't want to do; something that left alone it wouldn't do. "It is simply not a sufficient condition for aid to the disabled," he continued "to show that the benefits they...derive from any social expenditure is positive. The benefits must also be larger than he associated costs." That the "costs" would of course be greater than the benefits was a given for Epstein. He cited no data; he apparently thought he didn't need to.

By "aid to the disabled," Epstein simply means hiring them: in his view the only conceivable reason to hire a disabled person would be to "aid them" — because to him it's inconceivable that any disabled person would in any way actually benefit a business in the way a real worker would. Thus we see in Epstein the belief, which both liberals and conservatives seemed to share, that the correct public response to disability is to help disabled people, through charity. This was what Congressman Bob Stump had meant when he called the ADA "a retreat from a logical approach to the protection of the disabled."

Although alone of all civil rights laws, the ADA had a built-in formula protecting business against precisely the kind of "undue hardship" he worried about, Epstein nonetheless insisted that "these costs are ignored or systematically belittled under the ADA."

Like other law-and-economics theorists, Epstein cited no empirical data to back his contentions, positing conjecture as fact.

In his book, Epstein explains why disabled people, although they were inspiring, courageous and in need of help, were so terrible for business. It is a clear exposition, showing how those opposed to disability rights understand the disability situation. Based on the medical model, it has to do with personal loss:

> Having a disability is a source of an enormous level of personal loss. It requires extra effort just to tread water and still more

extraordinary effort to succeed against built-in deprivations. The sympathies of most people go out to those with limitations. If it were just a question of whether one wishes success to those who labor under disability, the popular sentiment seems clear: their exploits are the source of admiration and amazement, and the subject of plays, stories and movies that tug knowingly at the heartstrings....The entire apparatus of charitable giving and charitable service would be unintelligible if public attitudes were as harsh and archaic as Congress and the commentators so easily assume.

The losses that disabilities impose, however, are not restricted to people with handicaps. They also extend to those persons who have, or might have had, ongoing relationships, legal or social, with them. No comprehensive analysis can ignore those losses. Yet the rhetoric of the debate over the ADA sidestepped these issues by calling this common sentiment irrational or arbitrary, effectively ignoring the unmistakable costs that other people bear in doing business with the disabled....[H]aving to deal with X [who has a] disability is costlier than having to deal with Y, who lacks that disability. Business is harder to conduct as the pace of transaction slows. Customers may find it inconvenient, unpleasant or awkward to deal with persons who are deaf, blind, palsied or who have disfiguring marks or speech impairments. Their preferences should not be blithely condemned as irrational, for in their own personal life they may have to cope with difficult emotional or family problems, face powerful time and budgetary constraints, or even cope with disabilities of their own. It is wishful idealization to assume that anyone who is not disabled has an infinite store of emotional energy available for public consumption....

In light of the business realities of the situation, the popular treatment of the disabled cannot simply be dismissed as prejudice or bigotry. There is no contradiction between refusing to hire disabled persons for certain jobs, while offering them others at lower wages, and simultaneously making generous gifts to a charitable organization that specializes in the rehabilitation of seriously handicapped children.

Epstein's view of hiring the disabled was not much different than 1950s free-market economist Gary S. Becker's views on hiring Negroes, which he expressed in his first book, his 1957 *The Economics of Discrimination*. There he insisted that racist employers who refused to hire black workers would be put at such a competitive disadvantage that their businesses would fail; there was no need for federal civil rights law; the free market would solve blacks' problems. During the civil rights years the book was widely discredited. Yet as the Chicago School became the darlings of academia, Becker, now a fellow of the right-wing Hoover Institution, managed to win himself a Nobel Prize in economics in 1992, the year the ADA's rules on access took effect.

Epstein's views on the harm disabled workers caused business because they were so naturally costly to employ were an echo of Cato Institute economist Robert P. O'Quinn's 1991 Policy Analysis on the ADA: "For almost all employers, the costs and expected benefits of hiring a white or a black, a German or an Italian, a Christian or a Jew, or even a man or a woman, each of whom has equivalent aptitude and qualifications, should be equal"; but it was different with disabled people; they'd no doubt be costly to hire. Therefore, "any additional costs associated with hiring a disabled person…should be reflected in lower compensation paid to the disabled person." O'Quinn wrote that disabled people should pay more for using any public accommodations — a movie theater, for example — that had been made accessible for them, since they had forced the accommodation to spend money to help them.

Throughout the decade, article after article, including "A Good Law Gone Bad" in the May, 1998 *Readers Digest* and "Tunnel Vision" in the Sept. 19, 1998 *National Journal,* told readers the ADA actually hurt disabled people by making employers fear hiring the litigious creatures. Just as Howard's 1994 *The Death of Common Sense* had excoriated the ADA, the Manhattan Institute's prolific Walter Olson, in the 1997 book *The Excuse Factory: How Employment Law Is Paralyzing the American Workplace,* called the ADA a "spectacular injustice."

"The main result of the ADA is to provide disgruntled or former workers with another arrow in their quiver to challenge an employer's decision," David Copus of the law firm Jones Day in

Washington, D.C. told reporters. From these repeated statements of law-and-economics gurus that the ADA would make employers fearful of hiring disabled people, employers came to understand that they could simply ignore the ADA's employment mandates. They could point to such statements as proof that they were only part of a trend that had been warned of by experts when they now scrutinized — and dismissed — any employment inquiry from a disabled applicant. After all, who could prove otherwise?

In an August 1999 column for *Business Week*, Becker once again trotted out the "ADA hurts disabled workers" theory. It explained, he said, the "otherwise surprising results in separate studies by economists Daron Acemoglu and Josh Angrist of the Massachusetts Institute of Technology and Thomas DeLeire of the University of Chicago...[who] find that employment of disabled workers fell rather than rose since enactment of this law, mainly because of reduced hiring rather than greater firing of the disabled." To Becker this could only be explained one way: "To prevent costly lawsuits, many companies apparently avoid hiring job applicants whom [sic] they believe would prove litigious under the ADA." The "truly disabled" would likely be better off "if the ADA were scrapped altogether."

Doing away with federal guarantees of cash assistance to poor people, changing the federal tax structure, thwarting national health insurance moves, pushing for privatizing Social Security: The free-market radicals had a hand in all these; but their moves met vocal opposition. When they railed against disability rights, they generally had the floor to themselves.

They were correct in noticing that the Americans with Disabilities Act was different from other civil rights protections in that it did expect society to physically change itself in a number of ways. What they did not care for was its morality. Constrained to the Procrustean bed of their zero-sum analysis of society, deluded by the misplaced morality of the law-and-economics movement, they really believed that anything that regulated "free markets" took something away from "normal" people, only to give it to those who otherwise wouldn't have been able to compete and thus should have died off anyway. "Make them go away!" they cried.

Perhaps they saw, rightly, that the vision of the ADA called for retooling society into a more egalitarian one, where an individual's rights would have claim against corporate rights. *Anyone's* individual rights, in fact. But in viewing disability rights law as just another effort to thwart the holiness of the unfettered free market, they missed altogether its solutions to their own problems.

Down the wrong road: the courts take up the case against disability rights

About the time Christopher Reeve became disabled, law professor Robert Burgdorf wrote in a law journal that legal analysis of the ADA was proceeding "quite a way down the wrong road."

As ADA cases began working their way up from the lower courts, observers noted an odd phenomenon: Disabled people were losing cases in the courts of judges who were liberal on other civil rights issues, and who should have been expected to understand disability discrimination. In fact what was happening was that judges were simply stopping the cases before they even got started, telling people they weren't "disabled" as the ADA defined it, and that they therefore simply weren't eligible to use the law at all.

Because the ADA's passage was preceded by almost no public discussion about the reality or nature of disability discrimination, attorneys and judges were now faced with interpreting a law whose ideological underpinnings were mostly alien to them. The ADA is "based on a socio-cultural model of disability that judges don't understand," says Boalt Hall law professor Linda Krieger. Judges understood disability law as benefits law — things like rehabilitation or Medicaid — things one had to be "eligible" for. Judges were looking at cases to see if the plaintiffs were sufficiently "impaired" ("substantially limited," it was called) to earn eligibility for protection under the ADA.

A man with multiple sclerosis had been discharged from his job because, he was told in a written discharge notice, the multiple sclerosis prevented him from writing his reports in hand, something the boss required. The man had purchased, on his own, dictation equipment and had requested that he be allowed to have a secretary type his reports from his dictation. The employer refused to do it. But when the man decided to sue — even though he had, in writing, irrefutable evidence that the employer had terminated him because of disability and had refused to accommodate him in what could surely be seen as a reasonable way — he was told by the attorney he consulted that he would first have to prove to the court that he was truly disabled, getting medical evidence from doctors proving that he had a "substantial limitation in a major life activity" and that he was qualified to perform the essential tasks of the job he was doing. Because these matters were at issue, he was told, if he proceeded with his lawsuit he would have to grant the employer, as part of discovery, access to all of his medical and psychiatric records. The man felt that he, not his employer, would be on trial.

As a growing body of regulation from the EEOC and case law embroidered the ADA's definition of "qualified individual with a disability," things became ever more convoluted. What was a "major life activity?" How "impaired" did a person have to be? And just what was an "impairment?" How limited did one have to be to be "*substantially* limited"? Lists developed; rules grew. "Major life activities" came to mean "activities that an average person can perform with little or no difficulty: walking, seeing, hearing, speaking, breathing, learning, performing manual tasks, caring for oneself, working." Courts debated what was or wasn't a "major life activity" — all for the purpose of deciding if someone had a right to use the civil rights law that was the Americans with Disabilities Act. (When the law has attempted to define "race," it has been "not in laws protecting people from race discrimination, but in laws enforcing white privilege," says attorney Harriet Johnson. "Both before the Civil War and after the collapse of Reconstruction, southern laws made certain privileges white-only, enforced segregation and banned interracial marriages. This required legal definitions of black and white.")

The Fifth Circuit had ruled that a woman with breast cancer who was suffering side effects from chemotherapy and who had asked her employer for an accommodation had no right to one, because, in fact, she had no right to use the law. Since she had continued to work, said the court, she was not "disabled."

The concept of "reasonable accommodation" was the centerpiece of the law's employment section. An employee who was disabled had to be given accommodation, said the law, if the accommodation was "reasonable." It provided a list of criteria to guide employers.

Among the things the law listed as reasonable accommodations were "job restructuring, part-time or modified work schedules, reassignment to a vacant position, acquisition or modification of equipment or devices, appropriate adjustment or modifications of examinations, training materials or policies" and "the provision of qualified readers or interpreters." "Other similar accommodations" also qualified as "reasonable accommodations," said the law — "reasonable" being the key term — and therefore subject to the law's all-encompassing economic caveats. It was "reasonable," said the law, if it didn't impose an "undue hardship" on the business — and that, in turn, was defined through a formula that looked at the nature of the accommodation, its cost, and how much it would cost the company in both human and financial terms.

The Fifth Circuit had also ruled that a woman whose spastic colon condition was aggravated by multiple sclerosis was not entitled to an accommodation that would permit her to arrive at her clerical job 20 minutes late. Her condition, said the court, did not quality as a disability; therefore she couldn't use the law or its mandate that her company accommodate her. A law professor who had suffered a stroke resulting in a paralyzed left hand, arm and leg did not have a disability, said the Court, because he continued to work at his job. He couldn't use the ADA, either, it said.

In the years between 1990, when the ADA had passed, and 1999, many cases were simply stopped at the "summary judgment" stage — that is, they were simply thrown out of court because the person didn't meet the definitional standard of a "qualified individual with a disability," as interpreted by the regulations and the Court; they were told they were not allowed to use the law; the law was not intended for them since they weren't "disabled" according to what the court interpreted as the law's definition.

Many of the cases paraded by Bovard and Stossel were of this type; they had in fact never gone to trial at all; they'd been thrown out. When this happened, the issue of whether a company had behaved badly or not in firing or demoting someone, or in refusing to provide an accommodation, was never examined at all. The court was focusing instead on whether plaintiffs "deserved" to use the law — whether they were or weren't "truly disabled." That term, "truly disabled," was not yet any kind of a legal term — it was just how people understood the concept.

Of the many aspects of the Americans with Disabilities Act that irritated those from the Cato Institute and their ideological fellows, none seemed to anger them more than the law's definition of an "individual with a disability" that they saw being interpreted through the Equal Employment Opportunity Commission's regulations. The third part of that definition particularly flummoxed them: that a person with a disability could be someone who was simply "regarded as having an impairment." It meant, one of them said, that "a person who has had no medical problems can be considered disabled." This was true. To people like Burgdorf, it underscored the point that the law was about discrimination, not disability: if someone discriminated against you, giving you lesser service or refusing to hire you because the discriminator *thought* you were disabled, then it was a moot point whether or not you were, in fact, actually the bearer of some physical or mental condition or trait typically considered a disability: you had nonetheless been discriminated against *on the basis of disability;* and you still had a right to be protected from such discrimination. Those opposed to disability rights either truly did not understand this, or did not care to understand it.

"Experts consulted by *Readers Digest* agree that at the very least our lawmakers should narrow the definition of disability," wrote its senior editor Trevor Ambrister in 1998. This would "discourage marginal claims," he said.

In 1999, the Supreme Court took up three cases that had been appealed from lower courts: Those of Karen Sutton and Kimberly

Hinton, Hallie Kirkingberg and Vaughn Murphy.

Sutton and Hinton were twin sisters whom United Airlines would not hire as pilots because they were nearsighted. Commercial truck driver Hallie Kirkingberg functioned as though he had 20/20 vision, but he was dismissed by Albertson's grocery chain for not meeting the federal vision standard for driving commercial vehicles when his vision tested as "monocular" — that is, with functioning vision in only one eye. United Parcel Service mechanic Vaughn Murphy took medication for high blood pressure and could function fine. But because he had that high blood pressure medical diagnosis, he lost his commercial driver's license, which he needed to take a higher-paying driver's job at United Parcel Service — and was ultimately dismissed by UPS as a result. All of these people had sued their companies under the Americans with Disabilities Act.

The companies they sued all insisted these people had no right to bring a lawsuit under the ADA in the first place, because they were not truly disabled.

A lower court had ruled that Kirkingberg was "not disabled" because he had been able to compensate for the vision he had lost in the one eye. Yet Albertson's, using a federal commercial drivers license regulation that considered individuals with monocular vision to be "unsafe" drivers had, in fact, regarded him as "disabled" — that is, "unable"; it's why they dismissed him. Murphy faced a similar Catch-22.

None of this fazed the majority on the Supreme Court, who used the cases to set about the business of issuing behavioral injunctions against people who would claim "disability" status fraudulently. They were doing just what the experts that *Readers Digest* had contacted had wanted lawmakers to do — "narrow the definition of disability" to "discourage marginal claims."

By a vote of 7 to 2, they ruled on June 26, 1999 that people whose "impairments can be alleviated by medication, glasses or other devices are generally not disabled and so do not come under the law's protection against employment discrimination," as *New York Times* Supreme Court reporter Linda Greenhouse put it.

The question as to whether Vaughn Murphy's high blood pressure "substantially limited a major life activity" must be determined based on the "quality" of the individual's life with "mitigating measures" taken into account, said the Court. In this case the "mitigating measure" was the medication he took which controlled his high blood pressure.

"Thus Murphy could be considered disabled only if, with medication, his hypertension made him unable to continue working," wrote one scholar. "Unfortunately for Murphy, although his hypertension was not controlled to the level that permitted him to met federal safety standards, it was sufficiently controlled to permit him to perform at least some jobs, and so, the Court concluded, it did not interfere with the major activity of working." Murphy was not "disabled" under the ADA, although a federal standard had judged him "too disabled" to be a commercial driver. It seemed clear to disability advocates that both Murphy and Kirkingberg were those people whom the third prong of the ADA definition had been designed to protect.

Justice Stephen G. Breyer worried. Using this reasoning, wouldn't people facing discrimination on the basis of their disability who used artificial limbs or hearing aids be told they were not allowed to use the law, either?

The Supreme Court had "made the same mistake as many lower courts in treating the definition of disability under the ADA as analogous to eligibility criteria under the Social Security disability programs and special education programs," said Burgdorf, who continued to insist that the ADA's protection against discrimination on the basis of disability — like all other antidiscrimination statutes — had been intended to extend to all Americans who experience such discrimination.

Who had the ADA been intended for, anyway? Burgdorf's view was not shared by the majority of the Court, who did not truly seem to see it as a broad antidiscrimination law. "Congress did not intend to bring under the statute's protection all those whose uncorrected conditions amount to disabilities," wrote Justice

Sandra Day O'Connor. Congress found that "some 43,000,000 Americans have one or more physical or mental disabilities, and this number is increasing as the population as a whole is growing older," she wrote, quoting the law's "Findings" section. "Had Congress intended to include all persons with corrected physical limitations among those covered by the Act, it undoubtedly would have cited a much higher number of disabled persons in the Findings. That it did not is evidence that the ADA's coverage is restricted to only those whose impairments are not mitigated by corrective measures."

Justice Ruth Bader Ginsburg agreed. The law was not intended for — "did not reach," was how she put it — "the legions of people with correctable disabilities. The strongest clues to Congress's perception of the domain of the Americans with Disabilities Act, as I see it, are legislative findings that 'some 43,000,000 Americans have one or more physical or mental disabilities,'" she wrote, "and that 'individuals with disabilities are a discrete and insular minority,' persons 'subjected to a history of purposeful unequal treatment, and relegated to a position of political powerlessness in our society.'

"The inclusion of correctable disabilities within the ADA's domain would extend the Act's coverage to far more than 43 million people."

She continued,

[P]ersons whose uncorrected eyesight is poor, or who rely on daily medication for their well-being, can be found in every social and economic class; they do not cluster among the politically powerless, nor do they coalesce as historical victims of discrimination. In short, in no sensible way can one rank the large numbers of diverse individuals with corrected disabilities as a "discrete and insular minority."

Burgdorf was furious. The Supreme Court did not understand the law, he insisted.

"The ADA has a three-prong definition of 'individual with a disability,'" he said. "Only the first prong deals with people with an actual disability — and that is what the 43 million figure refers to." There were two other prongs to the definition — people who had a history of disability or people regarded as disabled. Those had simply been ignored by the Court, he felt. (Later, the DOJ would be strongly criticized by the National Council on Disability for what it called the DOJ's "egregious and pivotal failure to explain to the Court in the *Sutton* arguments that the '43 million' figure in ADA clearly referred to people with actual substantially limiting physical or mental impairments and not to people protected under the 'record of' or 'regarded as' prongs of the definition.")

"Any person who is disadvantaged by an employer because of a real or imagined physical or mental impairment should be entitled to claim the protection of the statute," Burgdorf continued. "It is not 36, 43, or 160 million people that the statute protects, but the entire 250 million or so people who live in America!"

Justice John Paul Stevens, the other dissenter, suspected the Court had been "cowed by [employers'] persistent argument that viewing all individuals in their unmitigated state will lead to a tidal wave of lawsuits."

The ADA was supposed to apply to all Americans, just like the Civil Rights Act, he wrote in an angry dissent. "Congress... focused almost entirely on the problem of discrimination against African-Americans when it enacted Title VII of the Civil Rights Act of 1964....But that narrow focus could not possibly justify a construction of the statute that excluded Hispanic-Americans or Asian-Americans from its protection — or as we later decided, Caucasians.

"[N]one of the Court's reasoning... justifies a construction of the [Americans with Disabilities] Act that will obviously deprive many of Congress's intended beneficiaries of the legal protection it affords."

But Justice Stevens's convictions failed to sway his fellow Justices. "I could not do my current job, I could not do many other jobs, without my glasses," Justice Antonin Scalia had lectured during the cases' oral arguments. "A lot of Americans wear glasses and couldn't function without them." Yet he did not consider himself disabled, he said. "This statute wasn't meant to apply to all Americans."

Special

> *'Special!' Such a pretty word! But what it*
> *means is 'segregated.'*
> — Cass Irvin

> If a plant is not already equipped with ramps and elevators, it
> may prove too costly to hire workers who can navigate only with
> motorized wheelchairs. But as long as there are other places for
> such people to work, why force the relationship?...Some plants
> could be made accessible to wheelchairs, others to the blind....
> The concentration of workers with specific disabilities, far from
> being seen as handicap ghettoization, will be regarded as a sensible
> effort to economize on public funds.
> — Richard A. Epstein, *Forbidden Grounds*

The real everyday world of public commerce and national discussion did not deal much with disability issues. When it did, it was
under the rubric of "special": special transportation, special education, special institutions, special housing. The "special" solution
was a logical one for a society which saw things in terms of us and
them, which acted as though it believed that anything given to
them necessitated something being taken from us. The case against
disability rights argued that segregating disabled people was an
appropriate response to the disabled's needs. But no one called it
segregation. It was called "special."

"Special" has been our country's sanctioned way of dealing with
disabled people, and a large part of the complaints of those against
disability rights is that many disability rights advocates are no
longer content with special, no longer willing to accept it, even
when others believe it is best for them. This refusal to accept what
has been deemed the appropriate way to deal with disabled peoples' problems is bitterly criticized — it is as if disability advocates
no longer know their place.

Special Transportation

Most of San Diego's handicapped population does not use public transportation, finding private conveyance — usually car or van service — more convenient than either the bus or trolley.

Yet, the Metropolitan Transit Development Board is mandated, under the five-year-old Americans with Disabilities Act, to spend more than $8 million per year — half of which is unfunded — to ensure that each of its 450 transit buses and 70 trolley cars is fully accessible to the physically and mentally disabled.

Now, no one objects to making it as easy as possible for these individuals to get from one place to another. The problem is that the federal mandate forces local government agencies, like the MTDB, to make specified modifications to accommodate the disabled with no consideration of whether there is a more cost-effective way to achieve the same goal.

As Christopher Reeve lay in his hospital bed recovering from surgery, the San Diego *Union-Tribune's* editorial writer was taking on the Americans with Disabilities Act's requirement that disabled people be allowed access to the same public transit systems nondisabled people used. The "unintended result" was that it would cost money — a lot of it.

More cost-effective, said the paper, would be to offer the handicapped a "special" solution. Just like JCDecaux had offered for public toilets in New York City, the San Diego paper thought it more sensible to "provide those of limited means with vouchers that can be used for door-to-door car or van service. Then they would not have to deal with the time, discomfort and inconvenience of commuting by bus or trolley."

The San Diego editorial writer's complaint — and solution — sounded all too familiar to anyone who had watched the fight waged by New York City's disability advocates over access to its buses and subways a decade earlier.

By 1978, wheelchair lifts on public buses had become a federal requirement, thanks to rules written by the Carter Administration. Carter's Transportation Secretary Brock Adams seemed to be taking seriously the 1973 Rehabilitation Act's Section 504, which mandated disability nondiscrimination in programs getting federal dollars. "Transbus," the bus every transit authority would have to buy after 1979 if they wanted federal aid in buying buses, would be accessible to wheelchair users. It was in the works from major bus manufacturers. Federal aid paid for 80 percent of a city's costs for new buses and subway systems; now, when cities bought new buses, said Adams, they'd be buying the accessible Transbus.

The American Public Transit Association, the trade association of the nation's public transit authorities, did not want the Transbus with its lift-outfitted doors. The group insisted it would be better to serve disabled people through paratransit, a separate system of special mini-vans equipped with lifts that would pick up the disabled persons and take them to the doctor or shopping.

On July 13, 1978, Theodore Lutz, General Manager of Washington, D.C.'s Metro system, handed his board an inch-thick document proposing that D.C.'s public transit authority buy 130 lift-equipped Transbuses, each estimated to cost $125,000. Buses that were not accessible reportedly cost a little under $100,000. Rick Dudley of the Paralyzed Veterans of America told the Metro board that the nation "didn't put a price tag on integrating other minority groups into this society." He opposed paratransit, he said. "It is inappropriate when we are offered a segregated service."

APTA said such integration was too costly, that most disabled people didn't want it anyway; they liked paratransit. At a series of Department of Transportation hearings across the nation held to discuss Transbus, APTA made its case again and again: expenditures for making buses accessible would divert money from other, more beneficial projects. Even if buses, subways and commuter trains were all made accessible, 90 percent of the "transportation handicapped" would still have "the inability to get to and from transit stops, the inability to wait out-of-doors, the inability to travel alone or in crowds and the inability to ride while standing." APTA pressed for letting a city's public transit authority have the "local option" of deciding whether to equip its buses with lifts or to offer paratransit instead.

One of the first things Ronald Reagan did once he got into the White House was to give the nod to local option. Segregated "paratransit" would be fine, said Reagan's new rules. All transit companies had to do was to promise to make "special" efforts to serve their "elderly and handicapped." They need spend no more than 3.5 percent of their funds on the effort.

Paratransit fell into the best of the category of special services. It was a program carved off of a regular public service — public transportation — and segregated, made "special" for the disabled. And many disabled people liked it fine. It was like a cab service that picked them up at their door and dropped them where they wanted to go. The problem was not what it did but what it didn't do.

Paratransit was never intended to be a complete service for all the disabled people in a community, but only for those who had been allowed to "sign up." In this way it was a benefit, no longer a true public service. It was a subscription service; and like most things associated with the public management of disabled people's lives, it was medicalized. In most cases it required a doctor's OK.

The transit system designed for the general public was available to anyone who could get onto its generally inaccessible vehicles. Its operators didn't care where you went, when you went or how long you stayed.

Not so with paratransit, whose riders' trips must be approved by the system operator. In many communities, only people who worked, or who used the service for medical needs, were allowed to use the paratransit system. Operators would refuse to take riders who canceled frequently (paratransit rides almost always must be scheduled a week or more in advance).

A paratransit service cannot transport every disabled person in the community; the more riders a paratransit system has, the more expensive it is to operate. Since it's really like a taxi service, every trip involves more gas, more time for drivers. A regular public transit system, on the other hand, has fixed routes and times; therefore its costs are stable. The more riders a fixed-route system has, the cheaper the cost per rider. With paratransit, just the opposite is true.

This is why paratransit operators set criteria for use, why they prefer to transport groups of disabled people from one place to another, why much of their time is spent running groups of people from one place to another: elderly people to nutrition centers or disabled people from special housing complexes to sheltered workshops or special schools.

The reason paratransit was considered a cheaper alternative to public transit was because, in truth, it didn't transport very many people. Most disabled people who used wheelchairs didn't use either the public bus system or the paratransit program: They paid out of their pocket for ambulances when they had to go somewhere, or they stayed home.

For those few lucky disabled people who got approval to be on the subscription service, paratransit could be quite convenient. If you didn't mind calling for your ride a week ahead of time. If you didn't mind coming home at 9 p.m. (or whenever the paratransit director told you you must). If you didn't mind riding for hours while your driver dropped off all the other riders, going first to the eastern suburbs of your city, then to the western suburbs, before taking you to the southern suburbs. Riders of paratransit could easily ride over 100 miles in one trip as they went from one rider's home to another. The convenience of the driver, not the rider, was the factor considered.

At 5:20 p.m. on a Tuesday, Arthur Campbell and Jackie Koch left a peer support group at Louisville's Center for Accessible Living. They'd both called TARCLift, the city's paratransit service, days earlier to reserve 5:30 rides home from the Center. Since Koch and Campbell lived in the same apartment complex, they figured one bus would be sent for both of them.

A while later, a lift-equipped minibus pulled up. As Koch was boarding it, a second minibus arrived. Its driver, Steve Jordan, called out to Koch that she was getting on the wrong bus; that his bus had come for her. She should get off the bus she was boarding, he told her, and get on his bus.

Koch got off the first bus and prepared to board the second bus, but its lift wouldn't work.

"Don't you move!" Jordan told Koch sternly. "I'm going after another bus." With that, the second bus left.

Campbell waited with Koch. The first bus — the one that had come for Campbell — waited for Campbell. Ten minutes passed. Finally, Campbell got irritated with the wait, and told Koch to get on "his" bus. As she was boarding a second time, Jordan returned with a new bus — the third on the scene.

"I told you not to move!" he shouted at Koch, seeing her preparing to board the first bus. "If I tell you to do something, I mean it!"

Jordan then told her that if she didn't listen to him, he would "have to stop picking her up."

The two drivers got together and talked, then told Koch and Campbell they'd decided to let the two ride the same bus. But which bus? The drivers decided it would be the first bus. The third bus left. It was now 5:45.

So Koch began the process of boarding again. The lift failed to work.

The first bus driver radioed Jordan and asked him to return. Five minutes later, the third bus arrived again.

When Koch and Campbell began to board this third bus, they discovered its lift wouldn't work, either.

At 5:55, a fourth bus pulled up. Koch and Campbell assumed it was for them and went over to get on. But the driver stopped them. "Oh, no, this isn't your bus. This bus is for Cass!" (Cass Irvin was scheduled to be picked up at 6:30.)

By this time, the driver of a large fixed-route bus sitting on nearby 8th Street at the end of his route had gotten curious about the four "handicapped buses" and come over. The drivers began talking among themselves.

Campbell, angry, went back into the Center, hoping to find a staff member who would write up a disciplinary report on Jordan. Finding no one, he came back.

The drivers called station headquarters and yet another bus — the fifth "special bus" — was sent to the scene.

When it arrived, Campbell and Koch boarded without incident, and the first bus driver took them home. They left the Center at 6:10 and got home — nine blocks away — a full hour and five buses later.

Before "local option" had become enshrined as law, New York City's Eastern Paralyzed Veterans Association had sued the Metropolitan Transit Authority over lifts on buses. And MTA Chair Harold Fisher had admitted to *The New York Times* that it was true that there was no publicly-operated transportation service in New York City for disabled people — neither accessible mass transit nor paratransit. But Fisher said the separate paratransit system would be better than the lifts on bus routes that the EPVA was suing for: it didn't cost as much. It would simply be too expensive, he said, to make public transit accessible.

By the late 1970s, the city of New York had finally bought some buses with lifts. Buses with lifts were running on 39 routes spread over the entire five-borough metropolitan area.

Only one route operated in Queens. That was the route Ellen Nuzzi kept trying to use to get back and forth to work at Long Island University.

Sometimes a bus with a lift came by; more often the bus pulling up at Nuzzi's stop had no lift.

Sometimes the lifts worked, sometimes they didn't. Sometimes the drivers knew how to operate them. Mostly they didn't.

Not infrequently, the driver of a lift-outfitted bus, seeing Nuzzi sitting at the bus stop in her wheelchair, would simply fail to stop altogether, leaving her and the others stranded. One day a dozen buses came and went at Nuzzi's stop, some with no lifts, others with lifts refusing to stop. Another day when Nuzzi boarded a lift bus, the driver, believing her wheelchair unsafe for other passengers, ordered her off. She refused to leave; sitting on the bus in her wheelchair until the driver, a long time later, reluctantly agreed to drive on with her as a passenger.

People on the bus called her selfish, she said. She did not see it that way. She rode the bus, she said, to make it easier for others in wheelchairs; to get bus drivers used to picking up people with their lifts. Besides, other people on that bus, unlike her, had the choice of taking other transportation or even another bus. But she had no other option. She needed a bus with a lift.

Nuzzi was not hailed as a hero like Rosa Parks, who had refused to give up her seat to a white woman, sparking the Montgomery bus boycott that would light the national fire of a civil rights movement. Nuzzi was simply called selfish.

When in 1979 the Eastern Paralyzed Veterans Association again sued New York's MTA, this time for planning to spend public funds on subway stations without making them accessible, they used the state's human rights law, which, nearly two decades before the Americans with Disabilities Act, had made it illegal to keep a disabled person from a public accommodation such as a bus or subway. From its bully pulpit, *The New York Times* editorialized on the wrongheadedness of giving disabled people access to the same facilities — in this case subways — the rest of the public enjoyed.

"After years of dirt and decay," wrote *The Times,* "the Metropolitan Transportation Authority finally has the money and the management to start remodeling New York City's subway stations — but can't. There's a wheelchair on the tracks." *The Times* fingered the state law as the problem: it had "stymied efforts to begin modernization on subway stations" with its requirement that disabled people be given access to public accommodations. Governor Cuomo, though he recognized "the tremendous cost of installing elevators or escalators in subway stations," refused "to recommend a change in the law."

It was the first verse of a song that *The Times* never tired of singing (another verse was sung when the JCDecaux company proposed inaccessible public toilet kiosks a decade later): Disabled people were causing problems for everybody with their laws requiring access. Officials should make exceptions for the city, grant waivers, find a way around the law. The law was misguided.

EPVA attorney James Weisman was unrepentant. "Once they decide to do something for the public, they have to remember who the public is," Weisman insisted to the *The Times.* "It is not just people who walk. There is no way you can spend $8 billion rebuilding the subways and ignore the needs of the handicapped."

When New York State Supreme Court justice Ernest H. Rosenberger ruled that renovations planned for 50 subway stations could not go forward without provisions for wheelchair access — meaning elevators — *The Times* was livid. "It's possible to sympathize with the desire for personal mobility without considering it a natural right unlimited by public cost," it lectured from its editorial page.

The disabled could "not prove that station elevators, average cost $1 million, will be used enough to justify the expenditure," it railed. "There are now 1,362 city buses on 54 routes equipped with wheelchair elevators. The next question is, how many disabled people use them? About 10 to 20 a day." An earlier story in *The Times* had reported that EPVA and the MTA had "not even been able to agree on the number of disabled people who might use the subways if they were accessible. The veterans say there would be as many as 117,000; the M.T.A. says there would be no more than 23,000." Alan G. Hevesi, the deputy majority leader the New York State Assembly, would tell reporters, "You're talking about hundreds of thousands of people who have mobility problems, not just those who are wheelchair bound," and later gave the figure of "350,000 people."

The New York Times did not accept any of those figures. "The subways in Washington "carry 29 disabled people a day, those in Atlanta carry five, though they were designed to be accessible."

"While elevators might benefit some," MTA chairman Richard Ravitch insisted, "it would be at a cost per ride that cannot be justified on any rational basis." Besides, the MTA argued in the paper, having disabled people on subways would be "dangerous." It did not elaborate.

"There's another, superior way to give mobility to the disabled," purred *The Times;* "special buses reserved for them alone." They were called "paratransit," *The Times* told its readers.

"There is no way that a door-to-door demand service is going to pick up large numbers of people and take them to work at 9 a.m. and take them home at 5," Weisman retorted. *The Times* insisted that the state legislature was "sympathetic" to access only because the organized disabled had convinced them that "the subway elevators would somehow end up paying for themselves — by making disabled people more mobile, more employable and thus more likely to pay more in the way of taxes."

Access would end up costing the city $2,000 a ride, said *The Times*. It was "an admirable idea" but "sumptuously impractical" for subways. *The Times* thought paratransit was "a very good public policy alternative" — "one that for $10 or $12 a ride can give disabled people door-to-door mobility" with "vans fitted for wheelchairs and dispatched like radio cabs."

Despite what *The Times* thought, paratransit was not the same as an accessible public transit system. But it was true that many disabled people wanted it. For all the tradeoffs — having to call a week or more in advance, having to let the bus company decide if your trip is "justified," having to ride around for several hours sometimes while the driver drops someone else off — paratransit in many ways plays into the view that disabled people can't handle something as rough and ready as mass transit. They need to be assisted by a special driver who knows their "condition." They need to be helped out of their home. They like a service that knows them by name; not a jostling rush-hour bus driver who barks at them to get out their change and get on the bus and don't block the aisle! which non-disabled people contend with riding home on the bus every day from work.

Disabled people have been conditioned to special services. Most accept them, even though they are far less satisfactory, and are not at all equal, or even equivalent, to services that the nondisabled public enjoys. But many disabled people believe that "special" services are better for them, and are their right.

"You have rights when you're disabled," a disabled activist once said. "Just not the same rights."

" 'Special!' Such a pretty word!" Cass Irvin had said. "But what it means is 'segregated.' "

Providing a "special solution for the handicapped" has been the typical response to disability in modern U.S. society — to segregate it, separate it, us from them, to make them go away and leave us alone.

Special buses. Special Olympics. Very Special Arts. Special education. No matter whether proposed out of genuine if misguided caring or for more selfish motives, it is always very clear, although we don't use the words, that "special" means segregated. Special solutions isolate disabled people from normal society, and nobody pretends they don't. But few seemed to think it should be upsetting to the organized disabled; when they complained they were called selfish. Or unrealistic.

Some of those who believe that "special" is the correct solution to the disability problem come by that belief from a generous heart. They believe someone disabled has problems that are different, perhaps unique; they believe that such an individual needs special, extra services or assistance. Almost always, such people see the disabled person's problems as being of a personal, medical nature, stemming wholly from their disability. They need help, assistance. They need something that likely wouldn't work for the rest of society — something special that works for them and their very different needs.

Although it was alarmingly reminiscent of the problem that had led to the lawsuit that resulted in Decaux's proposal for the coin-operated toilet kiosks, Suzanne Davis of the Kaplan Fund said the special toilets Decaux was proposing for the disabled would be kept locked, opened only when one contacted the person who had the key. Locked subway toilets had been the original problem; no one could ever use them. Now Decaux was proposing a locked-toilet solution for the disabled — but it seemed to occur to no one that this would be a problem. Because it was "special" no one questioned whether it would work well or not; that, perhaps, simply didn't seem important. What was important was that if it was locked it would appear "safe." To the public, that is. To the disabled person who could not find an attendant with a key, it was anything but safe, but that seemed a minor detail that no one other than the organized disabled worried overly much about.

Special education

"Can society afford to spend more on disabled children than it does on others?" *The Dallas Morning News* was talking about special education.

In the debate over special education, one can clearly hear the "they are hurting us" complaint. Special education students could cost almost three times more than the cost to educate other students, *Morning News* reporter Laurie Wilson wrote. Students with severe disabilities could drain the budget. The 1975 law now known as the Individuals with Disabilities Education Act had authorized the federal government to pay up to 40 percent of the average per-pupil expenditure for each child in special education. But Congress had never come up with the money. The federal contribution had never reached more than 8 percent.

An article in the Minneapolis *Star Tribune* a few months earlier (and a few month after Stossel's "The Blame Game" had aired) made similar points. "In the Anoka-Hennepin School District, a couple fight to get their retarded son a fitness program at the family's private health club. They win. In Minneapolis, the parents of a 9-year-old with visual impairments demand and get a $500 tandem bike so she can ride with other children for 'peer interaction.' A week later the family moves. The district is stuck with the bike." Like Stossel and Bovard, reporters Rob Hotakainen and Mary Jane Smetanka's stories showed greedy people who it was clear were taking more than they should. Because of people with "special needs" like these, "special education" in Minnesota had become "a $602 million-a-year empire that is choking taxpayers, crippling school budgets and creating a sorry competition."

> Special education takes a hidden toll. It consumes all of the aid school districts receive for special education and, when that's gone, requires districts to quietly siphon away money that is needed for other purposes.

"The Blame Game" had fingered people who simply claimed disability so they could get something for nothing. Using the same theme, Hotakainen and Smetanka wrote that "the number of children getting special help for emotional and behavioral disorders has more than tripled since 1980 and now tops 15,000." How much of our limited resources were we going to invest in these students "at the increased expense of other students?" Minnesota Rural Education Association director Vernae Hasbargen wanted to know.

"When the government wrote the IDEA, they didn't provide for a way out for states that couldn't afford the costs," Larry Bartlett, an attorney and professor of educational administration at the University of Iowa, told Wilson. "They didn't think about the most expensive kids. They obviously didn't consider an autistic child could cost $150,000. Congress didn't know the parameters of what they were getting into.

"No one is suggesting that disabled children should not be cared for," Wilson wrote, beginning with the obligatory disclaimer. "They are questioning whether expensive specialists should be provided for children who likely will need care all their lives."

Education was an investment in society's future, and what was the point of spending money on severely disabled students? They'd bring little return on investment, said Myron Lieberman, head of the conservative free-market Education Policy Institute. One had to look at the cost-benefit issues, he argued. "Special education should not be regarded as a black hole into which we pour large amounts of money without any idea of the expected or actual return."

The other problem, wrote Hotakainen and Smetanka, was integration. "Thousands of children with serious disabilities are moving into regular classrooms, forcing schools to hire hundreds of aides to care for them."

Teacher unions complained that "special education" students in "regular classrooms" caused problems: the children were sick; they needed "medical services" like catheterization or tracheostomy suctioning; they couldn't do typical classroom work. Teachers didn't like sharing classrooms with "resource" teachers there to assist the disabled child, either.

Commentator John Leo insisted that the mainstreaming of

"very serious cases," as he called them, was simply a way for schools to "save millions" by "dumping these students into regular classes without providing the support of expensive aides and special teachers."

Before the 1975 law passed, nearly two million students were excluded from public schools because of disabilities; over three million more received only the most minimal of educations. Many states had laws excluding blind or deaf children, or those labeled "emotionally disturbed" or "mentally retarded"; the District of Columbia legally excluded any child "deemed to be unable to benefit physically or mentally from school" (almost 200,000 school-age children with mental retardation or emotional disabilities were institutionalized). Schools could, and did, tell parents that their disabled child in a wheelchair simply couldn't come to school, and there was no recourse.

Congress passed the 1975 law overwhelmingly. It guaranteed a "free and appropriate public education" to any disabled child, saying that the child's education must be individually designed and the child be taught with peers — in the "least restrictive environment." Yet a 2000 report on nationwide compliance showed that in three-fourths of the nation, integrated education was the exception rather than the rule.

Many parents distrusted a school system putting their disabled child in a classroom of nondisabled kids who would make fun of her. Many wanted special classes. The word "segregated" wasn't used, though — when it was, it was put in quotes, sometimes by editors, to signal that it didn't, after all, mean the same thing as real, racial segregation. *Newsday's* Jerry Markon, writing that "federal officials have for years warned New York that it places too many children in special education and 'segregates' children from their non-disabled peers more than any other state," put quotes around "segregates" to indicate it was not the usual, typical use of the word, that it was not real segregation like racial segregation was.

At Sam Houston high school in Arlington, Texas, Brandie Bell was being "mainstreamed." Yet the 16-year-old, who used a wheelchair, found herself for most of the day attending classes along only one hallway. That hallway was separated from the rest of the school by glass doors. She didn't have lunch with the regular students either. To protect her from the jostle and bustle of a high-school lunch period, Sam Houston High made sure she and the other special students ate lunch earlier, by themselves.

One school, segregated classes, segregated lunch hour: this was Arlington, Texas's "inclusion" policy.

Before it was closed for good, Brandie had attended school at the Veda Knox school "for the profoundly disabled." It had been closed after the 1975 federal law said such separate education was illegal. And yet segregation went on. It was not called "segregation" but "special."

Arlington's approach to a "free appropriate public education" for children who had disabilities was like that of communities in over three-fourths of our nation. New York had a larger percentage of special education students in segregated settings ("isolated" was the word officials used) than any other state. Yet when proposals were made for moving children into integrated classrooms, school officials balked: their districts might lose money. The formula that dispensed separate, legally mandated special education money to school districts was based solely on the percentage of time each day a student spent in segregated, special-education-only classes.

The formula, giving districts from two to three times the aid for a regular education student, seemed to have been arrived at by means of a guess: "it was probably twice as expensive" to educate a "special education" student. The formula had been in place since 1980 with virtually no changes; critics said it gave local school officials an incentive to put children into isolated "special education" classes, in defiance of the federal law's "least restrictive environment" requirement.

Congress had pledged to pay 40 percent of the cost of educating disabled students, but has never done so. Critics charged that schools spent $15,000 per pupil a year on average, compared with

$5,000 a year "per healthy student." Washington spent under $5 billion in 1999 to carry out the law — $688 per child — "only a tiny fraction of the $50-plus billion a year schools spent on special needs children," wrote Scripps-Howard News Service's Mary Deibel.

The rest of the money came from state and local education coffers. Ohio schools spent $1.6 billion in 1998 on 230,000 "special education" students, only $120 million of it federal money. In Minnesota as around the nation, spending for "special education" increased at a much faster rate than spending for "normal" pupils. From 1982 to 1992, Minnesota's spending on "special education" went from under $227 million to $602 million, although state and federal aid increased by less than $112 million. The difference came from local school district coffers. In 1995, special-education spending hit $1.1 billion and accounted for more than a fifth of all school spending in the state. A reporter noted that Minnesota schools spent more than $12,000 a year on a "special education" child, more than twice what was spent on a nondisabled child.

A Missouri state law passed in the 1980s in backlash fervor said that "no additional funds would be provided for special education." Local school districts were forced to dig into reserves to pay for special education, which was considered a prime unfunded mandate.

Special education had been designed "to provide kids with equality in school," but the balance had gone "way overboard," a Massachusetts special education administrator told reporters. "Parents of regular education students...perceive that special education students are getting special treatment from transportation to discipline."

Special education teachers in New York were reportedly required to be certified in neither academic subjects nor reading; state officials continued to exempt special education from the "more rigorous academic requirements required of regular education students."

Per-pupil expenditures for special education students in Baltimore in 1996 averaged $8,940, complained the *Baltimore*

Sun, compared with the average for all students of $5,873. Severely disabled "special education" students in Maryland were required by state law to be taught in class sizes as small as six; in Baltimore, this translated into nearly three out of 10 of the city's 6,000 teachers being assigned to "special education" students.

Special education took money away from normal children and gave it to disabled children. One child's transportation needs could throw an entire school system into disarray. One child in Boston had reportedly cost the district $29,000 for travel to an out-of-district school called for in her Individualized Education Plan.

"There is no exclusion at Sam Houston High School," principal Ricky Kempe told the *Arlington Morning News*. The school included the disabled students in every activity "suitable for them — everything from pep rallies to guest speakers." They ate lunch by themselves, he said, so they could be "assisted as necessary." "Our regular education kids, especially the student council, spend time with the special education students," he insisted. "All our students love those kids."

If the segregation — "lack of inclusion," it's called — angered people, it wasn't because of the segregation so much as the money involved.

In San Diego, students like Frankie Husson, who had Down syndrome, rode on the special bus for three hours a day going to special education programs in special designated schools in the district, apart from regular students — what Maryland Disability Law Center attorney Winifred DePalma called the national practice of "consigning a really large number of kids to a setting where educational expectations are so minimal as to be nonexistent." In Baltimore, millions of dollars were spent yearly transporting students to one of 10 city schools devoted to special education, or to private residential or day school programs.

"When I was in school, the crazy kids took the little bus to class," comedian Chris Rock said on his stand-up comedy special on Home Box Office. "And they got out at 2:30, just in case they went a little crazy."

A group of special education students in a Georgia town, afraid of being teased, hid out at the end of each school day until all the regular school buses had left with their loads of "normal" students — so they wouldn't be seen boarding the smaller "special" buses.

Institutionalization and 'special housing'

At the time of the passage of the ADA, states still had laws on the books requiring people with mental disabilities to be institutionalized. Not even slaves had been so restricted.

"Spurred by the eugenics movement," write legal historians Morton Horwitz, Martha Field and Martha Minow, "every state in the country passed laws that singled out people with mental or physical disabilities for institutionalization." The laws

> made it clear that the state's purpose was not to benefit disabled people but to segregate them from "normal" society. Thus, statutes noted that the disabled were segregated and institutionalized for being a "menace to society" [and] so that "society [might be] relieved from the heavy economic and moral losses arising from the existence at large of these unfortunate persons."

"The state of Washington made it a crime for a parent to refuse state-ordered institutionalization," they wrote; "once children were institutionalized, many state laws required parents to waive all custody rights."

Justice Thurgood Marshall wrote in the 1985 *Cleburne* Supreme Court decision (the decision saying that people with mental retardation did not constitute a "discrete and insular" minority) that this "regime of state-mandated segregation and degradation [had] in its virulence and bigotry rivaled, and indeed paralleled, the worst excesses of Jim Crow. Massive custodial institutions were built to warehouse the retarded for life." Yet they continue today. In 1999, the Supreme Court in its *Olmstead* decision acknowledged that the ADA did in fact require states to provide services to people with disabilities in the "most integrated setting"; but institutionalization continued, because federal funds — Medicaid, mostly — had a built-in "institutional bias," the result of savvy lobbying over the years by owners of institutions like nursing homes: In no state could one be denied a "bed" in a nursing home, but in only a few states could one use those same Medicaid dollars to get services in one's home that were usually much less expensive.

Ongoing battles were waged to close down the institutions, to allow the people in them to live on their own or in small group settings. But parents often fought to keep them open. When they did close, other special facilities cropped up.

Despite opposition from the state's organized disabled, Illinois Governor George Ryan in 2001 approved $4 million for the construction of a four-building, 64-bed, 20-acre campus for people with "developmental" disabilities, run by Marklund, a for-profit company which at the time ran institutions in a number of Illinois communities. Critics charged that the "campuses," as they were now called, not only segregated disabled people but also siphoned money away from programs that helped people who were living in their own home to get supports like in-home help.

Syndicated commentator Mort Crim praised such places. "Special folks have special town," ran the headline to his piece in the June 13, 2001 *Detroit Free Press*. Writing about what he called an "incredible community in central New York" — Pathfinder Village — "created 20 years ago as the nation's only lifelong residential community for people with Down syndrome" — he said it gave its residents "independence, self-esteem and confidence." Crim seemed either not to notice its segregation or to see nothing wrong with it.

Pennsylvania's Western Center at one time housed over 750 people with "developmental" disabilities. It was closed in 2000, a decade after the ADA had become law, its remaining residents moved to homes in the community or to other institutions to wait for "community placement." Although the move to deinstitutionalization had begun in the 1960s in the wake of findings of abuse and horrid conditions in the large warehouses — people tied to beds, lying in their own feces; people covered with bruises and abrasions from beatings; people with sores infested with maggots — those who should have been most horrified at the conditions, the parents of those who were kept there, often fought to keep them open.

Critics charged that the parents simply wanted them open so they would not have to deal with offspring they saw only as burdens, that this was why they had put them there in the first place.

It was a fact that those wanting to keep the warehouses open were invariably the families of the people who were housed in them. The families downplayed the reports of abuse and foul conditions. Just as officials had insisted the special New York streetside toilets be kept locked for the safety of the disabled, the families worried that life in "the community" (which was how the organized disabled referred to the move to have such people live in small groups of three or four in a neighborhood, with helpers) would be unsafe for their offspring.

The Department of Justice was charged with enforcing the 1980 Civil Rights of Institutionalized Persons Act, but did little. Poor enforcement had led to Congressional investigations in 1983 and 1985; in a 1984 issue of the *Nebraska Law Review*, Robert Dinerstein wrote that "as a result of ...its utter failure to enforce CRIPA, The Department of Justice has manifestly failed to extend to institutionalized disabled persons the rights that are properly theirs." John Kip Cornwell, writing in the November 1987 *Yale Law Review*, leveled similar charges, as did the University of Minnesota's Mary Hayden in 1998, over a decade later. She said the DOJ relied too much on conciliation, showing "solicitousness for the prerogatives of state officials or parents who support institutionalization" rather than for the people who were being kept in the institutions.

In 1987 and again in 1990 the DOJ "formally advised Pennsylvania officials of 'deficient conditions' at its Ebensberg Center institution" — conditions that included inmates being blinded, getting gangrene from untreated wounds, infested with maggots, bitten by ants — but it took the DOJ five years to finally sue the institution.

DOJ took too few CRIPA cases and took too long to take the few cases it did. It accepted consent decrees and settlement agreements that did "not fully reflect and implement the rights of institution residents."

Residents in state institutions were also supposed to be protected under Title II of the ADA, which contained what advocates
referred to as an integration mandate: "A public entity shall admin-
ister services, programs, and activities in the most integrated setting appropriate to the needs of qualified individuals with disabilities," said the ADA. Investigations of Title II complaints fell under
the jurisdiction of the Office of Civil Rights at the Department of
Health and Human Services; the DOJ couldn't sue a state unless
it got a referral from HHS. In the ten years following passage of
the ADA, HHS had made no referrals.

Lois Curtis's and Elaine Wilson's attorneys had used Title II of
the Americans with Disabilities Act to sue Georgia Mental Health
Commissioner Tommy Olmstead when state policy would not
allow the women's Medicaid funds to be used to pay for help for
them in the community. Georgia's rules said the two women, who
had a history of mental illness, could get assistance only if they
lived in an institution. The Supreme Court agreed with the women
and ruled that "the unnecessary segregation of individuals with
disabilities in institutions *may* [italics ours] constitute discrimination based on disability"; that "the Americans with Disabilities Act
may require states to provide community-based services rather
than institutional placements for individuals with disabilities."

Note, however, that the Court used the word "may," not
"does." Like almost every Supreme Court decision relating to disability rights, the *Olmstead* decision was not unequivocal; there
might be some instances, said the Court, when it would be appropriate, necessary, to put people in institutions whether they wanted to be there or not. "[T]he states' need to maintain a range of
facilities for the care and treatment of individuals with diverse mental disabilities must be recognized." That might very well have to
do with money, said the Court. With disability, rights were usually allowed only when it was cost-effective to do so.

This view was supported by the DOJ, who, in arguing the case
before the Court, had brought up the "financial burden" defense,

and had also suggested to the Court the reasoning, which ultimately made it into the ruling, that "if there is disagreement about the need to institutionalize a particular person, the courts should defer to the state's treatment professionals."

Almost everyone — even states, in most instances — would argue that it was cheaper to provide services to people when they were living in their own homes, rather than having to keep open a large institution. Medicaid figures and countless studies said institutionalization was anywhere from three to four times more expensive. Yet critics of deinstitutionalization pointed out that while yes, it might be cheaper for the state to pay for services for a given individual allowed to live in her own home, that was not always the case. It depended on what the person was thought to need. For some people — someone believed to need constant supervision, or restraints, to prevent them from being a danger to themselves, for example — it was considered cheaper for the state to keep them in an institution. Officials also felt that if they made it a policy to pay for services so people could live on their own, where they wanted to, so many people would then want those services that, even were the services cheaper per person, the aggregate cost to the state would skyrocket, because people would "come out of the woodwork" asking for services — people who now stayed away from the system completely, fearing institutionalization. If services were more humane and attractive, in other words, too many people would want them.

In the *Olmstead* decision, the Court said only that states might have their financial reasons for wanting to institutionalize people. Under the ADA, said the Court, that was OK.

Parents of those who were kept in the Western Center used the *Olmstead* decision when they sued. The decision, they said, also required states to keep institutions open for people who were considered "inappropriate" for community living.

The National Association of Homebuilders liked special housing. Managers and owners of "seniors housing" complexes made up a portion of NAHB membership. Throughout the 1990s, the

NAHB and its chapters opposed mandates for access in "regular" homes. Access should not be legislated but market-driven, it insisted. The group claimed the third largest trade association political action committee in the country, and it systematically worked to prevent the passage of any legislation that might mandate any access feature in housing, no matter how minor.

In a February 5, 1998 letter to Georgia state representative Jim Martin, Jerry Ronter, president of the Georgia NAHB affiliate, complained about the proposed Basic Bathrooms Standard Act, an effort by Georgia disability activists to get minimum access features into single-family homes. The bill required only that new single-family homes have one bathroom on the main floor large enough to get into using a wheelchair, and bathroom walls reinforced to support grab bars, should they ever be needed. Still, the Association opposed it. "The Home Builders Association of Georgia, representing more than 9,800 member companies, adamantly opposes the passage of HB 1277 and any other similarly mandated legislation," wrote Ronter. He called the bill "well-intentioned but misguided." Ronter contended that private property rights would be harmed; that it would raise home costs.

The term "mandated legislation" was often used by the NAHB. It fought similar access bills in Texas and Illinois. It had fought the Americans with Disabilities Act and the Fair Housing Act. When HUD commissioned a booklet explaining the access requirements of the 1988 Fair Housing Act, NAHB went to Maryland Senator Barbara Mikulski to press that the booklets be destroyed.

"The way to do it is not through legislation," admonished NAHB legal counsel Rhonda Daniels. "It's a marketing issue. If there's a market demand, the builders will provide for that. A mandatory across-the-board requirement is not where the market is."

"Handicapped units" were not easy to rent, Robert V. Jones Co. attorney Herb told the *Las Vegas Business Press*. Waldman contended there weren't "enough handicapped people to occupy them." HUD had taken action against the Rock Creek Manor development, which HUD said was inaccessible in violation of the

Fair Housing Act. Unlike most disability rights laws, the Fair Housing Act, which was not a disability rights law but a civil rights law whose protections had been extended to people with disabilities in its 1988 amendments, did contain federal enforcement provisions. But in Waldman's view, federal enforcement of housing access was "out of sync with market realities."

Providing adequate space for wheelchairs in homes meant "that either the floor space devoted to other uses such as living rooms, dining rooms, bedrooms, and closets must be reduced or that the overall floor space must be increased. If space is added to kitchens and bathrooms [it is] at the expense of other rooms." The "adaptive design" would likely make the home "less comfortable for and desirable to the nondisabled. For example, requiring that all light switches, outlets, and thermostats be moved to heights convenient for wheelchair users may make them uncomfortable and unsightly for everyone else."

The lure of 'special'

People don't seem to see "special" for the segregation it is — perhaps because it is called "special."

Special Olympics has its "professional huggers." Sam Houston High School "loved" its disabled students. Like Sam Houston's perhaps well-intentioned but misguided belief that disabled children were better protected in their own part of the school, parents wanted to protect their disabled children by keeping them in classes "with their own kind." Ellen Schneider of Revere, Mass. told a reporter she feared son Mark would be taken advantage of at Revere High School because he was "so trusting."

Many parents wanted "special" for other reasons. Tricia Crane told *the Los Angeles Times* she withdrew 7-year-old son Rhys from his neighborhood public school when the district refused to put him in a special class for children with learning disabilities. She felt he needed more services than the integrated classroom setting provided. More parents were suing, using the Individuals with Disabilities Education Act, to get special services they said their children needed but public schools either would not or could not provide. Like most disability rights laws, there was no federal enforcement mechanism built into the IDEA; enforcement was up to parents, who, in order to get the law taken seriously by some school districts, had to initiate formal complaints or file lawsuits.

Using special education seemed to some parents a valid way to get things you knew your child needed for her education. If the label "disabled" came with it, then so be it. As Holliston, Mass. special education administrator Margaret Reed saw it, it was "far easier for parents to say their child has a disability than to say the child is a slow learner." That was one way of looking at it. Another way, though, was to look at the right the IDEA gave children and their parents. It was, in truth, a right every child in America ought to have: the right to a free, *appropriate* public education.

Mark Belyea, who grew up in Boston, remembered the stigma of being dyslexic in Boston's school. Now three of his children were in special education programs in a city north of Boston. Kathy Belyea told a reporter: "Special education is what is best for our children. It's going to help them get ahead in the long run."

People seek out "special" because it promises assistance in the form of accommodation, assistance individually tailored to meet individual needs. That is both its saving vision and its mistake. Running through the history of disability rights efforts is the thread of "individually designed" solutions: a wonderful idea that is inevitably doomed to run a collision course with public policy, which is designed for the masses: the masses who must fit its mold, not the other way around. When it came to people in that range of abilities we've designated as normal, even though variation occurred, it was variation not at extremes but in the vast middle. Door into the store a little heavy? Yeah, it might be uncomfortable, but most shoppers could handle it. It was only when people whose bodies fell outside this accepted range called "normal" began to demand that they, too, should be able to shop at this same store (the store whose heavy door had never slowed down the "regular shopper," even though everyone knew it was heavy) that problems arose, because then, the store owner had to change something. For people in the vast middle ranges of physical and mental capabilities in our society, it was simply accepted that one accommodated to whatever was there: a heavy door, a rather steep step, a sign in print so small you had to squint, a complicated instructional sign. It wasn't ideal, but it wasn't a problem — or, if it was a problem, it wasn't an insurmountable one. For the truly disabled, the problems with the door, the step, the tiny print, the incomprehensible sign, were insurmountable. Then the tables turned: At that point it was no longer the individual who had to accommodate to society, which was how it was expected to be (although we never really articulated this); now the society would have to change if it were to accommodate these truly disabled people, because they could not, simply *could* not, accommodate to the already-built environment, which was simply inaccessible to them.

Yet in our society, variation at the extremes was ignored, not accommodated. It was those people at the extremes that we wanted to simply go away. We wanted them to quit clamoring for society to change itself to accommodate them.

Disability rights movement adherents insisted that society was simply looking at the problem wrong. The right way to understand human ability is this, they said: Everyone has individual circumstances that can be best met by individually tailored solutions. This concept crops up again and again in disability rights law, and it works only because lawmakers understand that people who have disabilities, for whom they are passing the laws, are "special." In fact, disability advocates who help shape the laws, although they say that disability is widespread in society (a fact that those against disability rights dispute) also act as though the truly disabled are a tiny number, a number whose needs can be met individually. They say it does not cost a great deal; that costs are exaggerated, that meeting individual needs requires thinking but often can be done very inexpensively. It is this argument that has been rejected out of hand as ludicrous by those who argue the case against disability rights. But who is correct?

It is because parents wanted the best for their severely disabled child that they pressed in the 1960s and '70s for "special education" — to them, it meant getting their child the extra help he needed; the individualized way of teaching him that would help him learn best. My child's intelligence was fine, but he needed a voice output computer; he needed a keyboard adapted to typing with one finger. This was a different keyboard than my friend Anita's daughter needed. She could use a typical keyboard on a computer, but Josie needed a distraction-free environment to ensure that she could concentrate. Her need was different from my son Fred's need. Both, we said, had a right to a "free appropriate public education," but it couldn't be delivered identically or it wouldn't work for either of them. While neither child's disability was unique, it was in fact unique in the fifth-grade classroom of our neighborhood elementary school.

Most disabled people like paratransit. As one disability advocate described it years ago, it was the kind of service whose promise would make it attractive to anyone, disabled or nondisabled. It was a taxi service — a public one, free to the rider. "Go up and down the street," he said. "Just ask anyone you see walking around: 'Would you like it if the bus company would pick you up at your house and take you directly to where you want to go?' Who would say 'no'?" he asked.

But the rub of "special" was that it did not — often could not — deliver on its promise of individual solutions. It met the same fate all segregated programs met: because it was not seen as for "us" but for "them," it was resented. Any money put into it was seen as taking from us. It was stigmatized.

Those pressing the case against disability rights were fond of saying that the laws were "good intentions gone awry." In the case of "special" this seemed, unfortunately, true. But it seemed no one really examined why this was. They erroneously thought it had to do with people wanting more than they had a right to.

Although he called himself "wheelchair bound," David Klot was against the "expensive conversion" of subway stations, he told *The New York Times*. He thought the idea of giving disabled people vouchers to take taxis at reduced prices was a good idea.

Many disabled people who couldn't climb onto buses clung to

the belief that they couldn't ride them, even if they had had lifts. The snow might be too deep in the streets. They were nervous about getting out there in the cold and waiting. They were afraid something would happen. Many couldn't get to the bus stops because they couldn't get up and down the curbs on the sidewalks. The arguments weren't difficult to fathom; they were the very arguments the American Public Transit Association used to insist, perhaps not incorrectly, that most disabled people preferred special paratransit. Disabled people had to be convinced of their right to ride the public's buses, said disability rights organizers.

People often seem genuinely surprised when they learn that not all disabled people are happy with special. Public officials get particularly testy when the organized disabled complain about it.

Nowhere can this debate be seen more clearly than with paratransit, in which competing factions of the organized disabled managed to get provisions into the ADA that required not only that transit systems be made accessible, but that a city's transit authority *also* provide paratransit — ostensibly only to those who cannot make use of even accessible buses and subways, but in fact to any disabled person who has successfully lobbied to be given the OK to ride the special vans. And now that transit authorities by law can buy only mass transit vehicles that are accessible, it is they who are fighting against having to provide paratransit. In a 180-degree turn from their stand in the 1980s, they can be heard to complain that it's too expensive to provide paratransit; that disabled people should be using the regular system, which, they insist, is, after all, accessible.

There is a lesson in this, but we as a nation have not paid any attention to it as yet.

Both the disabled person who wants a paratransit ride and the parent who insists on "special education" for his child are seeking accommodation. They cannot conceive of it occurring without being "special."

What do they believe they are getting with "special"?

Paratransit offers protection from the hustle and bustle; the waiting at the bus stop. It's noncompetitive, easy. That you have to decide a week in advance where you want to go is a tradeoff many people are willing to make. What most of us would regard as an insufferable infringement on our "right to be abroad in the land" (as blind jurist Jacobus TenBroek put it) may not bother someone whose whole life has been a lesson in being a "patient," as the word so usefully means. The tradeoff? Personal attention, someone picking you up at your door, staying with you, helping you at the end. For some people afraid to join the mainstream, this is a "no-brainer."

No public transit service has ever deemed it their role as a nondiscriminating public agency to provide boarding assistance and help with directions, with maps and verbal guidance on and off buses at the correct stops — there has never been any alternative offered: for people who have cognitive impairments, it's special paratransit or stay home. Is it fair? No. Is it public? No. Is it special? Yes. Is it seen as the "appropriate solution" for what is perceived as a problematic group of people? Yes. Other options — city buses that work for people who are blind or cognitively disabled — have never been seriously entertained.

When law professor Sherry Colb took the 1991 New York State Bar exam, she ran into "special."

Colb, who would likely not qualify as "disabled" under the ADA after the Supreme Court's rulings limiting the law, found herself so labeled — and put into a special program — because she needed apple juice.

"Since childhood, I have suffered from a relatively mild form of hypoglycemia, a tendency for one's blood sugar to drop if too many hours pass without the ingestion of carbohydrates. As a result, whenever I have taken examinations that last more than an hour, I have brought with me a small bottle or two of apple juice, to avoid developing a headache and becoming very drowsy and light-headed. My need to bring juice to exams had never posed a problem for me or for anyone else prior to the bar exam," she wrote.

But two weeks before the New York State bar exam, she learned that food and drink would not be allowed into the exam room.

"When I called the New York Bar to explain that I needed apple juice in the exam room, I was asked why I had not petitioned for an accommodation prior to the deadline; I explained that I had not known beforehand that I would need to petition at all. I was told I would then have to petition both for a waiver of the petition deadline and for an accommodation for my hypoglycemia."

Colb got a statement from her doctor "proving" her hypoglycemia — her disability — and she was granted both her accommodation of apple juice and her waiver of deadline.

By virtue of being allowed to go into the special room because she needed to drink apple juice, she was now classified as one of "the disabled" — and removed from the class of regular persons. Although she considered her need to drink apple juice a routine part of her day — and had never had any problems in the past with being allowed to do so — in this case she had become labeled "disabled" and removed from the regular, "special" her only option.

In Colb's story, either we can regard her need for apple juice as the problem, or we can see that the system is flawed. If we are willing to believe it is the system that is the problem, we can realize that the problem was the bar exam proctors' belief that Colb's need for apple juice was "abnormal" and could only be allowed if she were labeled "special," removed from the normal test takers and told to go into the "special" room. But we are still a long way from that kind of understanding in society.

When Colb arrived to take her bar exam, "I was assigned to sit in a special room reserved for people receiving accommodations," she wrote. "Some had syringes because they needed to self-inject insulin during the exam; others had high-intensity lamps because they were vision-impaired. I felt somewhat ridiculous sitting there with my apple juice. At some point, the proctors asked that 'the special people' be seated — a label that bothered me."

The law exam was scheduled to begin at 9 a.m. But the proctors in the "special" room did not hand out the test papers until closer to 10.

I worried briefly that we might not get the full time allotted to complete the test, but no one seemed to be keeping an eye on the clock. The next morning, on Day Two of the exam, it appeared we would again be starting late. I asked one of the proctors whether perhaps we could begin our exam at 9 a.m. on that day.

With a puzzled expression on her face, she asked why. I replied that everyone else was taking the exam at 9 a.m., and that I did not know of any reason for us to be delayed. She smiled and responded slowly: "If you think you can take the exam with the normal people, why don't you go ahead and try?"

The nasty-nice paternalistic comment Colb got was no different from those that people who have been forced into "special" have been hearing all their lives. Many have become inured to them. Negro men in the South who had learned to remove their hats and lower their heads — or cross to the other side of the street — when a white person happened along the sidewalk knew this feeling well. In the South the action was driven by *animus*, by what we now call "racism." At the time, most who fell under its strictures, both white and black, simply called it "custom." And many well-meaning whites who felt no *animus* for their "colored help" whatsoever nonetheless thought the strictures of segregation enforced a needed decorum in society. Eventually society came to see it as wrong; as hateful.

We have not yet come to see the remark of the proctor as hateful — or, if we do, we do not believe such remarks are inspired by *animus*, hate, even if we concede that it may *seem* hateful to the recipient. *No one is against the handicapped,* we think.

Just as Colb "began to reply to this remarkable comment," she says she was taken aside by another woman in the "special room," one who was legally blind. "She observed that I must be newly disabled. I was embarrassed to tell her that I had actually been drinking apple juice for most of my life. She said it was not worth getting upset about the proctor's remarks and that she, the applicant, just felt lucky to be allowed to take the exam with her special lamp, since another state bar had refused to let her do so."

People who have had to accept special all their lives come to know its strictures. Even if they do not like "special," they know they cannot fight against it too much lest they lose the little they have gained.

Like the wheelchair users forced to accept special paratransit rather than gain access to a city's buses, like the deaf person who couldn't go to a movie with his hearing family but had to wait until the movie came out on video, where captions were placed (or go to the "special" viewing in the movie theater when a captioned version was running), the segregation of "special" is something disabled people have not yet been able to convince society is wrong. Most of society now agrees that disabled children should receive an education. We agree that people in wheelchairs should be allowed to go about in the community. What we do not concede is that they should do so in our children's classrooms, on our own buses and subways, in our own condominium complexes. Special, we say, is best for them.

E I G H T

The role of 'the disabled' in society

One of the reasons the ADA passed was that politicians close to the Bush Administration thought few disabled people would file lawsuits. The law could be enforced only through lawsuits. Not to worry, said lobbyists to the bill's detractors; few people would sue.

When people began using the ADA to charge companies and businesses with discrimination, they were considered spoilsports.

If people sued a company which had fired them (or would not agree to changes in their jobs when their disabilities made it impossible for them to do it the way they'd always done it), they were considered whiners, lazy, people who wanted special consideration they did not deserve. When people in wheelchairs sued places like Eastwood's Mission Ranch, they were "professional litigants" — or, as Eastwood would have it, victims themselves of greedy lawyers: meek individuals who, on their own, would never complain.

The week the ADA's access requirements for public accommodations took effect, 18 months after the law's signing, Doug Bandow called on Congress to "reconsider" the ADA. The immediate occasion for Bandow's dudgeon was disabled Washington, D.C. attorney Marc Fiedler, who was now filing lawsuits against a number of inaccessible businesses. Bandow called Fiedler a "legal terrorist" angry that "elevator buttons were too high, bathrooms were not configured conveniently for his wheelchair, ramps were not provided and that theaters did not offer seating for 'optimal viewing pleasure.'"

Fiedler's lawsuits also turned up in the stridently hyped April 13, 1992 cover story of the *Washington Times* weekly, *Insight*, under the title "Handicapping the Economy: The Downside of the New Disabilities Law." Though reporter Charlotte Allen tried hard and mostly failed to find businesses having much trouble with the law, *Insight* editors took pains so that headlines and photo captions made the law look as terrible as possible.

But the anti-ADA piece that drew the most attention as the law's access requirements were taking effect was by Susan Greenwald, a wheelchair user, who wrote on the opinion page of *The Washington Post* that she was helped by places remaining inaccessible. "My waistline surely benefits from the inaccessibility of the best ice cream shop in Georgetown," she joked. Greenwald didn't mind not being able to get into smaller establishments; she worried about mom-and-pop businesses having to put in ramps — one to cover three steps might cost $10,000, she stewed. "A suit against a small business might break the establishment."

"I don't want small businesses hurt," she said. "I wouldn't want to feel guilty for putting a family out of business."

Greenwald represented millions of disabled people who continued to believe that to demand a right to access was fundamentally wrong. She believed she didn't need to get in everywhere, that it wasn't fair to others to expect them to accommodate her. It was she, after all, not they, who had the problem; her problem was her disability.

Millions in society thought disabled people like Greenwald had the right attitude. James Kilpatrick, one of the few syndicated columnists to ever mention the ADA seriously during the early years following its passage, wrote that Susan Greenwald's message was "heartening." Kilpatrick wrote several columns, in fact, about Greenwald's heartening message. Though he seemed on a mission to promote the ADA as something that wouldn't really hurt business all that much, nothing in the columns suggested disabled people might have a right to be angry or to expect justice. Still, he couldn't get the name of the law right. He called it the "Disabled Americans Act."

President Franklin D. Roosevelt, who was disabled and ended up calling himself a "cured cripple," had struck a kind of implicit bargain with society, said historian Dr. Paul Longmore. Longmore said society was still exacting that bargain today:

The non-handicapped majority says, in effect, "we will extend to you provisional and partial toleration of your public presence — as long as you display a continuous, cheerful striving toward 'normalization.'"

"Cheerful" was the key word here, Longmore pointed out. Disabled people couldn't complain, couldn't whimper, and certainly couldn't protest or sue. That wasn't part of the bargain.

One could see this bargain's negotiations in progress whenever one observed an interaction between a disabled person and the larger society. It had much in common with the way relationships were conducted in the Jim Crow South. Disabled people who accepted their part of the bargain — and the vast majority did — went along with society's image of how they were supposed to act.

Roosevelt's bargain, said Longmore, could only be struck in a society that views disability as a kind of transgression, or personal failing, something the disabled person can, with effort, manage and control. Erving Goffman's characterization of disabled people as "failed normals" came from the same analysis.

Disability in the wake of Roosevelt became "a private, emotional or physical tragedy, best dealt with by psychological coping mechanisms," Longmore said. It was the medical model of disability, seeing disability itself as the problem, a problem to be dealt with in private — something between doctor and patient.

Although John Stossel had likely never heard Longmore's analysis, he was acting in accord with the bargain's tenets in dividing disabled people into two groups — the ones who didn't complain about rights or use disability rights laws, and the ones who did, whom Stossel labeled whiners and complainers; people who wouldn't deal with their problems but blamed society instead. Among the organized disabled, the inside terms that acknowledged this division were good cripples and bad cripples. Good cripples stuck to their part of the bargain; bad cripples didn't.

"School officials hate to see Gregory Solas coming," wrote *The New York Times*'s William Celis III. The ADA had been law exactly three years and the federal Individuals with Disabilities Education Act had been on the books for nearly two decades when

The Times profiled bad cripple Solas. Since 1990, Solas had "filed complaints against nearly 2,000 schools, colleges and universities over the absence of ramps for wheelchairs, signs for the visually impaired and other accommodations required by Federal law.

"At a time when budgets are stretched thin by recession and its aftermath, schools say resolving complaints like Mr. Solas's are forcing them into costly renovations, diverting money from other pressing needs," wrote Celis.

No one denied that the schools were breaking the law. But the law seemed inappropriate — there were pressing needs that should have been attended to before access for disabled people, it was said. Gregory Solas could not seem to understand that.

According to one study, reported *The Times*, "it costs $20,000 to $200,000 to equip a school" with ramps, elevators, escalators, barrier-free bathrooms and wider doorways, "depending on the age of the school building and the extent of its renovation. Federal disability laws spell out how public buildings should accommodate the disabled, from how far water fountains should be lowered to where signs for the visually impaired should be installed."

Although Solas was himself a wheelchair user, and his battle with schools was partly that he could not get in to his child's school for meetings, his battle was far more than personal.

"I just can't tolerate anyone getting ripped off of their freedoms. We pay taxes like everybody else and we should have the same entitlements. I just consider myself a regular guy who wants to get something done that's right." The former welder minced few words. "I've taken on an issue that happens to be very important to a lot of people."

It was true. In Solas's wake, parents of disabled children were increasing their demands "to an outrageous extent," said Gwendolyn Gregory, deputy general counsel for the National School Boards Association; after Solas had come on the scene, complaints had tripled.

"He's abrasive and aggressive," Henry S. Tarlian, Superintendent of the Warwick, R.I., school system, told Celis. Disabled students should be protected to the full extent of the law, he said, but Solas had "run amok." William Anderson, who himself had a disabled child, told the Providence (R.I.) *Sunday Journal* that he disagreed with Solas, and that access laws were too stringent. "To just spend money indiscriminately to do all this stuff, I just can't see it."

What Solas wanted seemed outrageous. It went against common sense. It wasn't fair to have to change all the schools. We wouldn't have to do it if it weren't for troublemakers like Solas, was the message his sources gave Celis.

Kornel Botosan was another bad cripple. Described as one of a breed of "greedy opportunists who are twisting the spirit of the disabilities act for their own financial gain," Botosan made headlines regularly. The wheelchair user "actively searches Southern California for businesses that fall below ADA standards," wrote *Orange County Register* columnist Gordon Dillow. Dillow reported that Botosan had sued Wilma's Patio, a Balboa Island restaurant, when he found he could not get into the restroom, and "demanded thousands of dollars in damages, plus attorney fees."

Wilma's Patio attorney Ron Davis called it "legal extortion," and Dillow seemed to agree. "No one should be allowed to turn anti-discrimination lawsuits into a money-making operation — regardless of whether it's a person in a wheelchair or just a lawyer who has to pay full price for his drinks," snapped Dillow.

The *Los Angeles Times* wrote about Botosan's lawsuits; CNN coverage of the 10th anniversary of the ADA featured him. When Stossel strafed Botosan on *20/20* just as Clint Eastwood was starting to make his move on Congress, *The Register* took up the cry against the man again, reporting that Botosan was "demanding thousands of dollars in damages." It seemed to anger those like Dillow that Botosan not only filed lawsuits but won them — "each time winning the $1,000 in damages allowed by law.

"He even made it onto TV's *The People's Court*, he won there, too," wrote Dillow.

Winning lawsuits was seen as no vindication that a disabled person's pursuit was a just one. Most who reported on "litigators" like Botosan made little of the fact that those who were sued had been breaking the law. Botosan was seen as part of a "legal cottage industry" devoted to filing ADA lawsuits. (He was in fact using both the ADA and California's civil rights law, but that didn't matter to critics.) Long Beach lawyer William Shibley charged that Botosan and his attorney had "conspired to use the Americans with Disabilities Act...as a cash cow."

Wilma Staudinger, owner of Wilma's Patio, told Dillow that there were a number of people with disabilities among her loyal clientele; none of them had ever complained about access, she said.

The ADA did not have any enforcement mechanism other than private lawsuits. Unless a business decided on its own to obey the law, the only way access happened was when it was forced through a lawsuit. Yet in bringing disability lawsuits, people knew on some level that they were breaking an implicit bargain with society, opening themselves to criticism and ridicule.

"I think it's important to realize that treating all disabled people as equal — with equal rights and responsibilities — is absurd," Dr. Kenneth Lefebre told a reporter for a disability publication. Lefebre's job at the Rehabilitation Institute of Chicago was to tend to the "stabilization," as Lefebre put it, of people undergoing the trauma of accepting disability in themselves for the first time. "Many of the patients that come through any rehab hospital are there because of their own ignorance, negligence, stupidity or criminal activities," he added.

Of those who criticized bad cripples, none seemed more vocal than those who either worked with disabled people for a living or had a disabled person in their family. And the implication was that they, of all people, should know the score.

Disabled people had to understand that it was up to them to figure out the best way around obstacles, Lefebre said. It was not society's problem, it was their own personal problem. It was "unrealistic and fundamentally stupid to expect either the state or the county or this city to make every type of public transportation available for the disabled." At the time, members of the activist disability group ADAPT had been protesting in the streets over the

Chicago Transit Authority's refusal to purchase lifts on the 363 new buses it had just ordered.

The theory was that "[r]ehabilitation helped disabled people fulfill their individual potential," writes social historian Ruth O'Brien. The "whole man" theory of rehabilitation, developed in the 1940s and championed by military doctors Howard A. Rusk and Henry Kessler, held that "an un-rehabilitated person could weaken and erode society's health." Disabled people, Rusk and Kessler believed, were "malformed and maladjusted," and "only...rehabilitation experts could show them how to strive toward normalcy."

"Disabled people had to counterbalance what distinguished them from the rest of society, carefully conforming to its notion of normalcy," writes O'Brien.

> Experts did not think that disabled people should have the autonomy to decide what would be in their best interest. So as not to be seen as "abnormal," they were encouraged to mask their physical or mental impairments, thereby exhibiting or expressing as little of their individuality as possible. Societal acceptance or rejection, according to Rusk and Kessler, depended on how well disabled people conformed to society.

Eileen Gardner had been appointed to the Reagan Education Department to oversee the office of educational philosophy under William Bennett. Formerly with the Heritage Foundation, Gardner had been a "teacher of handicapped children," she told *Washington Post* reporter Phil McCombs. In a policy paper, she insisted that the legal requirement that "the handicapped" be "mainstreamed" was damaging to "the normal child."

> Those of the handicapped constituency who seek to have others bear their burdens and eliminate their challenges are seeking to avoid the central issues of their lives. They falsely assume the lottery of life has penalized them at random. This is not so. Nothing comes to an individual that he has not [at some point in his development] summoned. Each of us is responsible for his [own] life situation. It is through accepting this responsibility that the individual learns....When one blames his problems on external sources and thereby separates himself from a situation he has created, he is

prevented from taking hold of and changing that part of himself which causes his difficulty. He becomes an ineffective malcontent.

"There is no injustice in the universe," Gardner had written. "As unfair as it may seem, a person's external circumstances *do* fit his level of inner spiritual development. The purpose (and the challenge) of life is for a person to take what he has and use it for spiritual growth."

It was accepted that nondisabled people knew what was best for the disabled. Gardner and Lefebre had many comrades who spoke from authority because they were involved in some way with "the handicapped." Rep. Mark Foley, who was pushing the ADA Notification Act, served on the board of his local Goodwill.

Marianne M. Jennings, professor of legal and ethical studies at Arizona State University, mother of a 14-year-old girl with what she called "significant mental and physical impairments," wrote that, though "touted as a magnanimous gift to the less fortunate," the ADA actually "deprives gifted souls of the self-exploration that comes from admitting you're not a golfer or university material." The golfer comment was an allusion to pro golfer Casey Martin, whose ADA case was soon to be heard by the U.S. Supreme Court.

Providing an accommodation to someone with a learning "challenge," as she called it, "deprives them of the right to explore why they were given the challenge of preclusion." Jennings served "on countless boards and committees for centers, schools and programs for the disabled," she wrote. And while she conceded that it was wrong "to deny otherwise qualified disabled folks jobs because of their disabilities," it was equally wrong to change the nature and demands of a job for their desires, she said. Karen Sutton and Kimberly Hinton, who had recently lost their case before the Supreme Court, were "ditzes...Mrs. Magoo in the cockpit." The idea behind the ADA's public accommodation requirements was "equally nutty": "What, pray tell, does a blind person see in a beer factory?" she wrote of a man who had sued to be allowed to bring his seeing eye dog while he took a public tour.

Jennings reserved her praise for Miss Iowa, Theresa Uchytil, "who didn't even have a hand" but who nonetheless "played the hand she was dealt." Jennings regarded Uchytil as a good cripple: "In addition to being in the Miss America pageant, the one-handed Uchytil is a baton twirler and a program manager for Gateway....Playing the hand you are dealt means not asking that the bar be lowered, but compensating and overcoming," wrote Jennings. "The rest of us mortals will watch in awe...."

The reason nondisabled people saw nothing wrong with their conviction that they knew what was best for disabled people was because society viewed disabled people not as a "distinct and insular minority," despite anything that Congress might have inserted into the wording of the Americans with Disabilities Act. They were no more than our daughters and sons, our brothers and sisters. While this might sound ideal — might sound exactly like what the organized disabled strove for with their "people first" language — in fact something quite different was happening. We viewed disabled people as just like us — but less: "disabled," as the word implied; unable; defective. They were "failed normals," as Goffman had put it, merely that. Not some minority with its own culture and traditions like African Americans, who maybe did have reason to view society from a different perspective. No, a disabled person was nobody but our uncle who had the bad luck to be injured on the assembly line, our sister who'd gotten multiple sclerosis.

A disabled person's role in society was not to criticize it from a minority perspective — for they were not a true minority — but to work at becoming normal, to be rehabilitated if not cured. Those who refused, or who were simply are incapable of it, were cut off as "hopeless cases," into the "Other" — to pity and care for, but to be given no say in the matter. What could they know? By definition they were defectives.

People like Greenwald ("my waistline benefits from the inaccessibility") were praised and used as examples because they seemed to agree with what most nondisabled people (including the reporters who profiled them) believed: that the problem wasn't so much society's failings as the body's disease or injury, which simply prevented full participation in society.

Those who argued the case against disability rights could always find disabled people who thought as they did.

"Deny as we may want to, at the point when a person can not be totally independent physically from others, one is no longer equal in body," wrote a woman with muscular dystrophy on an online forum. "At that point in life we are not equal to even our former self as far as physical ability is concerned."

"I do not want to be treated equally," she continued.

> I have to depend on others to drive for me and get me in and out of bed and all the day-to-day things I used to do. I can still think, but for the life of me I can't think of a way to get rid of the wheelchair. Therefore, I am not on the same ground I used to be on. To me that makes my way not equal…How can we bury our heads so deep and say we are equal to the able bodies around us? We are not. That's why it is called a handicap, because it is….We must be careful when we ask to be treated with equality. If we yell too loud about the wrong things, maybe the ADA will never be fully enacted.

People who stuck to their end of the bargain appeared on the telethons; they ran fundraisers in their hometowns, car washes and cake sales and 20K bike races to raise money for Jerry Lewis; they helped raise funds for local cure charities; they aided Mothers Against Drunk Driving by appearing on stage to serve as horrific examples of what could happen if you drank and drove.

Because they did, it was logical to insist that the bad cripples didn't represent most disabled people, and that, therefore, there was no real movement among real disabled people for the kinds of rights agenda being pushed by the organized disabled, as Foley called them. It was not hard, either, to dismiss the idea that they formed any kind of a true minority.

Those who pressed the case against disability rights relied on good cripples to endorse their message, and in truth there did not seem to be any cogent philosophy binding the thinking of those who would blame society for their problems. They seemed like isolated whiners. When someone thought of a spokesperson for disabled people, they thought of Christopher Reeve.

The anti-rights forces spent not an insubstantial amount of their effort in the media lecturing bad cripples to shut up about society's failings and realize that it was their own body — or their own unwillingness to work — which was causing their problems. They were to stop whining. No one, after all, held any ill will against them.

It was a way of putting the disabled in their place, reminding them of that bargain. And it was an effort to mute criticism from the bad cripples — for they were the only ones doing any complaining.

Almost everyone else in society either agreed with the case against disability rights or didn't see it as being of enough of a threat to their view of society to bother fighting over.

NINE

The 'silence of the good people'

The case against disability rights was primarily driven by free-market anti-regulation advocates. Its strength, though, came not so much from its arguments but from the fact that it encountered almost no public opposition from anyone other than individuals labeled whiners and malcontents, whose comments would appear occasionally in a letter to the editor.

The American Civil Liberties Union was rarely quoted supporting access. Access wasn't an agenda item for any of the dozens of other progressive public policy groups that could usually be counted on to speak out on a panoply of public issues from gay bashing to hate crimes to gender disparity in salaries to the glass ceiling to logging in old-growth forests to off-shore sweatshops to entrenched racism to lingering sexism to continued homophobia.

Jabs, slurs, condemnations of and bigoted comments about disabled people and their movement's goals encountered almost no public outrage. No articles in *Harper's* or *The New York Times Magazine* or *Mother Jones* examined the tenets of disability rights. No reporters delved into the issues from the disability rights perspective as though they might offer cogent lessons for society. Public debate, in the true sense of the word, was virtually nonexistent.

Martin Luther King, Jr. had once said that "the greatest tragedy of this period of social transition was not the strident clamor of the bad people, but the appalling silence of the good people." The comment fit the current situation — almost. The truth was that there had been far more heard during the 1950s from the "good people" about civil rights than there had yet been heard from them about the justness of disability rights.

To understand the silence, the public vacancy in the discussion about disability rights, it is useful to look at how we as a nation reacted to the injury of Christopher Reeve. It would be impossible

to find anyone who disagreed with what UVA hospital receptionist Wendy Ingalls had told a reporter who'd interviewed her right
after Reeve's accident: "It is a terrible thing to be paralyzed." That
sentiment was at least part of the reason why people like Eastwood
were so quick to point out that they weren't against the handicapped, why, indeed, "no one wishes to stint on helping the disabled," as the 1991 *New York Times* editorial put it.

It's also why disability rights is such a hard sell: because people
fear disability, view serious disability like Reeve's a horror almost
beyond imagining, a fate worse than death. This simply trumps the
idea of disability rights altogether. Next to such horror, the idea of
"rights" usually simply pales into insignificance.

Christopher Reeve had worked for imprisoned South American
writers. He'd fought to stop a coal-burning power plant in Albany,
N.Y. He'd helped Vice President Al Gore clean up a beach. Yet disability rights seemed to hold no interest for him.

"People say to me, 'why don't you give up on that [cure busi-
ness] and work for better conditions for people with disabilities?
Work harder for the ADA, bring up people on charges who fail to
meet the [access] codes?' I can't do both effectively, in my opinion."

"When they told me what my condition was, I felt that I was no
longer a human being," Reeve had told *Time* magazine's Roger
Rosenblatt as the two began to collaborate on the memoir pub-
lishers were urging him to write.

"Reeve did not want to become the poster boy for America's
quadriplegics," wrote Rosenblatt. "He wanted to be a symbol of
potential recovery."

"We were not meant to be living in wheelchairs. We were meant
to be walking upright with all of our body systems fully functional, and I'd like to have that back," Reeve said. "I never went out
and said I would take on the mantle of representing all people with
disabilities."

Disability rights seemed beside the point to him. "I'm not that
interested in lower sidewalks," he told a reporter. It was nice to
have access, he said, but people with disabilities should regard

those disabilities "as a temporary setback rather than a way of life."

People who heard Christopher Reeve speaking about his feelings found that those feelings resonated. It was how most people felt about life with a disability.

"Reeve decided to use the media to further his cause," wrote Rosenblatt, whose long cover story for *Time* magazine, appearing the week before Reeve was to address the 1996 Democratic National Convention, was itself showing just how effective Reeve's access to national mass media could be. "Every television show wanted an interview." Reeve had "become the most recognized person in a wheelchair ever."

Good Housekeeping magazine listed Reeve among the top 10 "Men We Admire Most" in its January 1997 issue. Reeve was one of *People* magazine's "25 most intriguing people" of 1996. "With what he has made of his tragedy, Christopher Reeve has lifted a nation," wrote one of the many freelancers who hurried to fashion books for youngsters out of Reeve's push to walk again.

As the most famous disabled person since Roosevelt, Reeve, perhaps inadvertently, bolstered the case against disability rights by offering a story of the disability experience that concurred with those who insisted that what people with severe disabilities faced were personal, medical problems, that what they needed was compassion — and a cure.

It's true that it would have been hard for any one person to advance both disability rights and cure. Pushing for rights implied that having a disability wasn't so much the problem as was society's failure to accommodate or provide access. The need for cure, on the other hand, was best advanced by preaching that disability was a personal, medical issue — which was what those opposing disability rights preached as well.

In focusing on cure, Reeve sanctioned a belief the American public already held: that a disabled person's defining problem is that his body is not "whole"; that what he needs — the only thing he needs, really — is to be cured. That without this cure, things will never truly be all right for a disabled person. For this is the message one sends when one pushes for cure to the exclusion of rights and access.

Scientists were standing by, ready. "They know how to put me back together," he'd say on TV. All was lacking was the money.

The facts in the speech he gave on *Larry King Live*, on *The Today Show*, to Barbara Walters were mostly invented: It was true that scientists were pretty sure *how* to repair the spinal cord, but they were a long way from being able to get the tissue to grow again. The government spent "$8.7 billion a year on Medicaid payments on people who qualify as spinal cord injured," he'd say, but they weren't being cured; they were just "sitting there, ticking over." "If the government were to spend $40 million a year, over the next 10 years," he'd point out to viewers, "you would have a cure. If the public will demand that the politicians spend that little bit of money, and make that investment, I'll be up and walking around again." "In his appearances, he evoked a clock ticking toward his 50th birthday," Rosenblatt wrote.

Reeve's first appearance before Congress, less than a year after he'd become a man seeking a cure, was reported in over 200 media outlets.

Despite the complaint that the search for cures was horribly underfunded, a lot more — a heck of a lot more — was raised with the cure stick than with the access stick. Almost none was raised with the rights/access stick. Few foundations anywhere funded disability rights projects; those that did gave only a few thousand dollars.

In 1990, the year the ADA became law, the year Jerry Lewis wrote in *Parade* magazine that if he had muscular dystrophy he'd be "half a person," Lewis's MDA Telethon raised $44 million in pledged donations; it was the 25th anniversary of the national telethon and the grand total raised by Jerry Lewis during those years for the cure of muscular dystrophy had surpassed one billion dollars. Reeve used phrases similar to Lewis's, talking about being no longer a participant but an observer, of no longer being whole.

"Be grateful you can walk and run and jump," he told viewers on *Larry King Live*. Research would "get us out of this," he told

King. By "this," he meant disability.

From the day he'd become disabled, Christopher Reeve's view of his own situation was widely reported. He did not talk about disability rights. And most people, including the media, took their cues about what was important for disabled people from Reeve.

Journalist John Hockenberry, whose own spinal cord injury had come 20 years earlier, had found the coverage of Reeve's injury superficial. Reeve's was "still a whole life," he had told his NPR listeners. When one became disabled, he said, one simply remade the world with what one had left. "It is simple. It is what humanity has always done."

People's reactions to disability, though, were another matter entirely. "People who are perfectly fine, sentient beings come up to you, and an enormous black curtain drops over their head," he said. "And suddenly they're not looking at you anymore. They're staring at some construct in their mind about, 'What does this mean? What happened to him?' or 'Is he in pain? I would have committed suicide if I were him.'"

What was going on, said Hockenberry, was that people were "measuring the real disabled person in front of them with their own category" — or mental construct — of disability. It was generally based not on real knowledge, but simply on what nondisabled people imagined it was like to be disabled.

When that black curtain fell, said Hockenberry, what was happening was that the nondisabled person was really wondering, "Could I have dealt with this?"

"It has lots to do with *them*," he said. "It has almost nothing to do with *me*. People wonder, 'is that beyond my threshold? Should I blow my brains out?'

"When I was in college, a professor came into the men's room. I was in front of the urinal dumping stuff in. 'Oh!' he said. 'I never thought that you went to the bathroom before!' Consider how far we have to go if that's actually the case."

Hockenberry had been thrown out of Broadway's Virginia Theatre in 1993, three years after the Americans with Disabilities Act, having lost his temper at being told he could not get out of his wheelchair and sit in the seat he'd paid for; that he would have to stay in the special handicapped section.

"People think our anger is bitterness about being in our chairs. Or we're bitter that we drove drunk into a tree. Or we're bitter that we went to Vietnam. Or we're bitter that we can't fuck anymore. They think that — and every other reason that might have to do with our being angry is actually just that, channeled through some silly incident in a bathroom, or some silly incident at a theater — some silly incident that masks the real anger that the disabled person must have — anger that they're no longer a human being."

When a group of pregnant women who had no real likelihood of bearing a child with a disability were asked in a survey about their images of disability and then about their attitudes toward actually bearing a child with a disability, "striking discontinuities were seen," reports the University of Oregon's Nancy Press. The women all expressed "upbeat, strongly positive and almost romanticized attitudes" when they were asked their general feelings about "people with disabilities." Many referred to disabled people as "triumphing," as Press put it; the women brought up things like the TV series *Life Goes On*.

When questioned about actually bearing a disabled child, though, responses changed dramatically. A woman who had told Press that "handicapped children were the most beautiful beings in the world" said that if a child born to her had a disability she would cry. The result of the interviews, wrote Press, showed "a dynamic and somewhat confused mix of old images of mental retardation and incapacity juxtaposed with new images of different but 'special' children — and absolutely no way to sort them out."

A Harris Poll survey taken shortly after the Americans with Disabilities Act became law found that the public both pitied and admired disabled people. An overwhelming majority agreed that the ADA should be law, but when questioned further, only a minority agreed with any of its provisions.

The complex of beliefs and attitudes that caused John Hockenberry's black curtain to fall has no commonly-recognized name: there is no word like racism or sexism or homophobia that is commonly used to identify such behavior; society doesn't seem to much recognize that the phenomenon exists. Some disability studies scholars refer to "the medical model"; others use the term "ableism." But these concepts are neither widely known nor accepted.

The idea that disability is normal and therefore doesn't need curing was simply an effort to "obfuscate an unpleasant truth with feel-good oxymorons," wrote *Salon.com's* Norah Vincent in a long article supporting the medical model of disability. Writing about the Society for Disability Studies (a group hopeful its SDS acronym might suggest a like militance to those who heard it), Vincent called disability studies "one of the most bizarre creatures the ivory tower has ever spawned," and disability pride a "surreal ideology":

> The human body is a machine, after all — one that has evolved functional parts: lungs for breathing, legs for walking, eyes for seeing, ears for hearing, a tongue for speaking and most crucially for all the academics concerned, a brain for thinking. This is science, not culture. How then can we make the case that blind eyes, or deaf ears, or mute tongues are serving the purpose for which they evolved? They are, in purely ergonomic terms, broken, dysfunctional and — contrary to what SDSers might maintain — in need of repair, if repair is feasible. When one is dealing with severe physical disabilities, it's difficult to accept that anti-medical definitions of disabilities do anyone any good. As SDSers themselves admit, such disabilities quite often entail a great deal of discomfort and pain, not to mention infuriating inconvenience.

The reactions that the disability rights movement provokes in people like Vincent, Bovard, Stossel and others are evidence that something is going on that we do not fully understand.

One can find virtually no public discussion that takes either the concept of ableism — or the word — seriously.

Writers who wouldn't dare ridicule racism, sexism, anti-Semitism or homophobia had a field day in the 1990s with ableism. It was a big joke with pundits bashing political correctness. In its salvo against political correctness, *Newsweek* called it a "most Orwellian category"; it was "a spoof of itself," said *Chicago Tribune* columnist Joan Beck — the watchword for political correctness run amok. When it appeared in stories, it was there almost without exception as a joke. In 1990, the year the ADA became law, *Newsweek* said the concept "does violence to logic and language."

"I remember my first reaction when I heard criticisms of *Amos 'n' Andy*, which was one of the radio programs I grew up with," First Amendment specialist Floyd Abrams told the *Columbia Journalism Review*. "I thought, 'This is ridiculous, this is absolutely absurd to be bothered by that.' And now it's inconceivable to me that anybody could have put it on without people reacting by saying, 'You can't treat our fellow citizens that way.'"

Comprehension about racial prejudice had evolved. There was still plenty of racism — but people recognized it as that: as racism. No matter how minor, that was still progress. That had happened with sexism and homophobia, too.

"I don't think there's any question but that there's a new level of sensitivity to racial, religious and perhaps sexually-oriented slurs," Abrams continued (saying nothing about disability slurs). Social censorship — the censorship that occurs naturally when the majority in a society itself comes to believe that certain ways of speaking about a group are morally indefensible — has taken hold. It hadn't happened with disability.

The New York Times called a National Federation of the Blind campaign for equal access "unreasonable insistence on a right that defies logic and common sense." In the 1980s, *Louisville Times* columnist Richard DesRuisseaux had written that "to claim that the stashing of blind people's canes during takeoff and landings is discriminatory is the most absurd notion to come down the pike."

U.S. News and World Report's John Leo could be counted on to provide a steady barrage of disparagement against the ADA and those who talked of "disability rights." His comments, like Bovard's and Stossel's, focused on the law's vagueness and insisted it offered an undeserved safe haven for slackers and malingerers. No Leo column against political correctness failed to include a jab at disability rights. "The disability-rights movement objects to all use of the words crazy and moron as insulting to the mentally impaired," he wrote.

One must grope through a fierce blizzard of euphemisms: the uniquely abled, the differently abled, the exceptional, the handicapable, the inconvenienced, the developmentally disabled, handicappers, injury survivors and people with differing abilities. A recent bulletin from the movement lets us know that Porky Pig, formerly a stutterer, should be listed as speech-impaired, whereas Mr. Magoo is visually handicapped and Captain Hook is orthopedically impaired.

For those who wanted to have fun lampooning political correctness, nothing seemed more fun than ridiculing disability terms. "What editor could resist the tale of academic orthodoxy in which cracked rules of civility require short people to be referred to as the vertically challenged?" wrote Anthony DePalma in *The New York Times*.

"People who are politically correct are pushing 'differently abled,'" Sol Steinmetz, Executive Editor of the Random House Webster's College Dictionary told *The New York Times*'s Richard Bernstein. "Differently abled" came in for its share of jabs. So did "people with differing abilities," selected in the spring of 1991 from over 50,000 entries to the Christina Foundation's Create-A-Word contest, for which Steinmetz was a judge. In truth, most of these terms were never used by anyone. "Challenged," though, was another matter: as years passed, more and more reporters began calling people "physically challenged" or "mentally" or "intellectually challenged" — although "vertically challenged" was used only as a joke.

People seemed to like to apply the terms "physically challenged" and "mentally challenged" to disabled people. The phrases implied that the problems a person faced should be used as an opportunity for personal growth rather than an occasion for irritation at the general intractability of an inaccessible society.

As to "differently abled," *Newsweek's* Jerry Adler wrote,

Well, many people with handicaps surely do develop different abilities, but that is not what makes them a category....They lack something other people possess. It does violence to logic and to language to pretend otherwise. If people could choose, how many would be "differently abled?"

Though they skewered it as the ultimate bad result of political correctness, in reality the politically-correct crowd mostly forgot about disability rights altogether when it came to anything other than its terminology. Political correctness mavens said they wanted to eliminate "racist, sexist or homophobic" speech. "In our own time we've seen... minority rights, women's rights, peace and disarmament and gay rights," wrote Barbara Ehrenreich, composing her 1991 litany of contemporary rights. Scholar Catharine Stimpson's litany included: "black or African-American studies; Native American or American Indian studies; Hispanic, Latino/Latina, Chicano/Chicana and Puerto Rican studies, Asian-American studies;...Women's, feminist or gender studies and...gay and lesbian studies."

Disability was routinely left out of everyone's listings.

In writing, disability served as a useful metaphor for "bad." A NOW ad in *Time* magazine asked for donations to "buy the government a hearing aid" — the point being that the government was clearly "deaf" to women's issues. "Our views don't mean a thing when they fall on deaf ears," read a direct-mail brochure paid for by the Washington State Republican Party mailed in the fall just after the ADA had passed.

Newspaper headlines routinely used "blind," "deaf" "paralyzed" and "crippled" as metaphors for "bad." "Legally Blind on the Hudson," "Hard Times Cripple A Football Legacy," "Copyright Fine Could Cripple MP3.com," "Primary Could Cripple Challengers." Strikers threatened to "paralyze" Seoul, "irate Cuban-Americans paralyzed Miami" and the Sept. 11 attacks "paralyzed the financial district." Headlines used "blind" and "deaf" to signal something bad: "Focusing on the Few, Blind to the Many," "Genetics: Blind Spot in Medical Training," "Turning a Blind Eye." Zimbabwe was "Deaf to Calls for Fair Elections," a song was "Falling on Deaf Ears."

One need only consider the uproar traditional civil rights and women's groups created when they complained about a slur to realize how different the landscape was when it came to disability rights consciousness. Andy Rooney had been suspended for saying that blacks "watered down their genes," but his comments about disabled people were considered just silly, just jokes. A newspaper labeled those who had complained about his 1995 column on handicapped parking "the walking wounded."

Dictionary publisher Merriam-Webster promised to make alterations to over 200 ethnic, religious and sexual slur words in the 1999 edition of its Collegiate Dictionary after receiving complaints that some definitions, especially for the word "nigger," were racist, reported *The New York Times*. Merriam-Webster had begun its review "after the National Association for the Advancement of Colored People objected to the dictionary's definition of the word 'nigger,'" said *The Times*, "even though a warning quickly followed saying it was offensive." The news article reported that the N.A.A.C.P. had "called on its members to protest the dictionary's definition of the word as 'a black person' or 'a member of any dark-skinned race.'" When Louisville's Council for Retarded Citizens developed a poster campaign depicting graffiti and the words "kike," "queer," "honkey," "nigger" and "retard" on a brick wall — the ostensible point being that "retard" was just as bad as the other words — the act provoked outrage from Louisville's civil rights community, which accepted it not for the message it meant to convey, but took it as racism and, insisting it was fanning the flames of racial prejudice, got the poster banned from public buses.

Groups traditionally supportive of civil rights — traditional civil rights groups, women's rights groups and gay rights groups — seemed to have little more understanding of disability rights than did the general society.

The Leadership Conference on Civil Rights in Washington, D.C. had lobbied for the Americans with Disabilities Act when it was in Congress, yet even after the bill became law a person in a wheelchair could not get into its inaccessible offices. It was far from being the only progressive group for which this was the case. Though its literature claimed to be interested in getting out the "disability vote," when HumanServe mounted its massive voter registration effort the first year the ADA was in Congress, 1988, it had done so without bothering to make its Manhattan office accessible to volunteers in wheelchairs. Habitat for Humanity routinely built inaccessible houses.

Among the organized disabled, the topic was a familiar one: Groups involved with civil rights, gay rights, women's rights didn't bother with disability rights. Didn't understand it. Didn't seem to want to understand it. Didn't bother with access. Were incensed when their lack of access was pointed out to them.

The organized disabled in Atlanta found the Fund for Southern Communities, a community-based progressive fund that made grants to social action and direct change groups, eager for proposals from disability organizations, but, when they went to pick up applications, found themselves unable to get into the office. Efforts from the groups got the Fund to ramp its entrance. But when it moved to new quarters, a number of years after the ADA had become law, they once again chose an inaccessible building.

"The way to piss off a liberal is to say, 'you're discriminating.' They've got this 'I'm better than you because I'm liberal and I contribute to all these good causes' attitude," is how one of the disabled activists in Atlanta put it. "But their solution to inaccessibility is to drag you up steps. They'll 'help' you." Liberals did not seem to really try to understand about rights when it came to disabled people, she said.

In the Oakland, Calif. offices of Pledge of Resistance, someone had written "weird — disabled" on the comments section of a list the group was using for phone outreach. The caller had reached a disability rights activist who had cerebral palsy, whose speech was hard to understand. The inexperienced phone bank worker had made the mistake of expressing feelings most people held, but kept to themselves.

Incidents like these were "so frequent and so subtle that they simply form the texture of my daily life," said the woman who reported it, who worked in the offices and had seen the note being written. Sometimes remarks like that were made about her, she said; sometimes about other disabled people. Recalling Erving Goffman's classic construct, she called it stigma. It was always present, she said.

Stigma paralleled class oppression, she wrote. "It's a constant flow of minor incidents, trivial incidents, unvoiced messages that we don't know our place, that we aspire to too much, that we dare want and ask for the things people around us take for granted, that we don't stick to our own kind, that we put people on the spot, simply by showing ordinary friendliness. We owe the world an apology for our distasteful condition. If we can't make our condition, our disability, go away, then we should go away."

T E N

The tenth year of 'a bad law'

Clint Eastwood and Mark Foley, talking to reporters about the lawsuit that was bringing Eastwood to Washington to testify at Foley's hearing, avoided suggesting that any fault might lie with Eastwood, Carmel's former mayor, in failing to obey an act passed by Congress a decade earlier. The fault lay with the law itself: nobody understood it, even though it had been the law of the land for a decade. "City and county officials don't even know what the law is. We have to have an education campaign," Foley told Matthews. "The Department of Justice doesn't even know how to advise cities as to what are the requirements. It is completely an open territory."

It was the same message that had been going out from the pundits for a decade now: The ADA was a problem; it was a law nobody understood; it caused "unintended consequences." Although no one was against disabled people, and things were, in fact getting better for them, the ADA was a bad law.

As the 10th anniversary of the bill's signing approached, those who shopped the case against disability rights chanted their ADA-is-a-bad-law mantra. It had cost business an enormous amount of money by interfering with the free market, they said, scaring beleaguered employers into hiring fewer disabled people than they would have done otherwise out of the goodness of their hearts had only the ADA not forced them to do so.

Editors loved the man-bites-dog twist of the story that ADA had hurt disabled people, who were now, it was said, hired less frequently than before the law. The story was originally Epstein's; when it made the rounds on the ADA's 10th anniversary it came from University of Chicago economist Thomas DeLeire, who wrote that the ADA had not worked, that it had had the kind of "unintended consequences" that occurred whenever government tried to regulate business.

"Contrary to legislative intent, ADA makes the disabled less employable," wrote DeLeire.

> The added cost of employing disabled workers to comply with the accommodation mandate of ADA has made those workers relatively unattractive to firms....Moreover, the threats of prosecution under the Equal Employment Opportunity Commission and litigation by disabled workers have in fact led firms to avoid hiring some disabled workers in the first place.

Taking figures the disability rights movement used to prove that the ADA had not been costly to business, DeLeire used them to prove that it had. "Providing reasonable accommodations can be costly for employers," he wrote. There was little evidence about the costs of accommodation, he said. A federal program, the Job Accommodation Network, and studies of federal contractors under the Rehabilitation Act like the one conducted by Berkeley Planning Associates in 1982, had all reported low costs to accommodation — JAN had reported that the median accommodation under ADA cost $500 or less; BPA had found that the average cost of an accommodation was approximately $900 (and that 51 percent of accommodations cost nothing). But "it would be wrong to conclude that ADA has little effect on employers," he said, because

> both sources underestimate the costs of accommodation by including only monetary costs. Allowing a disabled employee to work a more flexible schedule, for example, might not increase a firm's out-of-pocket expenses, but it does increase a firm's costs.

"The burden of ADA is not the less-expensive accommodations that very likely would have been made even in the absence of a government mandate but rather the more expensive ones," he went on. "According to JAN, 12 percent of accommodations cost more than $2,000 and four percent cost more than $5,000. The BPA study found that eight percent of accommodations cost more than $2,000, four percent of accommodations cost more than $5,000, and two percent of accommodations cost more than $20,000." Using these low statistical instances, DeLeire argued that the ADA imposed costs on employers so high that they now hired fewer disabled workers than ever before.

Investor's Business Daily reported that "DeLeire's analysis of federal data found an 8% drop in employment of disabled men, ages 18 to 65, from 1990 to 1995."

It was true the ADA had made disabled people less employable, Daron Acemoglu and Josh Angrist chimed in. The two Massachusetts Institute of Technology economists blamed the law "for a two- to three-week drop in time worked each year by disabled men." "The existing evidence suggests that although some accommodations are reasonably cheap, there are some quite expensive accommodations as well," Acemoglu told a reporter. "One possibility is that since employers aren't sure what the costs will be, they shy away from hiring disabled workers."

These kinds of statements appealed to business's very real desire to be left alone to run things as they saw fit, hiring and refusing to hire whomever they chose, for whatever reason, with neither public regulation nor moral compass. The arguments, quoted in the media, received little rebuttal.

The ADA forced employers "to provide handicapped workers with the accommodations they need to do a job — and it sets no dollar limit on the obligation....Just installing a ramp for a wheelchair can run as high as $10,000," wrote *Chicago Tribune* columnist Steve Chapman on the law's 10th anniversary.

"Since enforcement of the Act began in July 1992, it quickly has become a major component of employment law — one to which employers increasingly have had to respond," DeLeire wrote.

> Through the end of fiscal year 1998, 108,939 ADA charges had been filed with EEOC, and 106,988 of those charges had been resolved. Of the resolved charges, 86 percent were either dropped or investigated and dismissed by EEOC but not without imposing opportunity costs and legal fees on employers. The other 14 percent of the charges led to a finding of discrimination by EEOC or a private settlement at an average cost to employers of $14,325 (not including opportunity costs and legal fees).["Opportunity costs" was a term from economics: "the value of the next-highest-valued alternative use of that resource."]

The organized disabled would say that such figures actually proved that businesses were prevailing against most of the charges brought against them under the ADA. Critics of disability rights, though, saw them as cause for alarm, or at least something to yell about — all the easier to do since no one publicly challenged them.

Although the major complaint was economic, critics found other problems with the law. Even people like New Hampshire state legislator Robert K. Boyce, who "have been blessed with family members who have disabilities and who have taught us to be keenly aware of their legitimate needs and aspirations," did not like the ADA, wrote Manchester *Union Leader* columnist Bernadette Malone Connolly more than a decade after its passage. She could write "with clear conscience and firm convictions," she said, that the ADA was "a bad law." It was "disrespectful of able-bodied people's rights."

Linda Steir exemplified for Connolly what was wrong with the ADA. Steir had reportedly sued the Girl Scouts when her daughter, who had cerebral palsy, was kept from her troop's overnight camping trip because the campsite had no wheelchair access.

Mrs. Steir then sought out another troop with girls younger than her daughter, but the scoutmaster said she would feel unprepared to address the challenges of a Scout with cerebral palsy.

The volunteers at this private organization apologized to Mrs. Steir for any carelessly phrased communications and tried to invite her daughter back. But Mrs. Steir refused, is suing for an undisclosed amount of money, and is trying to force the scoutmasters into sensitivity training.

Connolly's column, like Bovard's five years earlier, offered up anti-disability rights touchstones — the ones then making the rounds of conservatives that summer included one about "an expensive wheelchair ramp" that had been ordered at "an AMC hut high up in the Presidential mountain range as though any wheelchair-bound person with the superhuman strength to propel him or herself to the top of the mountain range (a feat for any able-bodied athlete) would then require a ramp to enter a hut"; another about professional golfer Casey Martin, who "has circulatory problems and can't walk long distances" but who wanted the PGA Tour to "change its rule forbidding players to ride in carts during tournaments" — which proved that "the ADA runs roughshod over the rights of private organizations to make these determinations."

Things were getting better for the disabled, said Boyce. "No one can dispute that many improvements to access to public buildings and accommodations have resulted from the ADA, and on the whole it can be said to be positive," he told Connolly, pointing to "the new entrances to buildings like the Alton Town Hall and to the Alton Library, the many curb cuts and improved sidewalks."

He was not against access for the handicapped, he was quick to point out.

> Having had occasion to try to maneuver my wife in a wheelchair into restaurants and pushing another gentleman 10 miles in his chair during a fund-raiser on streets without curb cuts or even sidewalks in some places, brought home clearly the need for changes. I've watched people in wheelchairs struggle to call for an elevator in a major hotel where the call button was too high and large potted plants or ashtrays further blocked access. I've heard firsthand accounts of people unable to hold jobs for lack of minor accommodations.

Yet, he said, the law went too far. There were "those who are attempting, with some success, to redefine 'disabilities' to cover conditions that are at best questionable."

The complaint against disability rights continued year after year. Rarely rebutted, it was made with equanimity, with self righteousness, because after all, "no one is against the handicapped." The claim that disability rights cost too much, that it hurt non-disabled people, that it warred against common sense, that it allowed people who weren't truly disabled the benefit of its special rights, that it, yes, hurt disabled people themselves, was only made for the disabled's own good, said the critics. No one is against the handicapped.

This was paternalism, the particular cloak bigotry wears when it's bigotry against disability. Bigotry with a pat on the head.

PART 2
The Case For Disability Rights

E L E V E N

The Hearing

The hearing room of the House Committee on the Judiciary's Subcommittee on the Constitution was packed as Clint Eastwood prepared to testify on amending the ADA to require that 90-day notice be given to businesses before they were sued for failing to obey what was by now a ten-year-old law.

Over a dozen Subcommittee members had showed up. Mel Watt, Democrat of Charlotte, N.C., was there. So was Maxine Waters, Democrat from Los Angeles. Newton, Mass.'s Barney Frank and New York City's Jerrold Nadler were on the Subcommittee as well. Charles Canady of Fla., a Republican, chaired the group.

Although *The Wall Street Journal* had reported that Eastwood would solicit Christopher Reeve for the battle, Reeve was nowhere in sight.

The paralyzed celebrity was often in the news. When Eastwood was talking to *The Wall Street Journal*, Reeve was talking to *Newsday* health reporter Jamie Talan. Talan repeated for *Newsday's* millions of New York readers that Reeve had vowed to walk by his 50th birthday.

"I said that I *hope* that by my 50th birthday I'd be able to stand and thank everybody," he'd told David Frost earlier. Maybe not that quickly, he now said, but "within the next four to five years I should begin to start the process of recovery."

Reeve was like Nelson Mandela, Frost thought — imprisoned, but in his body.

"And you seem to have achieved what he achieved: to do it without bitterness?"

"Well, I have opportunities. And when you do, you need to help speak up for the whole disability movement, to push the researchers as far as they can go."

On Super Bowl Sunday, over a hundred million viewers had watched as Reeve appeared to "walk" — the $5 million McCann-Erickson commercial for Nuveen Investments showing Reeve rising from his wheelchair at a future gala to accept an award for his efforts to fund research for a cure for spinal cord injury. The spot aimed to show that people could do "amazing" things with their money if they invested with Nuveen. The commercial had moved many to tears, but others had felt it deceptive, misleading — spinal cord injury groups had even been getting calls from people convinced the ad was real and wanting the cure for themselves.

Reeve defended the ad as "a motivating vision of something that can actually happen," and when *Time* magazine commentator Charles Krauthammer, also a wheelchair user, criticized it as "nonsense" and worried that newly paralyzed people "might end up emulating Reeve, spending hours on end preparing their bodies to be ready to walk the day the miracle cure comes, much like the millenarians who abandon their homes and sell their worldly goods to await the Rapture on a mountaintop," Reeve retorted that Krauthammer, although trained as a medical doctor, was likely "unaware of the many published studies documenting the remarkable progress being made toward repairing a damaged spinal cord."

It was Reeve's celebrity — the fact that he *had* been seen by hundreds of millions in a Super Bowl commercial; the fact that his star still shone, despite the Nuveen controversy (or perhaps because of it); the fact that the public did indeed believe that he represented "the whole disability movement" as he put it — that had prompted Eastwood to say he'd get Reeve involved with the campaign to amend the ADA.

It wasn't surprising that Reeve wasn't there, though. Reeve had never been publicly involved with anything concerning disability rights.

Watt took the opportunity to make an opening statement. Thanking Eastwood "for taking time out of his schedule to be here and give us his perspective on this," he launched into a comparison: "I asked myself, if I had been traveling in Alabama or Mississippi and gone to a hotel or restaurant and been turned away because I was black, would there be, should there be, a requirement that I give somebody 90 days' or 60 days' notice to comply with the law before I could vindicate my right? Or before I could have a reasonable expectation of gaining access to that facility that is covered by the law?"

Rep. Foley took the floor. It was really his show.

He'd invited Donna and David Batelaan, both wheelchair users. "They started the business Access Mobility to give people like themselves a chance to have full employment, gain full access and share in the bounty of life that all of us may take for granted, and found themselves confronted by a lawsuit themselves."

The lawsuit against the Batelaans, reported first in the *Palm Beach Post*, had become fodder for those who pushed the case against disability rights. Turning up in the *National Review* and *USA Today*, it had done much to fuel this drive to amend the ADA. It had that kind of turn editors loved — a store owned by wheelchair users, selling wheelchairs to other users, being sued for wheelchair access violations.

The suit had been brought by Jean Pavlak of Jupiter, Fla., who had traveled to the Lake Worth store only to discover when she got there that the parking lot lacked reserved "handicapped parking" spaces, something clearly required under ADA rules for businesses open to the public. She sued.

Foley cared deeply about the Batelaans; he'd been former chair of his local Goodwill, he told the Subcommittee. Ignorance of the law was no defense, he admitted. "But we are talking about businesses that can barely afford clerks, much less lawyers, being expected to comply with very specific requirements of a Federal law that no one has made them aware of." That was not exactly true of the Batelaans, but no matter. "Let's not blame the businesses," he said.

He'd made sure that Joe Fields and his wife Tammy were there to testify as well. Joe Fields was an attorney from West Palm Beach. He had represented the Batelaans, and was a member of the board of the West Palm Beach Office of the Florida Centers for Independent Living, a disability organization. Tammy Fields was an assistant city attorney for Palm Beach County.

"Palm Beach County is one of the many areas of the country whose small businesses have been struck with lawsuits filed without notice under the ADA," Canady told the hearing room. Palm Beach had passed a resolution supporting the amendment the hearing was considering.

Foley turned to Watt. "A black person entering a restaurant and being denied access is reprehensible, but that is because the person is mean," he said. Most everybody understood the impact of civil rights legislation, he said, but "what we are talking about with ADA is ignorance."

Rep. Clay Shaw, the Florida Congressman co-sponsoring the bill, agreed. "Obviously, you do not give somebody 90 days' notice that they have to open their business to all races, regardless of any personal prejudice that they may have," he added. But the bill before the hearing actually strengthened the ADA, he said; it would get American businesses into compliance.

A celebrity, Eastwood would get his star turn first. "Mr. Eastwood came here today to be an advocate for common sense," Foley told the jam of microphones and cameras whose presence had forced the many disability rights advocates to remain out in the hall. "I am delighted that he is here."

On the West Coast the problem was much like Palm Beach's, Eastwood began. "I have experienced it firsthand.

"We have the same few lawyers that are perpetrating this case, and in my opinion they are perverting the law by going around and filing these broadside, sand-bagging type suits where they hit you broadside from nowhere, with absolutely no warning.

"I was hit by one in an old hotel I was trying to restore" — he was referring to Mission Ranch — "just on an allegation that somebody was there, and a year earlier they had been denied access. They waited a whole year to file this suit. They claimed that some employee told them that we did not have handicapped bathrooms. Well, the truth is we did have handicapped bathrooms.

"But once they file a suit on you, they keep adding everything. Every time they come back they keep upping the ante, adding many more problems to be solved which they can collect fees on. And it is really not very fair. The same lawyer-plaintiff combination has done Heritage House in Mendocino and they have done other places. And they have written me before on another restaurant that I was a one-sixth owner of, but nothing came of that because it was in compliance.

"I am here just to help out.

"I have got a lawsuit going. It comes up in the fall. We will go ahead and take it before a jury and find out what they think about this whole thing.

"But in the meantime, I meet the Batelaans and hear all these horror stories across the country, and you can't believe in America that these lawyers that cloak themselves under the guise that they are doing a favor for the disabled when they really are doing a disservice.

"Who in America gives these lawyers the right to be the self-appointed vigilantes to enforce the law? Why can we not just have some decency and give persons notice that there is some problem going on?

"That is all I am here for. I realize I am a bit naive on this, but with the same people perpetrating this over and over again, professional litigants, it is just not fair, and I am here just as a common person speaking of fairness."

Rep. Nadler had a question for Eastwood: Hadn't he been sued in fact under California's access law? That was true, Eastwood admitted.

"The bill you are supporting would not have affected your court case in any way, is that correct?" Nadler pressed. True as well. After a few minutes he added that he had been sued both under California law and the Americans with Disabilities Act, but that yes, the bill they were discussing would not in any case help him with the California law.

Eastwood stepped down. The tide of reporters flowed out of

the hearing room in Eastwood's wake. They'd get a few more soundbites from the star out in the hall. Advocates rolling in took the vacated seats.

The reporters had all left when Donna Batelaan began her story. The couple's parking lot and building were "totally wheelchair accessible," she insisted — they'd been sued only because "we had not painted the lines and posted a sign on the one handicapped spot that is required by ADA."

"An attorney from New Jersey, without notice, filed a suit against us. It cost us less than $100 to correct the infractions and $2,000 for attorney's fees," she said. Had she been aware she was in violation of the law when she'd been sued? Watt asked her. She'd known the parking lot "didn't have one blue parking space" and that the law did require one, she said.

But did the "one blue spot make a difference for people with disabilities? In my particular situation, no." Batelaan was incensed at what she saw as a personal affront.

Yet she made an odd witness for the prosecution. "The ADA is the most fundamentally important law passed to date," she said. Without it she and David would likely have not been able to get to Washington; not gotten an accessible hotel room. As she continued her testimony, her defense of the ADA became passionate — arguments against disability rights laws "were always based on dollar signs. Our rights are always too expensive" — and ended in a ringing denunciation of those who would attack the law. "Do not let media hysteria, greedy practitioners or poorly informed entrepreneur backlash weaken this great piece of legislation, the Americans with Disabilities Act!"

But her comments were not reported. The reporters had left with Eastwood.

"To understand why this seemingly modest notification provision would do such harm," Baltimore attorney Andrew Levy told the hearing, "you need to understand a very unusual aspect of the ADA." The dirty little secret of the law's Title III was that it "provides no damages when you break it. You can intentionally — knowingly — violate it for years — and you will not be held responsible for damages.

"Since there is no risk that a violator has to pay damages, the effect of requiring 'notice' is to encourage people to do nothing until they get a letter." The law was already difficult to enforce and widely ignored, he said; this bill would make it even more so — creating "a blanket nationwide exemption to the ADA."

The only incentive now in the law to induce private attorneys to take Title III cases, he said, was that if you brought a case and if you won, you could ask the judge to award reasonable attorney's fees. It was not true, said Levy, that "all a lawyer need to do is file a lawsuit and then send the defendant a bill.

"That does not happen in any universe that I have ever been in," he went on. "Judges takes these fee petitions very seriously. They are not just going around handing out money."

There was no incentive for bringing frivolous lawsuits that didn't win; "if you do, you're going to end up having worked for free." He reminded the Subcommittee that federal court rules allowed a defendant to recover his own attorney's fees if the lawsuit "was frivolous or brought in bad faith." Even when the plaintiff won, his attorney was allowed only "reasonable" fees, he reiterated — typically calculated as the standard hourly rate that clients in non-civil rights cases paid, "multiplied by the number of hours the judge finds the case reasonably should have taken to litigate."

This should not have been news to any of those on the Subcommittee; most had practiced law. Surely Foley and Shaw already knew all this, even if, perhaps, Eastwood did not.

The reporters covering Eastwood likely didn't know this. But they had long ago left the hearing.

That evening, on *Crossfire*, Eastwood would insist that "Once they sue you, then the clock starts, and they can — any other improvements you make they can claim fees upon. It's a racket. And there's people in prison all across this country for extortion and everything, but these guys get away with it legally."

Eastwood had repeatedly told reporters that he had been the

victim of a "sand-bagging type" lawsuit that had been dropped on him with "absolutely no warning." He had asked the Subcommittee a rhetorical question: "Why can we not just have some decency and give persons notice that there is some problem going on?"

But Eastwood, it seemed, protested too much.

Access consultant Fred Shotz had spent time on his flight from Florida, he said, doing something none of the media covering Eastwood's story seemed to have bothered to do: He looked at the legal papers filed in the Eastwood case, which he had gotten from the plaintiff's attorney. The papers revealed that Eastwood had indeed been sent an initial letter about the violations — three months after zumBrunnen had visited the resort, long before the lawsuit.

"Clint Eastwood did not tell you about the certified letter that was sent to him — that he refused to sign for, and that got returned to the plaintiff's attorney. That, I believe, is called 'notice,'" Shotz told the hearing.

"Nothing stopped Mr. Eastwood from building a ramp or widening his bathroom doors at anytime during the lawsuit, including the day he got served with the complaint," Levy was now telling the hearing. "Had he done so, the plaintiff's fees would have been in the hundreds of dollars, rather than the hundreds of thousands." Eastwood would tell *Crossfire* viewers later that evening that he had already amassed $576,000 in legal fees.

Eastwood's fees "could only have grown to the size they did because of his refusal to comply with the law voluntarily, and the scorched-earth manner in which his lawyer conducted the defense," Levy went on. "I've been trying cases for a long time, and I can't ever recall amassing a bill the size that Mr. Eastwood is complaining about in a relatively simple ADA case."

What it suggested, Levy said, was "that Mr. Eastwood vigorously contested his obligation to comply with the ADA"; that his attorney had "engaged in a great deal of pre-trial maneuvering"; and that "opportunities to settle the case at an early stage were ignored.

"This was certainly their right," he continued. "But defending a case in that manner has consequences" — and one of them was that you ended up with a big bill.

"That is a function of Mr. Eastwood's conduct, not some flaw in the ADA."

Dentist Steven Rattner saw Foley's bill as a threat to his future. A deaf man, he'd already lost out on one training class offered by a firm whose dental software he used; they'd denied his request for a sign language interpreter. By the time he'd gotten them to change their mind, the class had come and gone. "I had to wait six months for the next session." If this bill passed, and he had to wait 90 days to press any request, he'd never get an interpreter, he said.

As a business owner — he employed two other dentists and a staff of nine — he considered the ADA much like any other law whose rules governed his dental practice, he said. He had to comply with rules on disposal of biological waste, with tax codes, with license requirements, he told the hearing. None of them had a 90-day period to excuse a violator. When he'd opened his office, he'd had to pressure the landlord to make the waiting room fully accessible; but he'd done it. That was just the standard cost of doing business, he felt. "There is no reason why we should make an exception for the ADA." The law was 10 years old. "Ignorance of the law is no longer an acceptable excuse."

Christine Griffin, head of Boston's Disability Law Center, directed her comments to Watt when she insisted the situation was indeed analogous to race. "It is not always about a ramp or a physical access device that has to be in place. Why should a person who is blind and uses a guide dog have to wait 90 days after they have been denied access to a restaurant because they have a service animal with them? Why should a person with mental retardation wait 90 days to invoke a court's jurisdiction after being told by a restaurant owner that he will not serve him because he doesn't think the other customers want to look at him?

"Why should a man with cerebral palsy have to wait 90 days

after being refused service at a local liquor store and then escorted out of the store by police who call him 'retarded?' Why should a young man who uses a wheelchair have to wait 90 days to file a lawsuit after the taxi driver tells him that he does not pick up people that are crippled because he does not want to help them? Why should the parents of a 4-year-old child with Down syndrome have to wait 90 days to file a lawsuit against an afterschool music program that denied the child's access because the director of the program was uncomfortable with that child? And why should the working parents of a child with a disability have to wait 90 days after their child is denied access to day care because the kid has a disability?

"We had a case where a kid was in an after-school hockey program and they would not allow this kid to play hockey. The hockey team was starting; the season would have been over if we had waited 90 days and had to file something.

"There are instances when you do want to go right into court," she reminded the Subcommittee, "where you want to get a preliminary injunction to stop immediate harm." With someone with a serious medical problem being denied access to health care, "you would want to go in and get an injunction right away.

"You cannot wait 90 days," she said.

What about people denied insurance, or mortgages? Levy asked. Should they have to wait 90 days before suing? And sometimes, when medical care was involved, requiring a 90-day waiting period was dangerous. The bill would "rob people of their right to seek a preliminary injunction."

"I am skeptical of the aims of HR 3590," Maxine Waters said, referring to Foley's bill. "Any efforts to scale back the hard-won civil rights protections of members of the disabled community must be weighed carefully. Particularly when such action is being undertaken by this Subcommittee."

The Subcommittee had a history of attacking civil rights gains in the name of legal integrity, Waters said. "Efforts have been made to undermine the Fair Housing Act of 1988, affirmative action programs, and other civil rights gains."

In October Canady had held hearings on a bill called the "Justice in Fair Housing Enforcement Act of 1999." Much like the bill before the hearing today, that too had been an effort to roll back disability rights — to gut the access requirements that had been passed as part of the Fair Housing Act's 1988 amendments. The bill had been put up by Rep. Walter Jones, a Republican. The National Association of Homebuilders supported it.

Disability rights advocates had again trooped to the Subcommittee a week after Reeve had walked on the Super Bowl. On Canady's agenda that time was the requirement to make websites accessible, so blind people could get the same information from the Internet as sighted people. The federal Access Board would soon release rules requiring accessible design on websites of Federal agencies and departments; it was widely believed that these same standards would likely apply to the entire Internet sooner or later. The Justice Department said the ADA's Title III applied to all websites; that the Internet was as much a public accommodation as was a store or business. In November, the National Federation of the Blind had filed a class-action suit against the 20-million member America Online over what they said was an inaccessible e-mail interface, and insisted that making AOL accessible would not be that hard to do.

"In light of costs that application of the ADA would impose on that rapidly expanding segment of the economy, and the substantial First Amendment implications of applying the ADA to private Internet websites and services, the development of a legislative record on these issues" would "likely prove quite valuable," said the memo announcing the hearing.

Web access advocates knew that access was ridiculously easy to achieve. Default web page coding — text only — was in fact pretty much accessible; the graphic add-ons were what made it inaccessible. Most early academic web pages were accessible. It was when the Web caught the interest of business entrepreneurs that access problems developed. Designers began making fancier browsers and writing webpage coding that would be visually interesting to the vast television market, which they saw as relying on graphics rather than text. It was because of these graphic add-ons that the originally accessible Internet had now become pretty much inaccessible to blind people. As it bloated with graphics, requiring faster computers and faster modems and newer browsers to surf it, the Web became inaccessible as well to poorer people with older computers and slower modems.

Federal rules would likely require that "streaming audio and audio files have immediate text alternatives," Canady told the hearing. The "use of color to convey information" might be "restricted in some ways"; webmasters would likely have to "provide at least one mode that does not require user vision by formatting all information so that it is compatible with Braille and speech synthesis devices.

"Other provisions," he warned, "may ban touch screens, prohibit moving text or animation (unless the user can go to a static display with the same information)."

This time the celebrity making the case against disability rights was the Manhattan Institute's Walter Olson. Olson's 1997 *Excuse Factory* endeared him to ADA bashers; his own website was overlawyered.com, whose name pretty much said it all. He'd been pressed into service by access opponents who felt he'd make the case in terms interesting to the media.

True to form, Olson carped about the "ADA's application as a serious threat to the freedom, spontaneity and continued growth of the Web" and warned of the organized disabled lying in wait to file lawsuits — although to date the only one filed had been against AOL. AOL was big business, but "the principles at stake here will filter all the way down to many mom-and-pop Internet service providers.

"If it is easy pickings to walk down a town's main shopping street and find stores that you can hit with an ADA suit over their physical facilities, then it is even easier to browse the Web and find websites that are arguably out of ADA compliance." Suits would be filed "by the bushel basket." There'd be "an obvious temptation for someone to start doing this kind of thing once the idea of lawsuits over Web accessibility becomes a little more familiar."

Olson took the position that requiring access was akin to removing one's First Amendment right to free speech. If the rules were allowed to go into effect, he predicted, "hundreds of millions of existing pages would be torn down" and "the posting of new pages, by the tens of millions, would screech to a near-halt."

Much of this was simply wrong. It seemed most on the Subcommittee had figured that out by the time Olson testified, too — because Gary Wunder had testified first.

Wunder, a computer programmer at the University of Missouri — "a person who makes his living writing programs and getting information to medical doctors and hospital administrators," he told the hearing — was a member of the board of the National Federation of the Blind, the group that had sued AOL. He himself was blind.

Piece by piece, Wunder laid out facts that demolished Olson's arguments.

Wunder explained that most blind people browsed the Internet with programs called screen readers, "which look at the information sent to the screen and attempt to tell us, through speech or Braille, what is displayed there — both text and the little pictures and graphics known as icons. If there is a button we are to push to move to the next screen, our screen readers say 'NEXT - BUT-TON.' If we are presented with a form where we are to enter our name and address, the screen reader will say 'NAME' when we are in the name field, and when we come to the area of the screen where we are to enter our state, it will say 'COMBO BOX' and allow us to move through the choices until the two letter abbreviation we want is found. Those kinds of boxes, which usually appear in alphabetical order, leave me wishing I were from Alabama or Alaska instead of Missouri.

"Most of you make extensive use of a mouse when you navigate the Internet, but blind people cannot do this. We use the tab and arrow keys to move from item to item. Therefore, our request of website developers is that each item which can be accessed with a mouse also have provision for being accessed by the keyboard. This could mean a tab stop or perhaps a key sequence which could perform the same task as clicking with a mouse.

"In many ways, living in what has come to be called the Information Age is a dream come true for people who are blind," he went on. "Not so long ago, writing this testimony for you would have meant first writing a draft in Braille, writing a second Braille copy to perfect the draft, and then typing that Braille document so you could read it in print. Imagine the difficulty if, while trying to transcribe the Braille into print, I was interrupted by a phone call. Where did I leave off in the transcription? Had I made any typographical errors, and if I had, could they be corrected with white out? To ensure I had written a quality presentation for this Subcommittee would have taken the involvement of someone with sight to proofread my final product.

"Now, with the advent of the personal computer, speech and Braille technology, and the Internet, I can write my material myself, proof it myself, send it to others for their comments and criticisms, and eventually send the final draft halfway across the country for printing and distribution.

"Never in my wildest imaginings did I conceive of this possibility when I was typing my high school and college papers, but I would be hard-pressed to do without this now."

Despite the Internet's great promise, problems had developed. "One of our biggest difficulties comes when we try to shop on-line using pages where the creator of the website has failed to add text description in the code for the pictures. Computer technology is not yet sufficiently advanced to recognize a picture and tell us what appears on the screen. We still must rely on the creator of the page we're viewing to add a line of text which says, for example, 'Swiss Army Knife' or 'Queen Size Electric Blanket.' These explanations are easily added and are of tremendous benefit not only to the blind but also to people who see."

The presence of graphics on websites was is not the problem, he insisted, gently correcting Olson and others who had testified — "but the presence of *unlabeled* graphics and the design of systems which rely *only* on graphics."

"People who have things to market should make their pages as visually attractive and marketable as they can, in the same way they would design a store window. Making services available to the blind isn't a matter of deciding whether to make a screen visually appealing or audibly accessible. It means taking thirty seconds to add a textual description to the graphic you've decided to display." This expanded one's customer base to the ever-growing numbers of people who either did not see, or did not see well. Wunder did not add, but could have, that it also expanded the site's usability to the thousand of people in the ever-growing market for what are called "personal digital assistants."

"Some have suggested that labeling graphics and push buttons might constitute an undue burden on small businesses and Internet start-ups. But one could say with equal plausibility that choosing graphics rather than text is the burden." It took webpage designers far longer to create graphics than text; it took far more bandwidth to display them. "Either one — used exclusively — limits the audience that can be reached, and results in missed opportunities to communicate and sell products." Technology created for "special needs" ended up benefiting everyone. Some called this the "electronic curb cut effect." Wunder explained it in simple terms:

"In 1976, the first reading machine for the blind was developed which could look at ink print on a page, scan it into a digital image, recognize its ink shapes as letters, and then verbalize the resulting text in human-like speech. Now scanning devices are readily available to the general public. The recognition of text from a page allows many companies to store paper documents in their electronic data banks, and the text-to-speech pioneered in this first machine is now common in everything from simple children's toys to complicated telephone answering machines. Let us also not forget that the first efforts to get a computer to understand human speech came as a result of trying to give people who could not use a keyboard access to the world of computing. Now this technology is sufficiently advanced to allow the dictation of this very statement and its accurate transcription."

It wasn't true that access would make a site look clunky, he insisted. Nor would it take up a lot of bytes of Web space: Just the opposite: "a graphic displayed on a screen may take upwards of half a million computer characters to display, while its text description will take less than 100.

"What we are discussing when we talk about access is not whether it is technologically possible," he went on, "but whether we plan to use this technological revolution to include people who have all too often been excluded.

"Microsoft Project is a program which lets people manage the work tasks they've been assigned. Each project has a due date, and if it is large, as many projects are, it will have subtasks which themselves have intermediate due dates. When a manager looks at his projects, he is presented with a screen showing those projects which are most critical in bright red, and those of less criticality in lighter shades. It is intuitively obvious as he looks at the screen which projects need his immediate attention and which will wait. The calculations done by this program are simple and straightforward: check today's date against the due date of each project and assign a color for display based on the difference between the two.

"No matter how obvious the technique, that number is still inaccessible to me. If someone had thought about the nonvisual user when designing this system, it would have been easy to put out a list in order of due dates. A list with the most critical project first and the least critical last would have given me exactly the same information gained by my sighted colleagues, but a mechanism for making that program produce a simple list was not a part of its design."

He could give many other examples of inaccessible software, Wunder told the hearing. The point was "that the information which was needed was displayed with only one audience in mind — the visual user — although there is nothing inherently visual about two dates and the number of days which separate them. In fact, much more effort went into figuring out how to display those projects in a visually attractive color scheme than went into determining their order.

"The vast majority of blind people are over age sixty-five," he continued. "I think it would be a costly mistake for us to overlook the needs of this community — and the significant purchasing power they represent." It was an astute observation, given that the interests Canady represented always stressed the costs of access as being too burdensome.

"I've never seen any figures to indicate that the cost of accessibility is economically impractical," Wunder went on. "The issue may have more to do with ideological objections to government involvement than the real cost of implementing accessible systems.

"The Internet is not just a window on the world, but more and more it is the world. It is where people talk, where people shop, and where people increasingly make their living," Wunder told the Subcommittee. He urged them "to differentiate between the real-world needs of blind people" and the "hypothetical and yet unproved burden" to the business community of computer access.

"The effort required of the business community is minuscule when compared with the benefits to blind and disabled people and to the society in which we live. The cost of isolating the blind, the disabled, and the senior citizens of our nation is far too high, and the benefits to all of us will be immense if only we stay the course."

Now once again disability rights activists were gathered in the hearing room of Canady's subcommittee, this time to refute arguments that Clint Eastwood had championed.

"If this Subcommittee is serious about the bad acts of some lawyers," Maxine Waters said, "then let us have a hearing that would examine whether the state bar ethics boards are an effective vehicle to address such grievances. I cannot in good faith support an attack on the ADA because we want to go after bad-acting lawyers."

That did seem the appropriate solution. But Canady wasn't ready to end the hearing just yet. There was more to be heard from the Florida contingent.

Nearly a thousand cases had been filed in south Florida, said Joe Fields, "by a group of four or five associations represented by three or four different sets of attorneys." The attorneys were "using forms, over and over and over again." Fields had represented Baseball Dugout, who had fixed its problem within a week or two of being served with notice of a lawsuit. "The lawyer that sued this company came out there and said, 'yeah, everything is fine; I want some money.' He thereafter sent my client a letter saying 'I want $4,500' — $4,500 to do about two hours' worth of work."

The Palm Beach County Board of Commissioners had decided to back Foley's bill "after 38 lawsuits were filed by one law firm in a two-week period," Tammy Fields added. The suits were against "long-time established mom-and-pop businesses who unfortunately were not aware of the need to make certain modifications to their premises in order to comply with the ADA"; they were "located in a depressed corridor that is trying to revitalize." Dredging up the Batelaans' case again, Tammy Fields told the hearing that the suits hadn't even been filed by a local residents, but people from neighboring Broward County.

Most of the businesses "undertook immediate remedial action even though they had limited resources. In recognition of their remedial efforts, they received demand letters from the plaintiff's attorney in the amount of $5,000 in fees."

But none of the businesses being discussed had ended up paying more than $500 in legal fees, Fred Shotz reminded the Subcommittee. Lawyers may have asked for more, but judges weren't granting it. "That is how the system is supposed to work," he reminded them.

Shotz was also from Florida. He was a member of the Florida Paraplegic Association; his firm, ADA Consulting Associates, advised groups and businesses on access. He was the ADA consultant, he said, for the city of Lake Worth, where the Batelaans' store was located.

Shotz agreed that there had been a lot of lawsuits over access in Florida. "A lot of people who are disabled live in Florida. We have a flat state. We do not have snow and we do not have ice. We have probably one of the oldest populations on average in the country."

He thought it quite likely that there had been a thousand or more lawsuits over access. And yet, he said, it was also likely that fewer than one business in 10 was compliant with the law.

The Batelaans' parking lot, which had occasioned the original lawsuit that had started the chain of events that had led to this hearing, "is half paved and half gravel," he told the hearing. "I have tried to park on the gravel part of their lot and push my wheelchair across it. I am a former wheelchair racer, but I could not push across that parking lot."

The Batelaans had been quoted in the *Palm Beach Post* as saying they had "six employees that are disabled and qualified to park in accessible parking spaces." But even now, after the lawsuit, there were still "just two parking spaces for people who are disabled."

"There's been an undercurrent much of the testimony that somehow people should be embarrassed about filing lawsuits trying to enforce the law of the land," Andrew Levy had said earlier in the hearing.

"Congress intended private litigants to enforce this law. That is the whole structure of this statute." The fact that lawsuits were beginning to be filed simply meant that after a decade the law still lacked widespread compliance. If businesses bothered to comply with the law, they wouldn't have to worry about lawsuits, he added.

"Lawyers who bring ADA cases already assume the risk that they will lose and be paid nothing, with their only upside being that they simply get their normal hourly rate if they win," Levy had told the Subcommittee. The bill the Subcommittee was considering, "by making it even more difficult to get paid for enforcing the ADA" would "build into the statute more disincentives to enforcement, resulting in less compliance and accessibility.

"Just as cutting a horse's hay with straw eventually kills the horse, continuing to water down the incentives for enforcing the ADA will eventually kill it."

"I woke up this morning to the announcement that there finally were some indictments against the man who bombed a church where four little girls were killed — how many years ago? Little black girls in Alabama," Maxine Waters had said to the hearing that morning. She was referring to Thomas E. Blanton, Jr. and Bobby Frank Cherry, who had turned themselves in to authorities after being indicted by an Alabama grand jury. *The New York Times* had carried the story on its front page.

"Now what does that have to do with this hearing?

"Attitudes," she said. "Attitudes."

Correcting the record

Clint Eastwood's campaign to fix the Americans with Disabilities Act was the centerpiece of PBS's *NewsHour with Jim Lehrer* on the tenth anniversary of the law's July 26 signing.

"Clint Eastwood is off the wall on this one," Sid Wolinsky told reporter Spencer Michels. Eastwood and Foley were "just plain wrong." (The way disabled people sued businesses was "nothing more than harassment," Rep. Foley had told Michels.)

Wolinsky, head of the Oakland-based Disability Rights Advocates law firm, like many in the disability rights community, worked to rebut the case against disability rights, to correct the record, to change the tone of public debate. There was an important role for lawsuits, Wolinsky explained to Michels, just as there had been in other civil rights movements. Eastwood's "lawyers are trying to get rich" comments were simply divisive — and wrong, he insisted.

It was said that the problem with the ADA was that no one knew about it — "City and county officials don't even know what the law is. We have to have an education campaign," Foley had told *Hardball's* Chris Matthews — yet most disability rights supporters insisted the problem wasn't that businesses didn't know about the law but that they simply didn't bother to obey it.

James Raggio of the U.S. Access Board said as much to *Los Angeles Times* reporter Ted Rohrlich. People said Kornel Botosan had a cottage industry going in lawsuits for access to small stores, restaurants, bars; that both he and his attorney Mark Potter were getting rich off it. It was true he sued "mom and pop" stores, Botosan said — they were mainly the ones that were inaccessible. If he were only in it for the money, though, wouldn't he just settle the cases without worrying about the compliance issue? "The compliance issue was always the stickler," he said.

To John Parry of the American Bar Association's Commission

on Mental and Physical Disability Law, the real problem was that for years after the ADA had passed, few access suits had been filed at all. "Many disabled activists felt it was both fair and politically prudent to let businesses, which had opposed the law, have a reasonable opportunity to comply." The reason people like Kornel Botosan had begun filing suits as the '90s moved toward their close, said Parry, was because a sense had grown among disability rights activists that enough time had passed — nearly a decade — that a backlash against the bringing of suits would be unreasonable.

"The only way you open up society — other than through education — is through litigation," said the Disability Rights Education and Defense Fund's Stephen Rosenbaum.

Disabled people were "tired of hearing businesses complain over and over about why they need not make their facilities accessible because they don't have any disabled customers or employees," a pharmacist who used a wheelchair insisted to the *Los Angeles Times*. "Talk about circular logic!! The reality for disabled people is that a large number of businesses, both large and small, as well as public agencies, do not take the ADA seriously and have the attitude of 'so sue me' when contacted about their inaccessibility and noncompliance."

The fact that businesses were not "responsible for the condition" of their customers did not relieve them of a responsibility to accommodate them, Marc Fiedler had insisted, after he'd been reamed in the *Washington Times* by Doug Bandow for daring to file lawsuits. To Fiedler, Bandow's column was shrill and misguided. Businesses had restrooms for women, didn't they? Even though they weren't responsible for some patrons being women? The fact that businesses were not "responsible for" a customer's disability did not give them license to discriminate.

R. Richardson King's fulminations against the ADA's "absurd mandates" did not go unchallenged, either. "It is difficult to decide which is the greater injustice, that such illogical thinking is allowed to define the public debate or that the editors of *The*

Times-Picayune are willing to give it so much space," wrote Hiltraud Reeder. King failed to understand "that the ADA is not a business issue but a civil rights issue," he wrote. "Persons with disabilities are not 'unfortunate,' but are entitled to realize the opportunities available to every American citizen."

If King's kind of thinking persisted, added Joe Tagert, "women still wouldn't vote and blacks would still sit in the back of the bus." "All the Americans with Disabilities Act does is grant the same rights to disabled Americans that are enjoyed by the vast majority....We just want to be treated equally, like you."

It may have been that disability advocates spoke up every chance they got — but they got fewer chances than those pressing the case against disability rights. Often they were not interviewed for stories at all; reporters being either unaware of them or preferring to interview government officials and those they felt were more professional or less likely to be biased. They had no million-dollar foundations devoted to media work; they had no think tanks like Cato or Heritage. The sophistication of the case against disability rights lay in the fact that much of it was promoted by right-wing think tanks that had convinced the media that they were impartial and presented the facts of the issue. Mostly, the case for disability rights was presented piecemeal, in letters to newspapers and television news programs, as advocates tried to correct the perception that disability rights gave a free ride to whiners and malingerers.

Hundreds of people with heart conditions and emphysema wrote to CBS following Andy Rooney's excoriation of people who used "handicapped parking" with no visible sign of disability. "I'm sorry I angered so many people and sorry I added to the problem people with invisible disabilities have, but I haven't changed my opinion that a lot of people use the handicapped spaces who have no right to," he said after reading some of the letters on the air. "It was probably a mistake to make the official symbol on the license plate a wheelchair," he griped, unrepentant.

Much of what was floated out to the media about disability rights was simply wrong, but many of those who campaigned against disability rights didn't seem to care, even when they were caught.

It seemed Ed Hudgins, author of the fifth anniversary anti-ADA "Handicapping Freedom," had never actually researched any of the outrageous cases that his Cato Institute had floated into the public eye — cases which had been reported by Bovard and Stossel and had become part of our urban legend about the bad, bad Americans with Disabilities Act. When John Hockenberry interviewed Hudgins on *Dateline NBC* in 1998, Hudgins defended himself by saying only that he'd gotten his information from employers; they'd told him such things, he said. He himself didn't "have numbers on it."

Hudgins's stories had almost all been wrong. The ADA had worked as it was supposed to in each instance. The outrageous cases had been ruled just that — outrageous. The cases with merit had been won by those who'd sued for accommodation.

Stories about Mother Teresa's elevator had been wrong also. Plans for renovating the two buildings called for the operational parts — the dorm, the soup kitchen, the bathrooms, the counseling areas — to be on the floor a half-flight up from the street entrance; an elevator to those would cost only $25,000 or so — never the $50,000 that the *Washington Post* reported; certainly never the $150,000 *The New York Times*'s Sam Roberts worried about. In truth, money wasn't even the issue, as the Sisters had been told that sources would be found for the money and that they would not have to pay for the elevator themselves in any case.

Philip Howard had got things wrong, too. He'd repeated the erroneous information about Mother Teresa's elevator. He reported that city officials in Minnetonka, Minn. had "had to alter the municipal hockey rink to make the scorer's box wheelchair accessible." In fact, they'd planned simply to move the scorer's equipment out of the box were a disabled person to need it. None had, said city compliance officer Kathy Magrew. "You have to use common sense" — disability law, she said, was "flexible enough to allow for" that.

The New York Times had gotten it wrong when it reported that the MTA would be required to retrofit 88 subway stations for wheelchair access. The number all along had been only 27. Its editorial claim that subway renovation was being held hostage by "a wheelchair on the tracks" was also wrong on many points. The MTA had known for years of its legal requirement for access. It had simply ignored it. The money could have been found by using a bus barn in West Farms that was standing empty rather than spending $35 million upgrading a bus barn in the Bronx that the community opposed anyway.

Vincent Marchiselli thought it curious the way the case against disability rights always centered on cost. Marchiselli, in the New York state assembly as majority whip, had had polio as a child. The long debate over school busing to achieve racial integration had never been obsessively concerned about the price of buses, he knew; when people debated racial integration, it seemed that they understood that "more basic values were at issue. Yet," he said, "the debate over how to implement laws granting the handicapped accessibility cannot seem to be conducted without undue focus on the cost of compliance."

"Could it be," he wondered, that the case against disability rights raged so strongly because disabled people "have always seemed the least able to respond forcefully to the denial of their rights?"

If one looked consistently enough, one could see a clear case for disability rights and access being made in the margins — usually in the letters to the editor. One of the most interesting things about this case calling for disability rights — a case for the creation of an accessible society, actually — was that it was often unwittingly made by ordinary people who, had they been asked, would have not necessarily said they were disability rights advocates. They would have said they were simply advancing common-sense ideas.

In an editorial snippily headlined "The $6,000 Subway Token," *The New York Times* had insisted that "only a handful would ever use elevators down to the trains." This time, non-disabled New Yorkers wrote in to insist *The Times* was wrong; that they'd like elevators as well: "When the escalator from the Independent line to the Flushing Line at Roosevelt and 74th Street in Queens is not working — which is quite frequently — the 60 or 70 stairs that must be climbed are like Mount Everest."

"Why do we speak only of the disabled? As a mother with a stroller-aged baby, I would welcome easier access. To enter a subway station, I have to find a sympathetic person to help me in carrying babe-in-stroller down the stairs;…I crumple into a mound of despair when I encounter one of the revolving-door-type gates."

"Have you ever watched an aged person climb the steps out of a subway?" wrote another. "This issue affects every person in the city who does not have a car — unless one dies before becoming a senior citizen…"

It wasn't a small number, state assembly deputy majority leader Alan Hevesi said; there were well over 23,000 people in wheelchairs in the New York metro area, and far more people who would be helped by a more accessible system.

"If elevators now planned for just the disabled were opened up to parents with children in strollers they would surely be well used." Families with young children needed to be allowed to travel through the city with ease, too.

But "special," "reserved only for the handicapped" continued to be the order of the day. That was the plan for the subway elevators; that was the plan most of the time when things were planned for "the disabled." "It's not aesthetics, it's safety," was the way the J. M. Kaplan Fund's Suzanne Davis put it during the New York City toilet battle, explaining why there had to be special separate toilets for the handicapped — and why they had to be kept locked at all times.

"That's one of the most obnoxious, patronizing reasons we hear," New York disability activist Anne Emerman fumed. "We take risks every day in New York — we motor out of our apartments in our motorized chairs, we ride around in our neighborhoods. We had to fight to get onto the subways, too," she said, remembering that earlier battle that was still not won. "We live in the war zones. We live in the housing projects. We are everywhere.

We take our chances along with the other seven million people in this city."

The truth was that access was nowhere near as horrendous as it sounded, and there were many simple and practical solutions, Mary Ann Rothman, head of the New York City Council of Cooperatives, conceded when questioned in the early 1990s about New York disability advocates' push for access to New York City housing. Yet that point — "there are many simple and practical solutions" — never made it into a single article in any New York daily when "access" reared its ugly head, as it did with Celia Dugger's articles about the toilets, or Sam Roberts's reports of Mother Teresa's trials with bureaucracy.

Though she didn't like it, Rothman said she understood why disabled people were fighting tooth and nail for a requirement for full access. "They have lobbied for years to have available to them what the rest of us have taken for granted. And now that they have this law they say if all the condos and co-ops have to do it eventually housing will be available to them."

It was just that the idea of integration, of having things "for the handicapped" be open to all, was new to people, and it scared them, said New York disability rights leader Frieda Zames. "Once people make something accessible, though, they like it." About the Decaux toilets, she said, "If they just put up an accessible one, they wouldn't need paired sets and they'd save a bunch of money."

"It would be funny," said Emerman, "if it weren't so tragic."

Discrimination and the formation of a minority

*All we want are the same rights that the
majority takes for granted.*
— *Linda DiCecco*

Despite the fact that a 12-year campaign has been waged against
it, despite the fact that its provisions were but vaguely understood
even by many of the members of Congress who passed it (who
may have voted for it simply because they didn't want to appear to
be against the disabled), the fact remains that the Americans with
Disabilities Act, contrary to what its critics say, is a clear and specific prohibition against discrimination on the basis of disability. Its
problems are due far less to the wording of the law than to the fact
that it is simply "based on a socio-cultural model of disability that
judges don't understand," as law professor Linda Krieger put it.
And, of course, to the fact that it has been a convenient whipping-
boy precisely because it has been so little explained or defended.

Judges don't seem to understand the concept of discrimination
as laid out in the ADA nor the kind of society its framers envi-
sioned any more than the rest of society. Most of society still
believes, as Christopher Reeve put it, that to be disabled was to no
longer be "whole." Along with Reeve, as a society we have pushed
for cure, or, lacking that, a way to "help the handicapped," which
we have believed, along with Rep. Stump, to be "a logical
approach to the protection of the disabled." But we have not really comprehended the central tenet of the disability rights perspective: that people who "have something wrong with them" are not
as a result made less as citizens; that, disability or no disability, they
have just as much a right to access to all of society as does any other
citizen.

The ADA has been called "far-reaching." But it is more than
that. To understand its tenets, one must use a new model. Not the

medical model — it sees the problem as the person who has something wrong that needs to be cured or overcome — but a socio-political model, which sees the problem as the society which fails to accommodate to individuals and groups who are deemed different, abnormal, "they." The socio-political model says that separating people out into a group, labeling them and denying them access and accommodation on the basis of that label, has nothing to do with medicine. It says that it is simply a political act.

Just as one could understand the problems of Sherry Colb at the law exam as being either her own personal need to drink apple juice during the exam or the bar exam proctors' belief that Colb's need for apple juice was "abnormal" and could only be allowed if she were labeled "special," one can understand the problems people like Greg Solas face as being due to their body's own differences from the norm, or due to someone else's failure to provide the access and accommodation that should be anyone's due.

The next chapters look at the disability experience from this different, socio-political perspective. For it is only by viewing disability from this perspective that we can come to any true comprehension of why people with disabilities form "a discrete and insular minority" or understand the real nature of disability discrimination, which so many judges seem to miss. As long as we view the problem as the disabled individual's own body needing to be fixed — a view that people have found support for in Christopher Reeve's pleas to millions of television viewers and in best-selling books — we will continue to believe, along with many of our Supreme Court justices, that the problem is in the person claiming "disability," and not in those doing the discriminating against that person. We will fail to see, as the courts have often failed to see, that the ADA is not about disability but, like any other civil rights law, about discrimination.

What does disability discrimination look like? In the next pages, we will hear from a few of the many individuals who face it daily. But disability discrimination also extends to the entire group of people labeled "disabled" — we will see this in state policies on voting and "institutionalization" — a term peculiar to the history of people considered "disabled." It is only when we see these patterns of treatment can we begin to understand why those who drafted the ADA wrote that people with disabilities formed a "discrete and insular minority," "faced with restrictions and limitations, subjected to a history of purposeful unequal treatment, and relegated to a position of political powerlessness in our society.…" Finally, we will see that "disability" as used in the ADA and as understood by its framers (but not, so far, by almost anyone else) is not a medical term at all. It is a socio-political one, and it functions precisely as does race in our culture: to define for exclusion a group of people based on characteristics that we give undue attention as a way to discriminate. And that it is a term that can likely be applied to any of us.

Finally, we will look at a way out of this entire quagmire — a way to move toward the creation of a society that provides equal access and accommodation as a matter of course.

Linda DiCecco, who had a hearing impairment, cheered Greg Solas's push to make her local schools accessible. No matter what one thought of his methods, at least he was making it so parents like her had access: "Like other minority groups, we get tired of listening to bureaucrats rationalizing what they do to us. All we want are the same rights that the majority takes for granted."

An argument about who "deserved" rights undergirded the case against disability rights. The disabled weren't a real minority, went the argument; not like African-Americans. (What makes them a "category," *Newsweek's* Jerry Adler wrote, is that they "lack something other people possess." Goffman had called them "failed normals.") African-Americans, on the other hand, were a real minority. They had the legacy of slavery. They had suffered from segregation. They had been kept off buses. They had been denied the vote. They endured racism. Perhaps we did owe them some rights. But the disabled had no history of facing real discrimination. The truly disabled did deserve help; nobody contested that.

It was just that a lot of people who had something wrong with them but who weren't truly disabled ("I couldn't do my job without my glasses, but I don't consider myself disabled," Supreme Court Justice Antonin Scalia had said) seemed to claim "disability" to try to get something they didn't really deserve.

This might have explained why people fixated on cost. People didn't seem to understand the "more basic values" at stake, as Marchiselli had put it. The changes disability rights advocates wanted were unreasonable, taking away from nondisabled people, who, after all, as Bandow had said, weren't responsible for the disabilities of those who were seeking access and accommodation.

Bandow misinterpreted: although not responsible for people's actual bodily disabilities, nondisabled society surely was, in fact, responsible for the lack of access people daily encountered.

The disability experience in America: segregation, exclusion, overprotection, paternalism

"They see you as just nagging and complaining unnecessarily."

It was not like the Jim Crow South — at least nobody thought of it that way. Because, they said, no *animus* was involved. Yet disabled people were segregated in most things, and most saw nothing wrong with that. People were taught in rehabilitation "to be independent, but in a ritualized way," John Hockenberry had said once. "Choose your ritual for being independent. Crip sports. Radio dispatcher. Computer operator. Choose your ritual for independence and then perform it, and pretend like it's not a cage."

It *was* a cage, he said. But you were taught not to think of it that way. "Rehab teaches you to never go near the edge of the cage, and you will be fine." And you will behave in such a way that there is no cage. But it was a cage, nonetheless. A ghetto — an "individual ghetto," he called it. You were "committing yourself to a system that required you to live near a mall."

A disabled person was valued for "coping amidst the adversity." People would praise you; would say that you had courage — but this had nothing to do with the real experience of being disabled and "everything to do with the nondisabled community's need to be told that everybody copes." People who got angry about a lack of access were "being dysfunctional; weren't playing along with the game."

"When we got off the bus this afternoon, my son was in tears," one wheelchair user wrote. "The driver had made jokes about how maybe the wheelchair lift was not going to work today, either. I have no idea what it will take to get across that not being able to get on or off a bus is not funny. In the presence of my kid, bus drivers have called me a 'bad passenger,' a bad mother and a faker all for simply wanting to use the wheelchair lift. This morning the driver couldn't find the right switches to make the wheelchair lift work. When she did finally locate them, the lift did not work. Then, laughing out loud about this failure, she said, 'Is it okay with you, honey, if the lift doesn't work today? You didn't really want to go to work anyway, did you?'

"I told her that yes, I did want to go to work today. She refused to call in the wheelchair lift failure, and, still laughing, closed the doors and drove away without me, treating the wheelchair lift problem and the reporting failure as a pleasant joke between us.

"Another day, when I asked a driver to report that his wheelchair lift didn't work, he simply refused. As he was closing the doors, I heard him muttering about handicapped people going and thinking they could ride the bus like everyone else." Selfish, just like Ellen Nuzzi had been, for trying to ride the bus.

"I'm not free to sit where I want. I'm not free to use the bathroom when I have to."

"I have to keep a little map in my head of what places I can go and what places I can't go."

To political scientist Harlan Hahn, who had used a wheelchair for many years, being a wheelchair user in the inaccessible community was like "being in the midst of a vast desert with only a few oases."

Six steps up to the entrance of the San Rafael coffee shop. Theresa Camalo and her friend noticed the wheelchair lift to the side — it was being used to store table umbrellas. Discouraged, not wanting to turn getting a cup of coffee into a confrontation with the owner, she left. Coming back a few days later with a disability advocate, she called the shop owner out and talked to him about it.

"He was none too happy. He told us no one ever used it so he decided to use it for storage." If he kept it clear and posted a sign as to what it was, it would likely be used, she told him.

The next time she went by for a cup of coffee, the lift was clear. She went in and chatted with the owner. "Several months later when a friend and I went by to have a cup of coffee, the lift held a large garbage can." Camalo's friend went in and asked the owner to clear the lift. He "grudgingly moved the garbage can so I could use the lift" but made no apologies. "To this day he continues to store a garbage can in the wheelchair lift. It almost seems he is doing it to intimidate and embarrass — to say, 'your business is not wanted.'"

Said a man using a wheelchair: "I sometimes feel like a cockroach. I have to access the restaurant through the kitchen. Now if my dollar was worth half of your dollar, I could understand this, but my money is as good as the next person's money."

Art Blaser's Bay Club Hotel room in San Diego — accessible, according to the reservation printout — came with a bathroom doorway too narrow to enter in a wheelchair. The front desk clerk laughed nervously — "Oh! I'm sorry!" — but offered no alternative.

Marcus Young wore diapers because he could not get to the second-floor bathroom in his apartment at the Greenleaf Gardens public housing development in Washington, D.C. He'd been waiting years for the D.C. Public Housing Authority to obey the law and build accessible units. So had Jordan Cook. Paralyzed, he couldn't get into the toilet in his Richardson Dwellings apartment — he made do with bed liners, bed pan, catheter. Jordan nearly died when he was trapped in a fire in the public housing complex and family members could not carry him out.

For disability scholar Eli Clare, a flight of stairs posed no problem. But people assumed her "slurring tongue" and "shaky hands" meant she couldn't reason, either.

Todd Fernie stopped for the red light in the far lane. "My side window was down. A car pulled up in the other lane and the passenger in the front seat looked over and stared at me. Widening her eyes to look like Tweety Bird and dropping her jaw, she shouted out, 'It's drunk drivers like you that cause all the accidents on the road!'"

Fernie has cerebral palsy. "I just looked at her. After a minute, I replied, 'Excuse me, but I've been like this all my life!!'

"'Well!' she said, 'go to AA, you bloody idiot!'"

The assumptions people made about Clare and Fernie, Hahn's desert with few oases, Camalo's shop owner with the garbage can, Jordan's apartment in which he stayed a virtual prisoner, Hockenberry's cage with its decorations (that one was not supposed to regard as a cage): They were the "disability experience" — "a constant barrage of incidents so frequent and so subtle that they simply formed the texture of daily life," as one activist had put it. Segregation. Exclusion. Barriers. Menus one could not read. Signs with no audible equivalents. Announcements in airports with no equivalent announcements on monitors; a deaf person would miss them entirely. Steps one could not ascend. Doors one could not open. Virtually no one whom others considered "disabled" — even Christopher Reeve, who traveled to speaking engagements with a phalanx of aides to ensure that he got up sidewalks and into inaccessible buildings — could escape the barriers altogether.

Austin Community College's Brenda Lightfoot, losing her vision but still able to see a little, was undergoing mobility training with a white cane in a mall. A sighted woman, not watching where she was going, bumped into her. "You poor thing!" the woman gasped.

"Painted white, and tall as a ski pole," the cane provided independence but carried the stigma of blindness. Seeing you with it, people are "helpful but condescending....They call you by your first name — things they'd never do if you didn't have the cane."

"When you take that innocuous stick in your hand, the world changes," said UC/Davis history professor Kathy Kudlick, who had recently become legally blind and was also learning to use one.

"When I approach hearing people to ask for information, and try to speak, they give me a look, turn to another employee and speak to them, ignoring me — or search for pencil and paper before I can open my mouth again," said a deaf woman. "Twenty years of speech lessons, dismissed."

Stigma, not functional limitation, not anything that inherently "substantially limited a major life activity," was what made a person "disabled" in moral and political terms. And those were really the only terms that mattered in the case against disability rights. It was stigma that formed the identity of those we considered "disabled" in the United States. Stigma was what Art Blaser had been warning Christopher Reeve about.

Erving Goffman defined stigma as "an attribute that is deeply discrediting." People unable to conform to standards that society called normal were simply "disqualified from full social acceptance"; they "must constantly strive to adjust to their precarious social identities"; "their image of themselves must daily confront and be affronted by the image which others reflect back to them." The term can be used another way as well, to mean the attitude others hold toward someone with a stigma. Using it in this sense, one can say that what disabled people face in common is stigma.

Fat people with virtually no functional limitations faced stigma. Lisa G. Berzins, director of women's behavioral medicine at Manchester Memorial Hospital in Connecticut, wore a "fat suit" to make her look as though she weighed 250 pounds, to test the theory; when she removed the suit and revealed herself as her normal size 6, she found that those who had paid little attention to her before now saw her as credible.

Portland, Oregon gradeschooler Sam Lightner, whose face had been deformed since birth, encountered stigma routinely: "The girl stared at the little boy, pointed at him and then loudly told her mother to look at the ugly baby." Debbie, the mother, was asked what drugs she had taken during her pregnancy. Strangers told

Debbie they'd pray for Sam. When he was registered at the neighborhood school, "teachers worried about having the boy in their classes....Once a neighbor boy led his friends over to Sam's house and knocked on the front door so the others could see Sam's face."

When his mother took him to register for high school, the administrator "turned away from Sam, as if he were deaf." Another told Debbie that the school had "a great special education class for those who were mentally retarded students." Sam, neither mentally disabled nor deaf, would be assumed to be both. (And reporter Tom Hallman, who would win a Pulitzer Prize for his series about Sam, would never realize that in writing these things about Sam, whom he deemed OK because he was neither deaf or mentally retarded, was in his own turn stigmatizing students who *were* deaf or mentally retarded — labeling them as people one did not want to be, either.)

"When I was in school, the crazy kids took the little bus to class," comedian Chris Rock had said. "And they got out at 2:30, just in case they went a little crazy." If kids who rode the special bus were embarrassed, this was why. Even Chris Rock made fun of them. This was stigma.

The Supreme Court of Wisconsin had allowed a school system to exclude a boy with cerebral palsy because he "produces a depressing and nauseating effect on the teachers and schoolchildren." This was stigma.

"Well dear, it's quite expensive," was all the gallery saleswoman would say to Julie Washenberger, who'd gone in to inquire the price of a Terry Redlin painting she was considering purchasing. The saleswoman quickly turned to another woman who'd come into the gallery and inquired if she could help her. Washenberger, on the other hand, employed full-time, a homeowner with plenty of disposable income, was in a wheelchair.

A woman soon to be married wrote,

> I'd made an appointment and was looking forward to a fun day looking at lots of bridal gowns. I had no idea what kind of dress would accommodate a wheelchair but still look clearly traditional.
>
> The consultant went through my size area and picked out one dress that she thought would work, then left to wait on other cus-

tomers. My friend ran up and down the aisles, finding many dresses suited to wear in a wheelchair, and helped in the dressing room.

Each time I came out of the dressing room, I could see the
other girls trying on dresses and being oohed and aahed over by
the David's Bridal staff: "You look beautiful in that!" "How pretty!" I didn't get any reaction from anyone other than my friend.

Disability discrimination was about the paternalism, the segregation, the exclusion, the bigotry, the stigma.

It wasn't about disability *per se* at all. The Americans with
Disabilities Act — which should have been called the Disability
Antidiscrimination Act — had been written to "establish a clear
and comprehensive prohibition of *discrimination on the basis of
disability*" (italics added) — discrimination which "included outright intentional exclusion, the discriminatory effects of architectural, transportation, and communication barriers, overprotective
rules and policies, failure to make modifications to existing facilities and practices, exclusionary qualification standards and criteria,
segregation, and relegation to lesser services, programs, activities,
benefits, jobs, or other opportunities."

Those who had drafted the ADA had written in a "Findings"
section that disabled people formed "a discrete and insular minority." The status was one created not by the actual disability, but by
society itself — society's treatment. The "discrete and insular
minority," was created by us, nondisabled people: by society's reaction to disability.

The United States' disabled minority, said the law, being very
clear about it, was composed of people who "have been faced with
restrictions and limitations, subjected to a history of purposeful
unequal treatment, and relegated to a position of political powerlessness in our society, based on characteristics that are beyond the
control of such individuals and resulting from stereotypic assumptions not truly indicative of the individual ability of such individuals to participate in, and contribute to, society." That was what
constituted the minority — not the type of disability; not the severity of the disability; not the functional limitation it caused or how
"substantially" it "limited" any of what could be concocted by

bureaucrats as a "major life activity" — but the treatment by others. The restrictions. The limitations. The "history of purposeful unequal treatment." The conscious assignment to the "position of political powerlessness based on characteristics that are beyond the control of such individuals and resulting from stereotypic assumptions not truly indicative of the individual ability of such individuals to participate in, and contribute to, society."

The law was in fact very clear on the matter.

Asking the wrong questions

If Sam Lightner were turned down for a job after graduation, could he use the ADA? If not, why not? Were such people, who had no real functional limitations, less deserving of protection from discrimination than those who were called "truly disabled" — the "blind, deaf and wheelchair bound," as the Cato Institute had called them?

Did people who had multiple chemical sensitivity (which commentator John Leo doubted even existed) have rights? What about people who had learning disabilities? "Nobody is quite sure how to distinguish between people with genuine learning disabilities and those who are underachievers, lazy, not too bright, or just faking it to take advantage of ADA," Leo had groused.

If Sam Lightner were told he was not wanted because he would have a "depressing and nauseating effect" on others, would he have rights under the disability rights laws as they were now being interpreted by the courts? Why was it so important to the Supreme Court Justices that they continue to come up with ever more tortuous measures to determine if a person had a "disability" that was "substantially limiting" in a "major life activity" in order to be "qualified" for protection under the Americans with Disabilities Act? As we saw in Chapter 6, it seemed it was because the courts, or, more accurately, the businesses who fought against disability rights when cases were brought against them, wanted a clear, easy way to define people who they could then simply remove: Make them go away!

But disability could never be defined; it was too slippery. Any of us could move into it in the blink of an eye, the crash of a car.

If this same tactic had been tried with race — if the courts had tried to say that the Civil Rights Act only applied to people who were Truly 100-Percent Negro — the civil rights movement would have been outraged. Such interpretations would have been stopped. But the thinking of legal scholars from the disability rights community was not familiar to either attorneys who took on disability discrimination cases or the judges who heard those cases. As Linda Krieger had said, disability rights law was "based on a socio-cultural model of disability that judges don't understand."

If fears about the ADA "opening the floodgate to litigation" were revealing anything, it was that disability was an extremely common condition. When John Stossel and Sandra Day O'Connor argued that the ADA must not be allowed to let "everyone claim a disability," did they realize that the ADA's original framers had clearly intended both of them, Stossel with his stutter, O'Connor with her history of breast cancer, to be able to use the law in the event that they had found themselves faced with discrimination by someone who didn't like stutterers, who wouldn't hire someone who'd had a history of cancer? The law had been designed to protect you as well if a restaurant owner wouldn't hire you as a waiter because she suspected you had AIDS — whether you really had AIDS or not. Because the law was *not about disability — but about discrimination.*

Had the child who had trouble learning encountered "overprotective rules and policies"? "Exclusionary qualification standards and criteria"? "Relegation to lesser services, programs, or opportunities"? Had the woman with multiple chemical sensitivities encountered "outright intentional exclusion"? Had her employer refused to "make modifications to existing facilities"? None of any of this would have to be done if it would cause a company "undue hardship," but the law intended that it be done if it did not cause any undue hardship on the business.

As of the summer of 2002, no one was yet asking these questions. It seemed the courts only wanted to know if a person's claim of multiple chemical sensitivity was bogus, invented in order to force a business to remove its chemical-laced carpeting, or if a parent's insistence that his child had a learning disability was merely to get the extra edge of more time on tests.

There was little inclination to examine the substance of the problems such people raised. Rather than spending time on the essential concepts of what constituted discrimination, it seemed judges spent their time trying to define "disability." "Disability," though, wasn't the problem.

A 1999 posting for the job of coordinating Louisville's compliance with the ADA called for candidates "who had sufficient vision…to obtain information from written material and video display units" — a clear violation of the law itself, given that there was no need that such requirements be part of the essential functions of the job. It was no oversight, though: more than a half-dozen jobs advertised on the city's Internet site included similar language, seeking candidates with "sufficient" hearing, speech or vision for jobs ranging from librarian to park worker. When Louisville's blind community reacted with fury, the city's personnel department said they hadn't realized there was anything wrong with asking such questions.

With a 4.0 grade average from her technical college, Donna Fox thought her travel industry education would make it easy for her to get a job with the large travel agency in her city — several of her classmates had gotten jobs there, and their grades hadn't been as good. Fox had juvenile arthritis. Her disability was obvious to observers. Her physical mobility — in her hands, especially — was restricted by it. Yet unlike her classmates who had applied for jobs, Fox was asked to take a typing test.

A disabled veteran said,

> In Detroit, in 1966, I wanted to work on an assembly line I'd worked on before my injury, but I was told I'd be a "liability" — that I'd endanger my co-workers. Finally I found a job in Milwaukee — in a factory for minimum wage, 10 hours a day breathing carbon dust. Don't complain about the wages, the foreman told me: "This is as good as a cripple can do around here."

Other discrimination he'd faced was less overt:

A university that argued it could not make its 100-year-old classrooms accessible. Professors who would ask, in front of an entire class, if you were "a birth defect." The airline that would not let me board without a personal attendant (I don't need one) and tried to put a towel under me "in case you're incontinent." The total strangers who ask me if I am able to "have sex." Being asked to check out of resorts "because the wheelchair will damage the room." Being patronized, told, "you're so brave! I could never live the way you have to!"

Although some of the incidents happened 30 years ago, I can still feel the humiliation and anger. I would love to say that all the civil rights legislation has allowed me to be a part of American culture again, but I can't. I still encounter this stuff on a regular basis.

But most people, judges included — judges especially, it seemed — couldn't get around to focusing on the discrimination, so fixated were we on focusing on the disability. We wanted to make sure we certified as truly disabled only deserving people who really needed help and that we kept the others, the malingerers, the not truly disabled, away from the special help we thought disability rights laws gave people.

We fixated on the category "disability," just as we fixated on the category of "race." Which didn't really exist at all at the genetic level. Which UNESCO had in 1995 declared "useless as a tool for characterizing human populations"; which the American Anthropological Association had decried as "a worldview, a body of prejudgments that distorts our ideas about human difference and behavior." Even so, people in the U.S. focused on body color; we treated people differently because of it. The different treatment was the racism, and our country had nearly been torn apart by it. We recognized racism as a reality, "one of the single most important social variables in our society," as University of Michigan sociologist David Williams put it.

Its analogy was "ableism," said disability scholars. That was the "ism" for how we treated people we considered "disabled." Although the patterns of treatment were chillingly similar, pundits who believed racism alive and well joked that this "ism" wasn't even a word.

If race were not biologically real, if it were only a social construct, why was it that black people were considered a "real" minority in U.S. society? It was because of the history of our society's treatment of them. That was also the idea behind the ADA's "Finding" that people with disabilities were "a discrete and insular minority…faced with restrictions and limitations, subjected to a history of purposeful unequal treatment, and relegated to a position of political powerlessness in our society."

If disability were also a social construct, like race, why was it that we did not likewise see those relegated to its lesser status as being a minority? In fact, for this reason alone, people subject to disability discrimination should have by all judgments also been considered a true minority. But that was a sociological, a political explanation, and most people simply didn't see things that way. It had never been explained to us that way, and if it had, it was likely not many of us would have agreed with it. We thought, along with Jerry Adler, that what made them a "category" was that they "lack something other people possess."

Even if we agreed that disabled people were treated differently, few would agree that an "ism" was behind it. Few believed any real hatred underpinned it. There was no *animus*. "No one is against the handicapped," we said. This was paternalism; pity-coated bigotry, and its role was to insist that there was, in fact, no harm in treating disabled people differently, even as they suffered for it.

Denying the right to be abroad in the land: the ultimate segregation of institutionalization

It was Christmas Eve at the Oak Hill Living Center in Jones, Okla. Benjamin Sanders, quadriplegic, was being tormented by nursing home aide Nettie Agyeman, who kept poking at his bedsore. When Sanders thought he could take it no more, he cursed her. To punish him, Agyeman unhooked his catheter tube and stuffed it in his mouth. His throat clogging with his own urine, he cried for help.

But few people like Sanders got help, anywhere in the nation. Once you were institutionalized, you were at the mercy of staff. Incarcerated for no crime other than disability, people considered severely disabled or "feeble-minded" were historically segregated into special institutions, usually run by the states. They were not able to leave, no matter how much they wanted to. No other non-criminal group in America, not even slaves, had been so confined.

Although over 80 criminal cases were filed against institution workers in Okla. from 1998 to 2001, only three of the cases netted prison terms.

When aides finally checked in on Sheri Renee Herring in her room at the Albert P. Brewer Developmental Center in Mobile, Alabama, she was covered with fire ants. The 36-year-old woman had been bitten repeatedly throughout the night; the bites were "too numerous to count." Herring, with Rett Syndrome, was not able to move — or even call out for help. Taken finally to a hospital, she was found to have over a thousand bites. Brewer Center director Levi Harris told officials, reporters and the parents of the facility's inmates that Herring's case was an isolated incident. Later investigations revealed that the institution had had infestations of fire ants before.

Thomas Bayon had lived on his own with some in-home help for nearly three decades after becoming paralyzed at age 18 — until a brief illness put him into a hospital. When doctors gave him the OK to go home, he had no in-home worker anymore. County officials, who administered the Long Island in-home program Bayon had used, were taking their time hiring one. For eight months they stalled, saying they could find no one to hire. Bayon languished in the hospital the entire time. His story was not all that unusual. What made it unusual was that he finally sued the county, citing the 1999 Supreme Court *Olmstead* decision and insisting he had a right to live again at home.

"States have historically denied persons with disabilities the right to live in the community," said the friend-of-the-court brief of 200 historians and scholars filed in the summer of 2000 in the Americans with Disabilities Act employment case of *Garrett v.*

Alabama, in which Alabama was arguing that Congress had no real evidence of discrimination on the part of states against people considered disabled "sufficient to warrant Congress passing a law that superseded a state's sovereign immunity" protected by the Eleventh Amendment.

The forced institutionalization of persons with disabilities reached its peak in the early twentieth century, said the historians' brief. Official reports referred to people with disabilities as "defect[s]...[that] wounds our citizenry a thousand times more than any plague"; "by-products of unfinished humanity"; a "blight on mankind" whose mingling with society was "a most baneful evil."

Spurred by the eugenics movement, every state passed laws on institutionalizing people considered defective, so that "society [might be] relieved from the heavy economic and moral losses arising from the existence at large of these unfortunate persons." Statutes referred to them as a "menace to society." "Ugly laws," local ordinances that forbid people with "unsightly" or "disgusting" physical conditions from appearing in public...were part of the Congressional Record when the ADA was enacted.

A worker tossed cookies to a mentally retarded man housed in a state institution, who ran after them and ate them off the floor. "Watch this," said the aide to his co-worker. "Preston's like a dog. He'll chase 'em and eat 'em."

States instructed doctors, teachers and social workers to report all persons "believed by them to be feeble minded." Laws in some states authorized the removal of such children from their homes against parents' wishes and put into institutions. The state of Washington made it a crime for a parent to refuse state-ordered institutionalization. Once children were institutionalized, many state laws required parents to waive custody rights.

A 1996 General Accounting Office report revealed "serious quality-of-care deficiencies" in institutions "including injury, illness, physical degeneration, and even death."

At the Woodward Resource Center, run by the state of Iowa, Larry Tielebein was killed in 2001 by state workers who held him on the kitchen floor and bound his arms and legs in restraints until he suffocated to death. Although the Iowa medical examiner ruled the 45-year-old man's death a homicide, no charges were filed. Tielebein had been kept at the facility for 25 years — because he had mental retardation and cerebral palsy. Woodward continued to get federal Medicaid money to "care for," as the euphemism had it, other people like Tielebein — over 250 of them.

Between 1998 and 2001, at least half of the nation's 50 taxpayer-funded schools for the deaf were embroiled in controversies about sexual and physical abuse. When asked why it didn't investigate, the U.S. Department of Education insisted its job was only to ensure access to education — not safety of students.

Illinois's Equip for Equality had to get a court order to get its state Department of Human Services to release records of inmates housed in 10 state institutions; when it examined the more than 300 incidents where restraints had been used, over three-fourths of the reports gave no reason for the restraint whatsoever. Sometimes people were tied down simply because they did not cooperate with staff members, or because they'd said something considered insulting to staff.

State nursing home inspectors routinely missed violations regarding the care and treatment of nursing home residents, said a federal study. Commonly overlooked were violations involving improper use of restraints, physical abuse of residents and inadequate feeding and medical care.

A report released by the Democratic staff of the House Government Reform Committee said that none of the 25,204 violations of federal health standards found by state investigators from Oct. 1, 2000 to Dec. 31, 2001 appeared anywhere on the "Nursing Home Compare" website, maintained by the Department of Health and Human Services at www.medicare.gov. The site, which purported to offer the public a searchable database on the compliance status of nursing homes nationwide, got over 4.5 million hits a month.

A General Accounting Offfice report released in early 2002 noted that one in five of the nation's nursing homes had had cases of sexual or physical abuse that were not reported to law enforcement. Sen. John Breaux, D-Louisiana, chairman of the Senate Special Committee on Aging, told reporters that "law enforcement officials really don't want to go into a nursing home. They'd rather the institution handle it by themselves."

Violette King told *The New York Times*'s Robert Pear that she had found her father, Louis H. Papagianis, "with bruises, scratches and cuts on his arms, neck and cheek and behind his ears." Papagianis had been considered "combative." "Now I understand why," she told Pear. "He was trying to save his own life." Papagianis had been beaten by a nurse's aide; nothing had been done for months; the aide was fired only to be hired by another institution across the state line.

Over 1.5 million Americans in 17,000 nursing homes brought nursing home operators $58.4 billion in reimbursements from Medicare and Medicaid in 2001. The federal oversight agency for nursing homes, federal Centers for Medicare and Medicaid Services, did not require nursing homes to call police about a crime.

In an effort by the nursing home industry to protect itself, a bill was introduced in the Louisiana state legislature to restrict the use of state reports on institutions as evidence in civil lawsuits. Similar bills were introduced in other states. Owners of institutions worried that they were at a disadvantage when inmates' lawyers were able to introduce allegations made in state reports on a facility's use of restraints, incidence of bedsores and abuse of residents.

At Woodward, where Larry Tielebein had been killed, staff refused to talk to the state watchdog group for disability rights; under Iowa law, they didn't have to. Woodward head Dr. Michael Davis said that problems at the facility were related only to "documentation."

Herring's mother, Betty Lyons, who had put Herring in the institution where she was attacked by fire ants, was president of the parents' association. Eventually she filed suit against the institution. But initially she defended it to reporters, saying she was sure that staff had done all they could.

In 1924, the Virginia General Assembly adopted a Eugenic Sterilization Act as a way to "relieve the financial burden" on taxpayers. The law was also designed to protect doctors so they could not be sued for malpractice. That sterilization law opened the door to an estimated 8,300 people being routinely sterilized in Virginia between 1924 and 1979. Across the U.S., over 60,000 men, women and children are documented to have been sterilized against their will, most of them inmates of institutions housing people said to have "developmental disabilities." It is not known how many sterilizations were not documented.

When, on January 7, 2000, the body of Victoria Pepiakitah was finally noticed, she had been dead six days in her room at the Choctaw Living Center in Choctaw, Oklahoma.

"The things that go on out there, while they are not excusable," had to be "tolerated," Oklahoma former Deputy Health Commissioner Brent VanMeter said. "What are you going to do with these people if you don't keep them there and hope that that facility is doing the best that it can?"

Denying the right to vote

The right to vote is preservative of all other rights.
— *Supreme Court Justice Thurgood Marshall*

When I turned 18 I was very into politics and wanted to vote — but before the next election came around, I was institutionalized. When I got out, I was more concerned with not being re-institutionalized than with anything else, including voting; I was well aware that it would take very little to get me stuck back inside. But eventually I decided to try registering to vote.

I tried a couple of times, in different states. In every case, I was asked whether I'd ever been institutionalized. I have; but I've never been under guardianship. I've answered honestly, along with telling them it's none of their damned business. But I've been consistently refused the registration form.

In 1990 when the ADA became law, virtually every state had specific constitutional provisions, statutes, or case law that prohibited individuals with cognitive or emotional impairments from voting. Although the would-be voter in the incident above knew that the state law did not forbid institutionalized people from voting, but only those who had been under guardianship, which was a different matter, that fact made little difference: poll workers simply ignored her explanation, refusing to let her register to vote.

Registered voters had been turned away from polling places because they did not look competent. When one witness turned in the registration card of a voter who had cerebral palsy and was blind, the "clerk of the board of canvassers looked aghast...and said to me, 'Is that person competent? Look at that signature!'" The clerk then arbitrarily invented a reason to reject the registration.

A deaf voter was told that "you have to be able to use your voice" to vote. A blind woman, a new resident of Alabama, went to vote and was refused instructions on the operation of the voting machine.

Another voter with a disability was simply told to go home when she arrived the polling site and found the voting machines down a flight of stairs and no paper ballots available. On another occasion that voter "had to shout my choice of candidates over the noise of a crowd to a precinct judge who pushed the levers of the machine for me, feeling all the while as if I had to offer an explanation for my decisions."

When Fred Shotz, who had testified at Foley's hearing, went to his polling site, he'd had to jump over a threshold in his wheelchair. He could do it, because he was fairly athletic. But the place wasn't accessible. And the polling equipment had been placed "so close to a pool table in this city recreation building that I could not get to the table to register."

> After several minutes of my making a stink, two poll workers finally moved some of the voting equipment so that I could get in. After signing the election register, I asked for an accessible voting table and got stared at. I explained that I could not reach the table surface to read the ballot and put the pin holes in the proper places. A few minutes later someone figured out how to take the table out of the frame and placed it on a lower table for me, where several

poll workers were sitting. I asked, in a none-too-friendly way by then, if I did not have the right to vote in privacy. After some grumbling the four of them got up and walked across the room. While I was in the middle of voting, one poll worker who did not like having to stand called across the room, "Aren't you done yet?"

During her first years in her Oakland, Calif. neighborhood, Denise Sherer Jacobson, author of *The Story of David*, would go to her polling place, which she could not get into because of its steps. Rain or shine she would sit there "and wait to grab someone going in or coming out so they could notify a voting official in my party that I was there.

"The official brought out the ballot and would poke out the holes (we still had that primitive method in California) where I indicated my choices on the ballot card. California ballots have long, complicated propositions, and there were several I paused to think about. At one point the official tried to advise me on how to vote. To which I responded that he wasn't supposed to do that. Of course he thought my indignation was cute — he gave me one of those patronizing 'hee-hees.'"

A 1999 study of three upstate counties in New York found fewer than 10 percent of polling places accessible. Well under 500 of Philadelphia's nearly 1,700 polling sites were even minimally accessible for the 2000 election. At an allegedly accessible polling site in La Canada Flintridge, a ritzy suburb of Los Angeles, you have to go up two flights of stairs. "They're short flights but they're still steps," says the man in the wheelchair who can't get up them. An "accessible polling site in North Tonawanda, N.Y., is in an elementary school that does have a ramp, but the ramp entrance on Election Day, when school is out, is locked. "It's illegal, but no one cares."

People who have disabilities still faced insurmountable problems when they tried to exercise the U.S. citizen's constitutional right to vote with a secret ballot.

"There's no such thing as a secret ballot when you're voting at a table in the midst of other voters walking all around you, walking to and from their secure voting booths," said Shea Hales. The Bryan, Tex. polling site Hales used when in college "had no accommodations for wheelchaired voters. All they could do was hand me a ballot and send me to a table to fill it out. This was years after the enactment of the ADA, but they were still surprised to even see someone in a wheelchair, let alone someone who wanted to vote!"

"Because our polling place uses paper ballots, I have to have one election judge from each party with me when I vote," said Lolly Lijewski of St. Paul, Minn., who was blind. "One reads the ballot and marks it while the other watches. Usually the individual is an older person who reads in a loud voice and repeats my responses so that anyone in earshot will know who I've voted for. So much for privacy!"

News media had covered the controversial referendum regarding city benefits for domestic partners on the Austin, Tex., ballot for weeks leading up to the election, but when Ron Lucey, head of the Austin Mayor's Committee for People with Disabilities, a blind man, went to his polling site, and an elderly woman sworn in to read the ballot to him told him she had come to the end of the ballot, "I asked her about the domestic partners referendum, since she had not read it. 'Don't you remember, you voted against that one,' she told me."

"Of course I hadn't even had that item read to me. At that point I did not know whether she was dishonest or incompetent. However, from that day forward I have always had doubts about the accuracy and validity of my votes." Lucey has had neighborhood election judges who have sworn an oath not to show bias or influence in reading the ballot "give favorable or encouraging comments to me based on how I was voting while they were reading the ballot. One election judge attempted to recruit me for his local political party based wholly on the way I cast my vote. If I had been allowed to cast a secret ballot as called for in our Constitution, he would never have had the insight into my private political beliefs."

A final indignity for Lucey was having election judges "physically touch me in a condescending manner while assisting me. I do not need someone to wrap their arm around me and praise my every voting decision." Lucey longed for the day when Texas adopted an accessible voting system that could "free him from these indignities and restore my confidence that the vote I cast is accurate and valid."

The National Organization on Disability's Jim Dickson, blind since childhood, had never been able to vote by himself — nor have the nation's other three-quarters of a million blind people.

Not one of the polling places visited by the General Accounting Office on Election Day 2000 had ballots or voting equipment that would let blind voters cast their vote in secret. More than eight of every 10 polling places they visited had at least some access problems — in over two-thirds of them, wheelchair users couldn't even get into the polling place without help. In many places, accessibility was not even one of the criteria for selecting polling sites, even though at least three laws — the Voting Accessibility for the Elderly and Handicapped Act of 1984, the 1990 Americans with Disabilities Act and amendments to the Voting Rights Act — mandated access for people with disabilities.

After Florida's 2000 election fiasco with its paper ballots, the American Foundation for the Blind's Paul W. Schroeder told *The New York Times* that "the rest of the nation finally experienced what blind people have been experiencing all along: you never know if your vote actually counted."

While serving as a precinct judge, Andy Warber noticed "a lot of seniors and disabled voters used the tables that were in the room" rather than voting booths. None of the tables was equipped with a privacy booth. Later, Warber brought the matter to the attention of the election auditor. "From my conversation with him, I was never really was impressed that he was too concerned."

Sandra Williams, hired as the ADA compliance officer for the City of Louisville after the brouhaha over the classified ads seeking candidates with "sufficient vision," voted for the first time in the 1996 elections. She hadn't realized that she wouldn't be able to cast her ballot in privacy by herself. Her first inkling of trouble came when the poll worker asked the friend who'd driven her to the poll, "What's her name?" The friend told the poll worker that she did not speak for Williams, who was blind.

"'She can't do this alone; you'll have to go in and do it for her,'" the poll worker said — still to her friend rather than to her.

"I never even touched the ballot," said Williams.

A few years earlier an accessible polling machine had been on display at City Hall. But when Williams inquired as to whether the city had purchased any, she was told that "it was not a sound investment since there were so few blind people voting."

States denied Negroes the right to vote, requiring literacy tests and enforcing poll taxes. During the '60s, thousands of civil rights workers labored to end these practices, helping Negroes to register to vote, battling hostility, curses and beatings. People were murdered over the right to vote. When the Americans with Disabilities Act became law, many states had laws on the books forbidding the vote to people with cognitive disabilities. Virtually all states used inaccessible polling sites and made little effort to change, despite the 1984 Voting Accessibility for the Elderly and Handicapped Act which said polling places should be physically accessible. Few pollworkers took the requirement of a "secret ballot" seriously when it came to a disabled person voting. Yet in 2001 Chief Justice William Rehnquist would say it was wrong to compare disabled people's voting problems to those of Negroes which had led to the Voting Rights Act of 1965. Negroes had intentionally been kept from voting; most disabled people were not being intentionally barred from voting. To many disability rights activists this seemed a distinction without merit, since the results were the same.

Disability rights were "trivialized by people," was how disability rights attorney Steve Gold explained it. "The fact that a person using a wheelchair cannot get up two steps into a store, or cannot get on a bus, or that movies aren't captioned, is not looked at as a violation of that person's civil rights."

F O U R T E E N

Disabled 'R' us

To be regarded as "disabled" in the U.S. is to experience powerlessness on all kinds of levels — physical, psychological, political. To be considered disabled is to be put in a supplicant position, the position of the "patient," told to be quiet; if you need something, to ask kindly for it. These are the strictures of disability's Jim Crow. It is really about power: disabled people are considered powerless. Anyone with any savvy is sure to tell others that they don't consider themselves disabled. President Roosevelt called himself a "cured cripple" for that very reason.

"If I am talking with a person fairly ignorant of disability rights, and I want to impress upon them that we are legion, I will say, 'Thirty to 45 percent of the population of this country is disabled,'" professor David Pfeiffer says. "That is a way of getting to the discussion of 'what is disability' — so they will realize that everyone is, or will be, disabled.

"But 'disability' is an ideological term. To name a person as 'disabled' is to give them an inferior position. In our society people identified as disabled are second-class, third-class, or even worse-class citizens. We live in a constant state of discrimination. Identifying oneself or another person as a 'person with a disability' is an ideological act. There is no other way to describe it." Which is why not everyone with a functional difference will identify as disabled, he says. Being disabled "is a damning thing."

Sociologist Irving Zola had said,

> By agreeing that there are 20 million disabled, or 36 million, or even half the population...we delude ourselves into thinking there is some finite (no matter how large) number of people who can be termed "disabled." In this way, both [in] the defining and [in] the measuring, we try to make the reality of disease, disability and death problematic, and in this way make it at least potentially someone else's problem. But this is not and can never be. Any person...may be able-bodied for the moment. But everyone...will at some point suffer from at least one or more chronic diseases and

be disabled, temporarily or permanently....All of us must contend with our continuing and inevitable vulnerability.

Disability can happen to any of us. Shouldn't our civil rights be protected even then? Our right to vote with a secret ballot? To live where we choose? To ride the public's buses? To have a job? As jurist Jacobus TenBroek once said, to be "abroad in the land?"

If disability could happen to any of us, then how could "the disabled" be a minority? It seemed contradictory. In fact, it was simplicity itself: although anyone *could* become disabled — it was only *when* one *did* in fact find oneself the object of the discrimination that was so much a part of the disability experience that one became part of that minority which was protected by disability rights laws.

At least that was how it was supposed to be.

Most people don't think all that much about "the disabled." Uncle Joe has a bad heart. Christopher Reeve is a brave man, overcoming a personal tragedy by fighting to walk again. We see that they have met up with personal misfortune, and we want to help them if we can.

When we think about "the disabled" as a group, it isn't to view them as a "real" minority like African Americans. We feel sorry for the ones that we believe are truly disabled, who "can't help it." We're willing for those people to have special stuff like handicapped parking and bigger toilet stalls. But the vast group making up "the disabled" are not truly disabled, we think. They're like welfare queens, and we have to guard constantly against that group — "the disabled" — getting too big and too demanding of us. If we don't rein them in, their demands will continue until they bankrupt society. If we don't keep our guard up, there'll be no more standards for being responsible for one's own situation anymore.

We really wanted them all to just go away. They could do that either by getting themselves cured, becoming normal again — that would be best — or they could go away by stopping their whining about wanting us to change things for them. Even women, blacks and gays didn't ask that we change bricks-and-mortar things; didn't ask that we restructure our entire society, our job sites, our ways of doing business!! That was going too far. It was worse than affirmative action — and we didn't believe in that, either.

The problem with this reasoning was this: we were always falling into disability ourselves. In truth, there was no real "us" and "them." Each of us could slip into disability as easily as slipping into our shoes. And many of us had: an accident on the ski slopes. A heart condition flaring up in our 50s, so we had to slow down. High blood pressure. Our supervisor wondered whether we ought to be kept on the job when our physical came back showing macular degeneration had begun. Ten-hour days at the computer terminal at the office and repetitive motion injuries set in, inflaming our wrists, shooting pain through our shoulder, making it impossible to lift our arms high enough to pull on a sweater.

It was time for us to wake up. Sooner or later, it was likely we would find ourselves thought of as "disabled" in some situation or another. We would encounter stigma. We'd be excluded, shut out by a barrier that was illegal under disability rights law. Sooner or later, we would likely need some accommodation. Whether the accommodation was considered something "special" "for the handicapped" or something entirely normal, a typical option, depended entirely on whether society considered the item in question something for everyone — like electric garage door openers — or "for the handicapped" — like a house with a ramp.

Just as more of us are beginning to understand that protecting the natural environment helps all of us in the long run, it was time for us to see that creating an accessible society would help to erase the us-vs.-them zero-sum mentality that propped up the case against disability rights.

Marta Russell, author of *Beyond Ramps: Disability at the End of the Social Contract,* says,

> Society still perceives disability as a medical matter. [It] associates disability with physiological, anatomical, or mental "defects" and holds these conditions responsible for the disabled person's lack of full participation in the economic life of our society, rather than viewing their exclusion for what it is — a matter of hard con-

structed socio-economic relations that impose isolation and poverty upon disabled people.

Just as the point of the Civil Rights Act was not race but discrimination, the point of the ADA was not disability but discrimination. "The ADA is a mandate for equality," said Robert Burgdorf, which the courts were turning upside down by "focusing extraordinary attention on how disabled (i.e., how different from the rest of us) the plaintiff was, as a precondition of being protected by the Act and thus entitled to equal treatment.

"The focus of the Act was — and should be — on eliminating practices that make people unnecessarily different because of their mental or physical limitations," said Burgdorf. Period.

There was no real line where disability left off and one became "nondisabled" or "normal." Disability was a social construct, like race. Yes, there were people who had things "wrong with them" — but when one put them into a category, it was, as with race, an attempt to divide society into the "us" and the "them." We did it as a way to award benefits to the deserving; we did it as a way to move children into "special education" which would, we thought, both keep them from disrupting "regular kids" and give them the "extra help" they needed in school. But everyone looked down on them, stigmatized them — and we knew it, even as we said otherwise. People like Dan Massie and Judge Bob Thomas, wheelchair users who said they didn't consider themselves disabled, were making an effort, like FDR, to escape the stigma. The kids who rode the special buses knew they were inferior; they hid out after school so the regular kids wouldn't see them getting on the special buses. The "us" were always in the superior position, the "them" in the inferior position. Although there were efforts nowadays to keep people we considered "developmentally disabled" out of institutions and let them live "in the community," there were now as many horror tales of neglect, abuse and death in these "community settings" as in institutions. Because it wasn't so much about the setting as about the concern we had for the people in the setting. And few of us were truly concerned about such people — they were, after all, the disabled — not like us. Not really part of any society we were interested in creating.

As soon as Mom began having trouble walking, we thought she might be better off in a nursing home — a belief helped along by flacks for the nursing home industry: nursing home owners would get federal reimbursements for every "bed" they filled.

Much of the irritation which publications like *Newsweek* directed at terms like ableism sprang from the fact that there were getting to be fewer and fewer folks who would hold still for being put in a subordinate position. We couldn't do it anymore with ethnic (what we called "racial") minorities; we couldn't do it with women. Gays and lesbians as well had fought back against being condemned, done with being told they were morally corrupt for their lifestyles. The only group we could really kick around were "the disabled." So we made sure we instructed them soundly in keeping their place. "Could it be because the handicapped have always seemed the least able to respond forcefully to the denial of their rights?" Vincent Marchiselli had asked.

We spent a lot of time lecturing folks that they had no right to try to avail themselves of legal protections against disability discrimination. We said such folks weren't truly disabled but only whiners and malcontents, out to get some "special" treatment not available to the rest of us. Yet it was clear that we did consider such folks "disabled" because we refused to hire them and found excuses to fire them, for things like high blood pressure, or epilepsy, or bipolar disorder, or repetitive stress injuries which we caused in our factories by refusing to change working conditions or machinery to make it more ergonomically fitted to the work being done. We were happy enough not to accommodate such whiners — they weren't truly disabled, we said — except, of course, they weren't capable of doing the work either, because they were too disabled. Those of us who ran companies tried to have it both ways. And hardly anyone paid any attention to what we were really doing. After all, no one was against the handicapped.

Such people were a "discrete and insular" minority for the same reason blacks were: because of our society's past and ongoing treatment of them. This idea had never really made it into any public discussion about disability rights. Judges ruled as though the idea had never been presented to them, although it had, in countless friend-of-the court briefs filed by disability rights groups. It was much like the America of the early 1950s when it came to race: "The notion of drastic change for the benefit of Negroes," writes historian Taylor Branch, "struck the average American as about on a par with creating a world government, which is to say visionary, slightly dangerous and extremely remote. The race issue was little more than a human interest story in the mass public consciousness."

Most of society simply paid no attention to what was going on when it came to disability rights; understood very little of what continued to come down from the courts, including the Supreme Court, about who was or was not "disabled." Because disability rights had never seemed important, not as civil rights had come to seem important in the 1960s. We didn't see disability as an important issue — or, more accurately, as a "social" issue. It was always considered a personal issue, a medical matter.

It never occurred to us that the Supreme Court, in continuing to make pronouncements about what amount of what kinds of "limitations" did or did not constitute a truly disabled person (the only kind of person, it said, who had a right to use the Americans with Disabilities Act), was doing something quite analogous to setting rules as to how "black" one had to be before one could use the Civil Rights Act. Had the courts tried that in the decade after the 1964 Civil Rights Act had become law, there would have been a national outcry. But when it happened to "the disabled," we didn't even seem to notice. Businesses saw it as a way to "keep the lid on ADA litigation," as the American Trucking Association put it, no matter how wrong it was. It was really a coward's way out, a way to avoid being called to account for whether one's business had obeyed the ADA or not.

Even as our wrists hurt from typing on our too-flat keyboards, even as we tried to turn off the graphics option on our Internet browsers because we got sick of how long it took the graphics-bloated Web pages to load (and then fumed when we discovered that much of the information we needed was delivered through the graphics, and no alternative text had been provided by the Web designer); even as we put the TV on "mute" and just read the captions when it got too noisy in the bar; even as we guiltily ducked into the "handicap stall" at the airport because it was big enough to accommodate us and our rollbag and computer bag safely as we used the toilet, we groused that the disabled were ruining things for society; wanting special treatment at work because, they said, they had carpal tunnel syndrome; wanting accessible restrooms everywhere, wanting more captioning on television, wanting wanting, wanting, always wanting special accommodation.

The Americans with Disabilities Act — and the disability rights movement that spawned it — has at its core "a central premise both simple and profound": that people called "disabled" by society are just people — not different in any critical way from other people. In order to address disability discrimination the right way, Burgdorf said, as a nation we first have to "come to grips with the underlying realities of human abilities and disabilities.

"Though we are conditioned to think otherwise, human beings do not really exist in two sharply distinct groups of 'people with disabilities' and 'people without disabilities,'" he went on, echoing what he wrote in the 1985 U.S. Commission on Civil Rights report, *Accommodating the Spectrum of Individual Abilities*. Disability is "a natural part of the human condition resulting from that spectrum — and will touch most of us at one time or another in our lives. The goal is not to fixate on, overreact to or engage in stereotypes about such differences, but to take them into account and allow for reasonable accommodation for individual abilities and impairments that will permit equal participation."

Creating the accessible society

*Disability rights holds the power to change
the trajectory toward a cookie-cutter
society. It has the potential to transform
society itself.*

— *law professor Matthew Diller*

While the civil rights model had some positive effects for the disability rights movement, it came with baggage as well: that "equal rights" equates with "equal treatment." In fact, the ADA presents a set of new ideas for people — that equality means, in fact, that sometimes people have to be treated differently, given different accommodations, in order to achieve equal rights. The real goal of the disability rights movement in the U.S., which culminated in 1990 with passage of the Americans with Disabilities Act, is actually to provide equal opportunities for all Americans — not to identify a particular group of individuals who are entitled to some kind of special treatment.

Yet judges had ruled that neither a law professor with a paralyzed left hand, arm and leg as the result of a stroke nor a woman with breast cancer could use the law because they weren't "disabled," since they continued to work; that an employee with AIDS who had gotten Social Security disability benefits couldn't use it because he had thus proved he couldn't work.

It is an "absurd way to apply a civil rights act," says Georgetown University law professor Chai Feldblum, who had lobbied for the bill in Congress. Because cases are stopped before they ever get started, the real disability rights questions that would begin to open the way to an accessible society never get asked: Is firing a worker who couldn't lift her hands above her head, rather than modifying the equipment so that she could reach it, discrimination on the basis of disability? Would changing the equipment be "reasonable" for the company to do? If it were changed, would it not help other workers as well? Is running a non-ergonomic factory a kind of disability discrimination? The question never gets asked. The real ideas behind the Americans with Disabilities Act never get explored.

What concepts must we get clear before we can begin the work of fashioning an accessible society? There are five: Reasonable accommodation, demedicalization, universal design, customization and integration.

Reasonable accommodation

Companies are quite content that their practices never get scrutinized by a court or a jury. But the point of this major disability rights law — to make life easier for people, to figure out what could be easily changed through what the law called "reasonable accommodation" — never gets dealt with. We don't talk about that kind of thing.

We never get to it because we are too busy hectoring the disabled, warning them not to try using legal remedies to try to better their lives.

There is some truth to the fact that people who could actually get by without an accommodation at work or from a public service do sometimes try to get one — to "cash in on the ADA," as its detractors maintain. And it is true, mostly, that when people complain of disability discrimination, it is because they are seeking an "accommodation" which they feel they need but which is not being provided. When this happens, we scrutinize the complainers, trying to find a way to prove they are simply being whiny malcontents.

But if we allowed such cases to go forward, we would be forced to look at the substance of the complaint: what was it, in fact, that they wanted? Was it, in fact, a reasonable thing? Would it really hurt the rest of us so much that it was unreasonable? If it were found to be unreasonable, it would be denied — just as people who filed suit over racial bias, who complained that affirmative action policies had been ignored, lost their cases, too. Most disability discrimination cases, though, never get that far.

The ADA's original framers knew that cases could be lost; but they never expected that the issues raised by those cases would never get examined at all. They had intended for the law to look at these issues, to open up society. To make us pay attention to things we'd simply ignored before: Was it reasonable that a library be up a flight of steps, when that meant it excluded a portion of the population? Was it reasonable that a McDonald's have its menu on the wall overhead, with no alternative available for people who couldn't see that far away? Was it reasonable that one should have to ask nicely, and hope to find counter help that would not be irritated that one asked what was on the menu? That one would not be ridiculed or simply ignored? Was it reasonable that a subway that had to serve nearly 14 million people have entrances down flights of 60 to 70 steps, with no alternative for people who could not clamber down them easily? "Why would San Francisco set up its visitors' center in a plaza that has absolutely no access to people with disabilities?" Disability Rights Advocates' Larry Paradis had asked. Was it reasonable that a public lecture have no alternative for someone whose hearing didn't work well, but who also wanted to learn what the speaker was saying? Was it reasonable that a multi-million member e-mail service be "upgraded" in such a way that blind people could no longer use e-mail?

Disability discrimination "cannot be eliminated if programs, activities and tasks are always structured in the ways people with 'normal' physical and mental abilities customarily undertake them," Burgdorf said.

Disability rights activists see a woman in a wheelchair and often have no real interest — or only a passing interest — in knowing why she's in the wheelchair. If they want to know, it's because they think they may have some comradeship around an issue specific to the disability — if the woman has muscular dystrophy, for example, she will have been affected by the Jerry Lewis Muscular Dystrophy Telethon one way or the other, they think; they may want to see what she thinks about that.

But they aren't usually looking around for an individual cause of her problem. They're more likely to wonder: can she get into her house? Does she have ramps, wide doors? Does she have someone other than her family who helps her get dressed, do what she needs to have done — someone she has control over, so they work for her?

To these activists, the woman's problem is not that she cannot walk, any more than a 5-ft., 4-inch-tall woman's problem is that she isn't 5-ft.-10, or that an African American's problem is that she does not have white skin. They simply accept that she can't walk as a given. Yes; some of them would say if asked, it would be fine if she were "cured," but that's not going to happen tomorrow — and meanwhile, while people wring their hands wanting the cure, this woman's life could be much better — she could be having a much higher quality of life, if only certain things would change — things that it's easily within society's power to change. Sidewalk curbs could be cut; steps could be ramped. Doors could be automated.

When disability rights activists meet a woman who uses a wheelchair, they want to know: How can her life be made better? To figure that out, they want to know, specifically, how her life is being made worse today because of the negative attitudes society holds about being in a wheelchair, attitudes which result in difficulties obtaining a decent, normal lifestyle.

The charge that the ADA has encouraged vast numbers of people to "claim disability" in order to get its special rights says something about the nature of what we think the ADA entitles people to. What it entitles people to is "accommodation" — but only if the entity granting that accommodation (or a court, if the case is taken to court) deems it "reasonable." In fact, in far too many cases, the accommodation is viewed as "unreasonable" because it is perceived as "special." And the reason it's seen as special is because most of us have come to believe that individuals have no real right to individual accommodation if it is something that is not already routine in society.

Companies don't want anyone telling them how to deal with their workers — they never have; they never will. Stores don't want anyone telling them how to design their entrances; how many steps they can have (or can't have); how heavy their doors can be. Yet they accept their city's building and fire codes, dictating to them how many people they can have in their restaurants, based on square footage, so that the place will not be a fire hazard. They accept that the city can inspect their electrical wiring to ensure that it "meets code" before they open for business. Yet they chafe if an individual wants an accommodation. Because, it seems, it is seen as "special for the handicapped," most of whom likely don't deserve it.

Accommodation is fought doubly hard when it is seen to be a way of letting "the disabled" have a part of what we believe is for "normal" people. Although no access code, anywhere, requires them, automatic doors remain the one thing, besides flat or ramped entrances, that one hears about most from people with mobility problems: they need automatic doors as well as flat entrances. Yet no code, anywhere, includes them; mandating them would be "going too far"; giving the disabled more than they have a right to. A ramp is OK. An automatic door? That isn't reasonable. At least that's what the building lobby says. Few disability rights groups, anywhere, have tried to push for that accommodation. Some wheelchair activists are now pressing for "basic, minimal access" in all new single-family housing, so, they say, they can visit friends and attend gatherings in others' homes. This means at least one flat entrance and a bathroom they can get into.

De-medicalization

No large grocery or hotel firm, no home-and-garden discount supply center would consider designing an entrance that did not include automatic doors. They are standard in hotels and discount warehouses. Not, of course, for the people who literally can not open doors by themselves — for such people are "the disabled": them, not us. Firms that operate hotels, groceries and building supply stores fight regulations that require they accommodate "the disabled." Automatic doors that go in uncomplainingly are meant for us, the fit, the nondisabled, to ensure that we will continue to

shop at the grocery or building supply center; to make it easy for
us to get our grocery carts out, our lumber dollies to our truck
loaded with Sheetrock for the weekend project. So the bellhops
can get the luggage in and out of the hotel easily. When it is for
"them," it is resisted; when it is for "us," however, it is seen as a
design improvement. Same item; different purpose.

This all has to do with the "medicalization" of disability.
Medicalizing a product stigmatizes it, signals it as being for "sick"
people, "failed normals." People resist things they perceive as looking as though they are for "the disabled."

At the end of 2001, designers unveiled what *Time* magazine
called "the most eagerly awaited and wildly, if inadvertently, hyped
high-tech product since the Apple Macintosh" — "the tech
world's most-speculated-about secret." The product, called a
Segway, had been developed by Dean Kamen, who had also developed the iBot wheelchair. It was a wheelchair itself, of sorts — for
nondisabled people. Kamen called it a "human transporter." *USA
Today* called it "a gyroscope-stabilized, battery-powered scooter
that ...will revolutionize short-distance travel."

> Developed at a cost of more than $100 million, Kamen's vehi-
> cle is a complex bundle of hardware and software that mimics the
> human body's ability to maintain its balance. Not only does it have
> no brakes, it also has no engine, no throttle, no gearshift and no
> steering wheel. And it can carry the average rider for a full day,
> nonstop, on only five cents' worth of electricity.

"Cars are great for going long distances. But it makes no sense
at all for people in cities to use a 4,000-pound piece of metal,"
Kamen told reporters.

Kamen did not like the Segway being compared to a wheelchair,
even though it served exactly the same purpose as a personal
mobility device. He had designed the iBot wheelchair, and he bris-
tled when people called it a wheelchair, too — insisting it be called
a "robot."

The association of a product with "the disabled," marketers
insist, puts people off. A whole line of personal mobility devices
developed in the last 30 years were called "scooters," not wheelchairs, although they are purchased exclusively by people who

"have something wrong with them." Older people who find it difficult to walk avoid the traditional "wheelchair" in favor of these newer vehicles, because they seem less "medical."

Dislike of the medical image is part of what is behind the National Association of Homebuilders' resistance to designing houses that look as though they have ramps — and the industry's insistence that, while they might reinforce bathroom walls so grab bars could be installed later, they will not build a house "on spec" — that is, to sell to the public — with grab bars already in place. To them it looks "medical" and thus undesirable; it looks as though it were "special for the handicapped," not for regular people.

Frieda Zames had thought that it was simply because the idea of accessibility was new that it was resisted. But she also recognized that because it was associated with disability, it "scared people."

"Once you make something accessible, they like it," she said. That seemed completely true. The problem came in getting to that point.

Sherry Colb was told she had to get a special permission to drink apple juice at her bar exam. Getting permission, she was classified as "disabled"; only if she were classified that way would she be permitted to go into the "special room" where all the other people who had asked for "special accommodations" were segregated, like the woman who needed a bright light to see the exam.

An understanding of disability discrimination would ask us to see the problem not as Colb's need for juice, but as the exam officials' insistence that her condition be medicalized by a doctor's note (to prove she wasn't cheating) so that they could turn down the reasonable request for juice if she did not have a dispensation. But what is wrong with drinking apple juice during an exam? What is wrong with using a bright light to read an exam? Why must one be segregated from others in order to use such tools? Because one might cheat with the lamp or the apple juice?

Today, students do math problems on their calculators. Years ago, they did math problems by shaping their fingers around pencils and writing. A person who could not hold a pencil was disabled, deemed educable, if at all, in a special school for "the handicapped." Today one need not have the ability to hold a pencil to do math problems; one need only be able to push buttons (a numeric keypad) on a computer or calculator, or speak the numbers into a voice input device (although the latter, still being a somewhat new technology, often gets classified as "special," designating the student as "special" as well.) What has changed? The tool has changed, that's all.

With its changing, though, the designation of who is "disabled" also shifts. Disability is, in fact, a function of the tool, the accommodation, not the other way around. This in a sense was what the Supreme Court was trying to get at when they said that people whose disabilities could be "mitigated" — like Karen Sutton's with eyeglasses — were not really disabled. The converse was true, too: In a world in which eyeglasses did not exist as routine fashion accessories — which is really how we regard them — many more people would be truly disabled: They would be able to see only fuzzily. (Where the Court was wrong in this ruling was not in its understanding of functional impairment, but in insisting that none but the truly disabled could use the law.) Because we so routinely think in terms of us and them, "the disabled" and "normal people," we cannot see this point so easily. It is obscured by the hegemony of that medical model.

Everyone has individual circumstances needing individually tailored solutions. We see this concept in disability rights law, but we misunderstand it, believing it a point being made only about "the disabled" who have "special" needs. It's accepted when it's seen as being only for the "truly disabled" — a tiny group. But when people not "truly disabled" seek it out, they engage the ire of people like John Stossel. In this case, disability rights are "good intentions gone awry." Does this have to do with people wanting more than they have a right to? It is only when the people are "the disabled" that the things they are asking for through the rubric of "special" are considered "more than they have a right to." The request is automatically "medicalized." In any circumstance other than a disabled person asking for "special," though, the accommodation is seen not as an "accommodation" so much as simply a choice. What people seeking "special" want is not more than others have a right to, but simply those choices nondisabled people regard as their natural right.

Customization: the expansion of consumer choice

Companies continually increase accommodation as a way to increase profits. They do so cheerfully, seeing it as a way to "expand market share." Of course, they are doing it with normal people in mind. And that makes all the difference in the world.

Individuals can and are provided a blizzard of accommodation in the most prosaic of items.

As an article in *The Boston Globe* noted,

> For decades, a toothbrush was just a toothbrush. It had bristles, it had a handle, it came in a few colors. It performed its function admirably, didn't call attention to itself, and slipped obligingly into the porcelain holder that protrudes from bathroom walls. Now check out the "oral care" department in your pharmacy. Toothbrushes come with power tips. Gum bumpers. Pivoting heads. Gum massaging bristles. Zig-zag bristles. Multi-level interior bristles. Flared side bristles. End rounded bristles. "Indicator" bristles that fade so you'll know when to change your toothbrush. They come in right-handed versions and left-handed. They are sculpted, amorphous, multicolored, and multitextured. They come with rubber grips and "squish" grips, curved handles to offer "better hand action," and flexible necks that bend to absorb brushing pressure. "Mouth-friendly," they're called.

"Cathy" comic-strip creator Cathy Guisewite often pokes fun at consumer culture run amok: 80 kinds of shampoo; six dozen varieties of coffee drink, the 46 accessories for the basic computer. The serious point to the comic is that all these choices are "accommodations" to fit individual needs — and increase profits. No one mandates these accommodations; they're just ways to sell product. If demand doesn't exist, marketing creates it.

"Mighty Coca-Cola, the ultimate global brand," writes Seth Stevenson, is "inventing hundreds of faddish new drinks and gim-

micks to sell them." Consumers are becoming more sophisticated
and demanding. We want more options. We want bottled water.
We want health drinks. We want a brand-new thing we have never
seen before, and three months later we want another one. We want
endless choices, in dozens of categories."

Coke's "old corporate strategy," he writes,

> is no longer viable....The new approach is something more akin
> to "How may we surround you with a broad range of products,
> one of which may happen to catch your fancy?"...Coke's new
> products...will be based on the idea that there are "32 possible
> beverage occasions in each day."... [Coke] needs to find a drink
> for every conceivable demographic (trendy or staid, health nut or
> slob, man, woman or child) in every different society Coke sells to
> for each of the 32 beverage occasions. If [Coke] doesn't have the
> right drink on hand, [they'll] buy one or make one
> up....Consumer demand drives Coke to invent new products and
> scrap old ones at a mind-boggling rate. Coke maintains about 200
> brands in the market [in Japan] at any moment.

What happens when people begin asking for accommodation? If
it is perceived as being requested because of disability — a "medical need" — it's resisted. If it is perceived as being for trendy people, celebrities, it is embraced.

Imagine the difference if children with "special needs" were
viewed by the local school board in the same way Coke views the
Japanese teenagers they're marketing their drinks to for the 32
daily beverage occasions. What is different? Not the accommodation of individual desires, needs, tastes, but the perception that one
is for "the disabled," the other for an upscale market. When the
desire to accommodate is strong, as it is in the case of Coke wanting to dominate market share in the beverage industry, solutions
can be found that are exciting and individualized and, yes, cost-
efficient. The reason "special" does not deliver on its promise of
individual accommodation is that because it is segregated, for
"them," it is stigmatized. Money spent on it is seen as taking from
"us."

Amazon.com serves up millions of individual pages, tailored so
that when you log onto their site, you'll be presented with book

choices selected by Amazon's vast database based on what your prior purchases indicated you'd be looking for. That is accommodation, and amazon.com thinks it more than reasonable. It sells books.

At the start of 2002, the Mountainview, Calif. start-up company MobileAria made headlines with the announcement of what it called "a hardware and software kit that makes hand-free office work a reality." They were not aiming their pitch at Stephen Hawking, although it would have worked for him. Using voice recognition, it would let you make hands-free phone calls while driving, and, if you had your laptop along, send and receive e-mails as well. MobileAria was negotiating with auto makers to get its technology built right into the cars. It would add about $200 to the sticker price — plus a $30-a-month service fee. A few weeks later, Cybernet announced it had gotten a patent for a low-cost technology that let one use one's eye movements to control a cursor on a computer screen.

Two trends — the move to diversity of product (exemplified by the ever increasing variety of toothbrush and the individualized page views of the amazon.com website) and the move toward uniformity of product (exemplified by the cookie-cutter design of new housing) — exist in tension in today's consumer society; but they are not seen to have anything to do with disability or "special." In fact, they have quite a lot to do with it: they point the way toward what might result if we were to do away with the political and social category of disability altogether and its concomitant solution of "special."

In today's society, variation at the extremes is ignored; variation in the acceptable midranges — people who like each of those 72 varieties of coffee drink — is celebrated. But everyone has individual preferences. The most successful products are often those that accommodate the widest variation of human difference.

The basic architecture of the initial Internet drew from this purest of disability rights concepts: that the best structure was one that could be used by the most people, infinitely tailored by the end-user, a design that was "platform independent."

Universal design

Those preaching against disability rights say it is for the most part "good intentions gone awry," creating an expectation in people for more than they have a right to, that they haven't worked for and thus don't deserve. Yet when someone wants something they do not yet have — an accommodation — instead of impugning the morals of those asking, would it not be wise to look at the substance of the request? Given the range of human variation, it is likely the request signals that a product might be better, in fact, were it redesigned to be useful to more people; that a policy can be changed to create a better working environment for both workers and management.

Instead of impugning the motives of those asking for the accommodation (which is essentially what is being done in our nation's courts when a company tries to prove a plaintiff not disabled enough to deserve the legal right to ask for accommodation) what if we simply stopped and examined was being asked for? And then asked ourselves why it wasn't being provided, and what could come from it being provided as a routine accommodation for everyone? This is virtually never done, but when it is done, what results? Often, "universal design" results — design that accommodates the widest possible range of people.

"It wasn't long after sidewalks were redesigned to accommodate wheelchair users that the benefits of curb cuts began to be realized by everyone," says engineer Steve Jacobs. "People pushing strollers, riding on skateboards, using roller-blades, riding bicycles and pushing shopping carts soon began to enjoy the benefits of curb cuts! These facts are a prime example of why sidewalks with curb cuts are simply better sidewalks."

Gary Wunder had made a similar point at the hearing; he'd called this the "curb cut effect." What happened with curb cuts happened on an infinitely larger scale with electronic technology.

"TV manufacturers will tell you that their caption decoders for the deaf wound up benefiting millions more consumers than originally intended. Televisions with decoders are simply better than those without. Captioning can help us search for and retrieve video content, by word, through the use of multimedia databases, or watch programs in silence while someone is sleeping or in noisy environments like sports bars. Captions have also been crediting with helping children read more effectively, and at an earlier age, by enabling them to see the words being spoken at the same time they hear them. Captions have also helped immigrants learn to speak and read English."

Jacobs wrote,

> In 1802 Pellegrino Turri built the first of what we came to call a "typewriter" — he built it for his blind friend Countess Carolina Fantoni daFivizzono, to help her write legibly. In 1987, Alexander Graham Bell was granted U. S. Patent No. 174,465 for the telephone, a device he had developed in his work to help deaf people communicate.

> In 1964, when deaf orthodontist Dr. James C. Marsters of Pasadena shipped a teletype machine to deaf scientist Robert Weitbrecht in Redwood City, and asked for a way to attach it to the telephone system, who would have guessed that by the turn of the millennium over 100 million people, in all parts of the world, would be communicating with each other, over the Internet, using basically the same technology? Instead of calling our devices Telecommunications Device for the Deaf (TDDs) or TTYs, we call them Internet chat rooms!

> In 1972, Vinton Cerf developed the host-level protocols for the ARPANET — the first large-scale packet network. Cerf, hard-of-hearing since birth, had married a woman who was deaf, and communicated with his wife via text messaging. "I have spent, as you can imagine, a fair chunk of my time trying to persuade people with hearing impairments to make use of electronic mail because I found it so powerful myself," Cerf said, early on. Had it not been for this experience Cerf may not have used text-messaging to the extent that he did — and may not have integrated e-mail as part of the functionality of ARPANET, the precursor to the Internet.

The ADA required that public telephones be equipped with a volume control and a shelf, a phone jack and a power outlet. Cranking up the volume on an "accessible" phone made phone conversations easier for anyone using one in a noisy environment. And how often have you seen a business traveler hook a laptop modem up to an "accessible" public telephone to retrieve her e-mail messages?

"Another benefit of the ADA is the lowering of pay telephones so that wheelchair users can access them. It also means children are now able to access these same phones," Jacobs said.

McDonald's and other fast-food giants began using cash registers with pictures of the fast-food item in lieu of words. It made for fewer mistakes on the part of the entry-level, sometimes uneducated staff. It was also accessible to people who, because of functional limitations, were unable to understand the written word. Thus it expanded the pool of potential workers able to handle the job. This was important to McDonald's, which needed lots of unskilled workers who could be easily trained to operate its cash registers.

Integration

When middle-class parents in affluent suburbs seek out "special" education for their children, using the law to pay for their son's education in a private school, they are using "special" in its best sense: individually tailored to fit an individual's specific needs — in this case, needs pertaining to learning.

But what people who advocate "special" don't seem to truly understand is that, no matter what it might potentially give people in terms of advantages ("potential" because, in study after study, just as with racially segregated school, special education programs are shown to be a vastly inferior experience to that of an integrated classroom), at heart it is a segregated system, and it denies choice to those who want to be integrated. This has always been the problem with segregation, and it is no less a problem for being called "special" rather than what it is: segregation.

In the 1954 Supreme Court decision, *Brown v. Board of Education*, the Court, once and for all (one had hoped, anyway) had insisted that separate, when enforced as policy, was inherently unequal. This is no less true when those being segregated are cat-

egorized by disability rather than by race. That we refuse to believe
this fact is simply more evidence of the paternalistic thinking that
occurs when the subject happens to be disability rather than race,
and the indifference we as a society show about its pervasiveness.

People who seek out "special" for themselves, whether in education for their children or for services that society calls "special"
— "special handicapped parking" as it's called; special transportation; special accommodations like Sherry Colb was told to ask for
on her bar exam, are not trying to get something "more" than the
typical citizen gets, even though that's how it's often interpreted.
In fact what such people want is simply *access to the same services*
nondisabled people enjoy. That, however, they are frequently told,
is not open to them: Sherry Colb would not be allowed to take her
bar exam alongside other normal students; the only avenue open
to her was "special." For such people to be then accused publicly
of wanting "more" is blaming the victim, and it goes on all the
time.

In a truly accessible society, people have choices and options —
nothing is reserved for one group that another group is excluded
from. Although one would think that such a solution would be the
delight of the free enterprise system, the libertarian's dream, in fact
people like Richard Epstein, who you'd think might espouse such
a future, tout special segregated solutions as the appropriate solution for "the handicapped" — "other places for such people to
work," as he put it, rather than a company's regular plant, which
is not "already equipped with ramps and elevators."

Decades of prodding by advocates, most of them parents of
children who could not learn in the cookie-cutter way, parents who
had some influence over policy, have begun to get school systems
to understand what its advocates insist the Individuals with
Disabilities Education Act was about all along: both integration
and individual attention, which, as they have repeatedly said, does
not hurt anyone and ends up helping the group itself.

"Ultimately, the enforcement of the IDEA's civil rights protections will benefit every child, not only children with disabilities,"

says the National Council on Disability, which called for "a unified system of education that incorporates all students into the vision of the IDEA." The group's 1996 report, *Achieving Independence*, outlined a system "in which every child, with or without a disability, has an individualized educational program and access to the educational services she or he needs to learn effectively" and called for a fully integrated system of education in schools that "readily responds to the individual educational needs of all children."

Like most policy proposals from disability rights advocates, the report got little national attention at the time. Yet some people understood. Sometimes their comments even made it into the news.

To talk about special-ed reform separate from education reform didn't make sense, Jan Nisbet, head of the University of New Hampshire Institute on Disability, told *The Boston Globe*. "The whole system needs to be unraveled. It's time the state stopped blaming kids with disabilities for their special-education funding problems."

There were not two problems — "a special education problem and a general education problem" — insists education expert Mark Mlawer. "There's one major problem: What is wrong with general education and how do we fix it?"

"Every kid has a quirk that could be diagnosed as special needs....It's almost laughable," Vincent Cowhig, supervisor of special education in Revere, Mass. told *The Globe*. "If there were more opportunities in the mainstream, it would vastly decrease referrals to special education in any district," Janice Patterson, director of the special education program for the Mineola, N.Y., schools told *Newsday*. If money earmarked for special education simply "went into the schools, we would have 15 to 18 children in the classroom," Lorraine Skeen, the principal for 17 years of P.S. 171, an East Harlem elementary school, told *The Globe's* Jordana Hart. "We would no longer need special education. We would no longer need support services." The reason the special education supports were needed in the first place, she insisted, was "because we are not providing a good education for children."

Because the mandate for educating "disabled" children is so much more specific than the mandate for educating nondisabled children, and because the federal law does not allow the lack of money to be an excuse (as it does in so many disability laws), parents of nondisabled children resent what they see as the extra things that can be gotten for children under the rubric of "special education." That is why special education has grown 65 percent nationwide since the law was passed, said critics. "For a long time there was the message that special ed. was the only game in town; if your child needed some sort of help, go there," Christine M. Chambers, director of special services for the Wilton, Conn., public schools, told *The New York Times*.

Sherman Oaks lawyer Valerie Vanaman, who had represented disabled children for more than two decades, first as a lawyer with the nonprofit Children's Defense Fund, told the *Los Angeles Times*, "If you probe deeply enough, the money may not be nearly as much an issue as the fear that if this really worked" — "this" meaning the IDEA's mandate for individualized education plans — "then we are going to have all these other parents clamoring for the same thing for their children, and not inappropriately so."

Even though at public hearings people tend to paint special-education students as "a drain on the system," and special-ed costs as "out of control," data often do not bear this out. The problem sometimes occurs because of how special-education expenses and reimbursement are reported. Special-ed costs show up in school budgets, while reimbursements from the federal government turn up in town budgets. "What most people see is only the expense," New Hampshire State Senator Ned Gordon told *The Globe's New Hampshire Weekly*. "And they're unaware they're receiving funds as an offset against their taxes. For most special-ed students, the cost is nominal."

And there is no question the children fare better in an integrated system.

The preschool at Zeh Elementary School in Northborough, Mass., "teaches both special-needs children and normally developing children three to five years old," reported *The Boston Globe's*

Peter Schworm. "By providing pupils with individual instruction, special-education expertise, and increased interaction with their peers, the school enhances children's social and intellectual development."

Attending school with "more advanced pupils...boosts them beyond what they would have probably achieved in a segregated setting....Normally developing children benefit by attending small classes with as many as four teachers, all of whom hold degrees with special education training. While all pupils receive a good deal of individual attention, more advanced students are encouraged to work more independently than in typical preschools."

The truly innovative thing about the program was that the teachers had degrees in "special education," which meant, among other things, that working with children different from the norm did not faze them as it often did regular classroom teachers. One of them told Schworm that in her classroom students were "learning very young not to categorize people." Parents ranked the program's "excellent teacher-pupil ratio and diversity" as its primary draws.

Reasonable accommodation, demedicalization, universal design, customization and integration: simple enough concepts to understand, but hard to implement when the society you live in continues to see people with disabilities as having something wrong with them, or as whiners and complainers trying to get some special rights they don't deserve, creating expenses for the rest of us, rather than simply as members of the same society we all live in together.

S I X T E E N

The disability rights vision:
beyond 'marketplace morality'

> *'It costs too much' can be the end of a*
> *discussion about whether certain people*
> *get access, or it can be the beginning of a*
> *discussion about how we can work*
> *together.*
>
> — *Cal Montgomery*

Critics accuse the Americans with Disabilities Act "of doing both too little and too much," said U.S Commission on Civil Rights chair Mary Frances Berry: "too little because it has not increased by a large enough margin the number of people with disabilities in the work force; too much because it has forced employers to hire people whose disabilities render them unqualified to perform job functions; too little because it has made employers wary of taking a chance on people with disabilities; too much because it has encouraged frivolous lawsuits from people whose disabilities are not genuine.

"One wonders whether critics who wield numbers and statistics," she said, "have ever considered it worthwhile to place the ADA within a framework apart from that of marketplace morality."

The problem of cost

"Oh, no! No no no! It's not for me! I don't have to ramp *my* entrance," the Bike Shop Man said to John Hockenberry. The ADA "requires local governments and private enterprises to pay the costs of accommodation out of their own pockets," which adds to the costs of doing business with "few if any offsetting benefits," said Cato's Ed Hudgins. "These costs are ignored or systematically belittled under the ADA," said Richard Epstein.

The reason the issue of access and accommodation devolves into a complaint about cost so quickly is because it has been allowed to do from the beginning by those who allegedly support disability rights — the law's initial backers in Congress. By allowing the insertion of "undue hardship" and "reasonable accommodation" language into the law, they made it acceptable to believe that the simple moral imperative of giving people access and individual accommodation was not something important enough, morally significant enough, to require. Whether the law's Congressional supporters really felt so half-hearted about the concepts, or whether they merely felt it better to pass a law with loopholes than no law at all, is by now moot. The intervening 12 years have shown the kind of bigotry that can legally run unchecked as a result of that faint-heartedness.

Just as warning a four-year-old never to play with matches will ensure that the idea, never before considered, now lodges itself firmly in her brain as a possibility of something new and interesting to do, allowing cost to provide an excuse for the denial of rights has assured that it now routinely does so, and that what public discussion there is about disability rights is rarely devoted to the moral imperatives of access and accommodation but instead to "how much it costs." Our nation's discussions about civil rights for racial minorities focused on issues other than cost because Congress simply would not allow cost to be factored in when racial discrimination was at issue.

DeLeire wrote that people "underestimate the costs of accommodation by including only monetary costs. Allowing a disabled employee to work a more flexible schedule, for example, might not increase a firm's out-of-pocket" expenses, but it does increase a firm's costs," he said.

It is true that accommodation does come with opportunity cost. "If you accommodate, you're *not* doing something else," agrees disability activist Cal Montgomery.

She explains:

Having a standard way that things are done streamlines the process of bringing new employees into a workplace. It also standardizes the cost (in dollars) of bringing new employees in. If all employees go through a particular training program, regardless of whether or not they already know most of what's in it, then you know exactly how much you're going to spend on wages while they're being trained, on training materials, and so on. You could probably spend less on some new hires and get away with it, but then you'd have to spend the effort figuring out exactly what each new hire needs, which would also raise the cost.

When you bring in an employee who doesn't fit the standard way of doing things, you're going to spend money altering things; you're going to spend time and energy on accommodation. The money you spend installing a ramp for a wheelchair using employee could have been spent on a pizza party for your employees to reward hard work and improve morale. The time you spend moving items stored on high shelves down lower for an employee with dwarfism could have been spent retraining poor performers so that they do their jobs better. And so on.

But, she adds, *everything* in our society has opportunity cost.

When you spend time, money, and effort ensuring that the people who're training new hires are sufficiently comfortable with a diverse array of workers that they aren't going to assume cultural differences translate into incompetence, you're spending time, money, and effort that you could have used on something else if you'd only hired people from the same cultural background as your trainers.

"The reality is that employers are willing to accept the costs of dealing with certain kinds of employees, including a fair amount of individualized attention in order to recruit and retain the most desired employees," she says. "And a fair amount of effort and investment goes into making jobs demand as little thought and training as possible, so companies can employ very low-wage workers and deal with high turnover. Companies are willing to spend time and money and effort ensuring that there's no blatant racism and sexism in the hiring process and that hostile work environments don't arise," she adds. "And they are willing to tolerate all kinds of disruptions so that employees they think might come back and shoot them aren't provoked."

In the first case, they think it's worth it in order to get and keep the people they think are really desirable; in the second case, they think it's worth it in order to deal with a strong economy (which means that they have to lower their standards and that their work-

ers will have more chances to get better jobs) or to fail to deal with
abominable working conditions; in the third case, they think it's
worth it in order to avoid lawsuits, losing out on government contracts, and bad publicity; in the fourth case, they think it's worth it
in order to avoid lawsuits, bad publicity, the loss of valued employees, and death.

The first woman in a formerly men-only area meant a jump in
the need for restrooms — just as the first wheelchair-user in a formerly "walkie-only" area did, she points out. The first person of
color hired by a merchant in a segregated Southern town meant a
lot of customers considering defecting to the competition. "The
only reason that these things look free now is that these early initial costs have receded in our memory, and because we've now got
a society in which — in theory, at least — some of these costs are
now a normal part of doing business and not some 'special' cost
associated with particular groups."

" 'It costs too much,' " she says, finally, "can be the end of a discussion about whether certain people get access, or it can be the
beginning of a discussion about how we can work together."

There are other things to keep in mind about the discussion of
costs of access and accommodation. The first is that people lie
about costs — either inflating the cost or blaming access for costs
that are attributable to things like overcharging and construction
snafus. The cost given for installing an elevator in Mother Teresa's
New York City homeless shelter (Chapter 3) was twice the actual
cost. The cost cited for the Burlington city hall ramp included the
additional cost (borne by the architectural firm, not paid for out of
the city's public funds) incurred when a mistake had to be corrected.

The second thing to keep in mind is that there is very little of
an objective nature to the "real cost" of access. Much depends on
whether access is viewed as something benefiting everyone or
something extra that only benefits a few (and, were it not for those
few, would not have to be done). An automatic door should cost
the same, whether it is being installed "for the handicapped" or as
the main entrance into a grocery store. In the latter, it's never mentioned. In the former, though, it's noted as an "extra" cost.

The third thing to remember about the discussion of costs is that costs are increased artificially through "medicalization" and "special." That same automated door, with a "special" button mounted on the side of the building embossed with the wheelchair access symbol, might actually have cost its store owner more than the same door sold by a grocery-store contractor, if it was sold through a contractor who wasn't above making a few additional bucks when he bid on "handicapped access" projects if he thought he could get away with it. It would have been cheaper to install accessible public toilet kiosks on the streets of Manhattan than inaccessible ones plus "special" ones for wheelchair users. It was natural with this arrangement to target the cost of the "special" toilets as the problem. When the issue of access to mass transit arose in New York City, *The New York Times* pressed not for making the public systems accessible but for "paratransit."

These "special buses reserved for them alone" were a "superior way to give mobility to the disabled." In fact, the only reason paratransit has ever been "cheaper" is because it has transported so few people. Once forced to make their regular public transit systems accessible, cities are now trying to discourage people from using paratransit — because it costs too much. In 2001, Philadelphia's public transit officials said they thought it likely that 10 percent of the 6,000 people who used paratransit could take a regular city bus instead. (A federal judge had ruled SEPTA was violating the ADA's requirement that people with disabilities who used paratransit be given service equivalent to what riders of its regular bus system got.) Getting rid of 10 percent of its riders would save the transit system nearly $7.5 million a year, officials figured.

The problem of 'Ron' and the disability rights vision

It is one of the most difficult-to-resolve arguments in the case against disability rights: that "special education" for some children is horrifically expensive and takes away from normal kids. *The Willamette* (Ore.) *Week* made that point in March, 2002: that some children, who would clearly never amount to anything ("some of these kids are so severely disabled you wonder what the point is") were costing the school system exorbitant amounts of money. The argument that "they" were taking from "us" occurred in arenas other than public education, of course. It was a central point of the case against disability rights. But "special education" offers as good a jumping-off point as any to look at how the us-vs.-them perspective blocks pursuit of viable solutions.

The Willamette Week's example of the "20-year-old with the body of an adult and the cognitive skills of a newborn who needs to be syringe-fed through a tube in his stomach every hour" works nicely for this purpose. Since the story did not name him, we'll call him "Ron."

It was true that kids like Ron had a limited educational horizon. "People might look at these kids and say they are a waste of tax dollars," said Shirley Burns, a program director at one of Portland's special ed. schools. "But we're enhancing their lives, and they have a right to that."

One could, like those against disability rights, simply discount Shirley Burns's statement as ridiculous. Or one could examine it for signs of how to go about creating the accessible society. People who discount Burns's statement likely hold a zero-sum perspective of community: providing for Ron is a waste of resources. Ron will never provide anything to society; he is only a drain. Looking at it this way is both a political act and a moral one. Too little has been said about the morality of the case against disability rights. The fact is that the case against disability rights is morally bereft; it is selfish. Selfishness is supposed to be good for capitalism; altruism passé, perhaps faintly ridiculous. But why? Simply because the free-market ideologues who have held public sway throughout the '90s have said that it is so does not make it correct.

There is a case to be made for an expansive vision of community, in which Ron fits simply because we choose to have him fit; because we as a society believe it is the right thing to do. This makes as much economic sense as the crabbed and selfish view, and who is to say it will really hurt society in the long run to hold it? Perhaps it will, in fact, help society.

For that is the other issue: whether it is better for society to carve off the "them," to make them go away, labeling people as "disabled" — either in order to certify them for special benefits or to tell them they are not able to work in our factories — or better to see them as, simply, part of us. To take the latter view requires that we go beyond the liberal directives of merely including the "less fortunate" in our society, for that is the charity model.

The disability rights model takes a different direction. The accessible society approach means that we include the Rons in the accessible society with us, just as we include ourselves. For doing this, ensuring that Ron is part of us, not them, is a way of ensuring ourselves that we ourselves will remain included in our families, our neighborhoods, our communities, when we ourselves become that "less fortunate" person by acquiring ALS, having a stroke or bearing a child like Ron. This approach is fundamentally different from "inclusion of the less fortunate," which presupposes a power inequality, the power and control belonging to the ones who give, the gratitude — and dependency — required of those given to.

The accessible society approach is essentially a kind of environmental investment strategy: we invest in the accessible society to ensure that it is available to us as well — that our own lives are afforded the same accommodation we have always had, and that we maintain the same power in our homes, neighborhoods and communities that we have always had, whether we remain unencumbered by stroke or paralysis, or whether we succumb to them or any of the other conditions that continue to befall humans and will continue to befall us all, whether Christopher Reeve gains his cure or not.

Understand Ron's situation as part of this investment approach to creating an accessible society, and things change.

Peel away the problems one by one. This book can offer only the most simplistic discussion of this. Ron will need to be cared for; this creates jobs; many people enjoy caring for people like Ron. Vast sums of money will need to be expended. But is that really true? How much of the cost is due to the medicalization of Ron's disability? How much is because those who produce "durable medical equipment" — like the wheelchair and bed Ron uses —

sell them to "special institutions" at exorbitant prices simply because Medicare will pay for it? Why must Ron live in a "special facility" — an institution? Why can't he live at home? Ron has the right to have his own life, his own things, his own choices. Ron has as much a right to control his life as you do. This idea seems implausible, in any case a harder problem to solve because we do not believe people like Ron can possibly know what is best for them. If we are to create a truly accessible society, though, that understanding must change, and it can only change with the help of disability activists who have been in Ron's position at one time themselves.

Willamette Week reporter Nigel Jaquiss wrote that Ron had the "the cognitive skills of a newborn." That may be true, or it may not be. Enough people with severe disabilities whose cognitive abilities are intact have been written off as having little or no cognitive ability to make us suspicious when we hear such a statement. It might be true, but it might not be. Even if it is true: Many people whose ability to move, feed oneself, bathe oneself is no better than Ron's do have the cognitive skill to plan and control their own lives. (It's just that few of them are allowed to.) It is to these people that we would ideally turn to learn what to do make Ron's life a decent one for him.

There are plenty of those people; but we as a society rarely notice their presence and make virtually no effort to seek them out and put them in policy positions that would let them show us how we might create an accessible society for people like Ron.

When solutions to problems like Ron's start being offered, they seem at best impractical, in reality simply unworkable. Yet they are no more impractical than a host of other endeavors society engages in. The reason their application has thus far been so marginally successful is because there is no public will behind it, not that the ideas in and of themselves are unworkable. It is because we do not care to figure out how to solve the problem of Ron in a decent way that we do not do so; not that the problems themselves are unsolvable. That is only what we like to say, to avoid doing anything. Adhering to the medical model of disability has its benefits: If we believe that the only real thing that can help Ron is cure, and cure hasn't been found, then we're off the hook about doing anything else for him.

Ron's life will always create problems. Will they been seen as manageable problems different from non-disability problems only in type, not in degree? Or will we view them as horrible tragedies requiring hand-wringing, blame, guilt and institutionalization? Viewing Ron's problems as tragedies is what drives us to lash out at "them" for taking our resources and pity them for having to "suffer." It is what we tend to do with our "disability problem," true. But it does not have to be this way.

Viewing Ron's problems as different in type but not degree from other problems will make us want to come up with a solution that will work well for Ron — for, in finding a solution that works well for Ron, we will have found one that will likely work well for us if and when we need it — or one that can be modified for our situation, just as the solution to Ron's problems may have been modified from solutions some other school found for someone somewhat like Ron in another community in another part of the country, perhaps developed by an education expert who had a childhood much like Ron's.

Once we see Ron as one of us, the entire proposition shifts. For most people, though, it is intensely hard to see Ron as one of us. That is the central impediment to creating a truly accessible society: the us-them problem. Getting to the place where we can see Ron as one of us requires that we discard the emotional baggage that Christopher Reeve and Jerry Lewis would have us cling to, the belief that there are two kinds of people, those who are "whole" and those who are not; those who are normal and those who are "failed normals." John Hockenberry had talked about a black curtain that fell, he said, when someone saw someone in a wheelchair. "It has nothing to do with me," he had said. "It has to do with them."

People have to deal with their own constructs of disability, in their own minds. As a nation we have barely begun that work; barely recognized, even, that it is work desperately needing to be done, and that, contrary to everything we have been taught, this is public, not private work. We need to talk about the experience of disability as a political and cultural one, not a personal, medical one. Only if we do that work will we be able to grapple with the policy implications inherent in Robert Burgdorf's contention that people do not come in two "sharply distinct groups of 'people with disabilities' and 'people without disabilities,'" but reside at all points along a spectrum of capabilities.

But the second part of what he had said was even more important: that we must not fixate on, overreact to or engage in stereotypes about people having functional disabilities — whether it is we or someone else who has them — but simply to take them into account as we go forward with the work of seeing to it that all of us are able to participate in our society equally. Achieving that equal participation sometimes required very different accommodations, disability rights advocates insisted. That was central to the disability rights message.

Would Ron be able to achieve equal participation? To the extent of his abilities, yes; if we permitted it — if we allowed him an education, to the extent that he could acquire one. He was getting that "education," but only because a law had been passed in 1974 — the Individuals with Disabilities Education Act — a law we argued about and ridiculed almost incessantly, failing to press Congress to fund it, while complaining that it took money from our "regular" children in our local schools.

The case for disability rights said that we needed to approach this issue without stereotype or fear, but simply in an open-minded way, seeing a solution of access and accommodation for Ron.

None of this offers any solutions. What it offers is a way toward solutions. All this book can do is point out that if such an attitude is not adopted, true solutions will never be found. Solutions must be crafted individually, for individual situations — just as disability rights advocates say. But the solutions will never be equitable, or viable, unless an attitude shift is brought to the table. This book has been a look at why the attitude shift needs to occur, and why it has been prevented from occurring. We are also now discussing what that attitude shift must do.

As a kind of exercise, let us look at the costs incurred by the Portland school for Ron: $100,000, says the article. Equipment for people like Ron "is custom-built," and "incredibly expensive." Maybe that is a cost that can't be lessened. But perhaps it can be. It is likely no one has examined the cost too closely, accepting it as a given, because it is specialized and medical. If medicalizing disability has any sure outcome, it is that it will raise costs. Diapers in nursing homes, costing $15 a package at the CVS (about 30 cents apiece), but billed to Medicare as "female urinary collection devices" for $8 apiece, is a cost that has to do with greed, frankly; it has nothing intrinsically to do with people who wear diapers.

The Diaper Cost Analysis can be fruitfully applied to every aspect of Ron's "education," including the "registered nurses" the *Willamette Week* reported that he needed. Christopher Reeve also said he needed nurses, round-the-clock nurses, he said. Registered nurses must be paid at the going rate for registered nurses, even when they are hired for jobs that do not require a registered nurse's training — changing catheters, suctioning tracheas. Most states' nursing associations have gotten laws passed requiring the presence of a registered nurse for such tasks. This has to do with money and job protection, not skill. We pay little attention to this, just as we don't much question Ron's special equipment cost. It is easy to see how costs for Ron can shoot up to $100,000. A lot is due to political decisions. It is *because* we "medicalize" costs for Ron that they rise. A General Accounting Office study found that nursing home therapists' $25-an-hour salaries had been billed to Medicare for $600 an hour.

"Typically, facilities charge separately (and exorbitantly) for supplies such as diapers, catheter tubes, and rubber gloves, as well as for special services like incontinence care, pressure-sore treatment, hand or tube feeding, even turning and positioning. Doing a resident's laundry often generates a separate charge," reported *Consumer Reports.* The monthly cost for such items can run to more than $900, it found in the facilities it surveyed.

This is not to say Ron doesn't need assistance in turning over or

being "suctioned," being diapered or catheterized. It is to say that
the costs associated with such things are magnified because we
allow them to be magnified by approving legislation at the state
and federal level that allows for costs to increase around things
considered medical. Despite oversight hearings, exposés and pon-
tificating from politicians, little changes in the medicalization of
costs; to change it would require a Herculean effort of national will
that we will likely not see any time soon. Even so, we should
understand that the cost issue is a function of political will. It's not
intrinsic to Ron's actual needs. And so it could change, if we had
the political will to change it.

Ron's is an extreme case. More typical are the hundreds of thousand of us who, like Ella Williams, are becoming disabled by the
modern workplace, acquiring what we call repetitive motion
injuries. We need changes and support as well. Although we are
considered too disabled to work — and thus we can perhaps draw
benefits — we are not considered disabled enough to use the ADA
to get employers to change the ways they run their factories and
offices so that we can continue to work.

It can hardly be expected that the nation's owners of commercial enterprises and large companies would suddenly change and
become benevolent supporters of the little guy, the worker, the
consumer. But what could happen, and has not yet had the faintest
stirrings of even starting to, would be that those who have traditionally been advocates of a more inclusive and welcoming society
for the masses begin to understand disability rights in this sense —
understand it, perhaps, in the same way they understand the push
for environmental regulation in order to protect our biosphere,
our plants and animals, and our own ecological futures. For disability rights is in truth more akin to environmental rights than
anything else.

Instead of assuming that any accommodation requested by a
"disabled person" will end up taking away from the rest of us,
would it not be to our society's benefit to abandon the lifeboat
mentality and consider that the accommodation, provided not
simply as a "special" accommodation to the one disabled person

but as a routine matter to everyone, might in fact help the rest of us, too?

This is precisely what business interests are resisting as they wage war against the Americans with Disabilities Act, using tactics that stop cases before they get started by getting the courts to bar plaintiffs as not disabled enough (read: unworthy) to use the law.

Those who push for the disability rights vision of access and accommodation have as their aim the increased humanizing of society. They would like to stop businesses from arbitrarily shutting out people simply because of something simple, like the storage of supplies too high for some workers to reach, which has "always been done that way" and which a company does not want to be forced to change.

Those who argue the case against disability rights are correct in seeing that the ADA wants society to change in fundamental ways that the Civil Rights Act had not required; but they do not respect the morality behind it. Disability rights is not seen as a moral issue, as civil rights had been. It is seen only as an economic issue: what helps the disabled hurts the rest of us. Nor do they seem willing to entertain the idea that retooling workplaces might be a solution to worker morale problems, and might increase productivity — preferring to adopt a "you can't make me do it" stance arguing against regulation, or, that failing, beating up on those who would press for more humane workplaces by accusing them of moral turpitude in trying to unfairly claim "disability."

Thomas DeLeire, intent on proving that the ADA had hurt disabled people by making companies afraid to hire them, simply dismissed studies saying costs for hiring disabled people were modest. (The Job Accommodation Network "reports that the median accommodation under ADA costs $500 or less." he wrote. "The BPA [Berkeley Planning Associates] study found that the average cost of an accommodation is very low — approximately $900 — and that 51 percent of accommodations cost nothing.") The studies, despite what they reported, he said, "underestimate the costs of accommodation by including only monetary costs."

But what if DeLeire is wrong and the Berkeley Planning

Associates and the Job Accommodations Network are right? Neither DeLeire, Epstein or anyone else making the case against disability rights ever offered the slightest shred of real evidence to support their contentions. Like Philip Howard, they seemed to simply invent outrageous remarks and float them as fact — with very little rebuttal. Neither DeLeire nor any other disability rights detractor offered proof — they just yelled louder.

All data that came to light showed that access cost very little. Yet none of it fazed disability rights detractors. They called such data "anecdotal" and continue to press their case, as filled with hubris as ever.

It has been 12 years since the ADA was passed, and more than that — at least two decades — since state and federal laws began mandating access and accommodation. With built-in loopholes, to be sure, but mandating it, nonetheless.

And yet still people continued, with little guilt, to claim that they did not know that they should have provided either physical access or a level of accommodation to a person considered disabled who wanted to take part in something they offered the public. "City and county officials don't even know what the law is," Foley had told *Hardball's* Chris Matthews. Maybe.

Some activists refer to this as "laziness-induced long-term ignorance."

"If 2001 was really the first time anyone had told the folks at the workshop I was attending that captioning wasn't any good unless you provide a screen that the people using the captions can actually see, well then, maybe it's true that they didn't know," said one activist. "But when you sign up for the same workshop a year later, and bring up the captioning issue again, and they react to the same information with the same 'but we didn't know,' then at that point, I think the barrier itself, and not the mental states of the people erecting, maintaining, or defending the barrier, is what's relevant."

It is no longer acceptable for a business to say that it never intended to keep women out of management positions if in fact it becomes clear that few women ever achieve such posts in the company. Such a company's intent is irrelevant; it has behaved illegally. When it comes to access and accommodation, however, "intending" to help disabled people — even if you end up failing to provide any access or accommodation whatsoever — is usually accepted as an excuse. Because, it's said, no *animus* is involved in disability discrimination: no one is against the handicapped.

If I don't intend to keep wheelchair users out of my building, but I have my entrance up nine steps, the intent is irrelevant.

The persistence of the medical model

Although much of the resistance to access and accommodation can be blamed on allowing businesses to use the cost excuse, another reason change is so slow in coming is due to the persistence of the medical model.

We are conditioned to believe that what needs to be done for "the disabled" is to help them get themselves "fixed" — through medical intervention, or, if they can't be cured, then to help them adjust psychologically to being a good cripple through rehabilitation. Most of society is simply not conditioned yet to believe that something like a ramp, or an interpreter, or having someone type up case notes that your organization's quadriplegic social worker could only dictate, will really help what is wrong with that person. And so it simply does not occur to us that access and accommodation might be that important in the life of someone who has become disabled.

Christopher Reeve's own sentiment, when he had said that he himself was not that interested in lower sidewalks, and that while access was all right, he intended to consider his disability "a temporary setback rather than a way of life," sums this up nicely. On some level, those who fight access are not simply being obstinate. They actually don't see much good coming from access, not for them (it adds to the costs of doing business with few if any offsetting benefits, said Epstein) or even for the disabled person, who, as long has he continues to have "something wrong with him" can never have a decent life, no matter what, because, after all, it is the man's body that is causing his problem, far more than the lack of an automatic door or a ramp.

The medical model's grip on society prevents the disability rights vision from taking hold. And as long as people do not understand the disability rights vision, they do not try very hard to understand the morality of access and accommodation, either.

If you think of yourself as a good guy, as Hockenberry's Bike Shop Man clearly did, and then are suddenly confronted by an accusation that you've done something wrong (or failed to do something right), "you get to choose between thinking you're not such a good guy as you previously thought, or thinking there's something wrong with the accusation," says Montgomery. "And the latter is by far the easier one for most people."

Then what? You can then rationalize that what you've done — not ramping your step, for example — isn't really all that bad. Or you can be angry at the accuser.

"Eastwood kind of *has* to hate us now, because it's the only way he can save face," says Montgomery. "To preserve Clint Eastwood's sense that he's a good guy, we agree that it's okay, when certain people want to get in, to tell them to just wait."

Interlude

Being able to get on a bus may seem like a small thing to many people without disabilities. But people with disabilities are still struggling to get to the back of the bus. Years after the Americans with Disabilities Act passed in Congress, we are still just trying to get on the bus.

Without the civil rights of fair treatment on and basic access to public transportation, the right to almost everything else stays theory only. And, just as the Montgomery Bus Boycott of 1955-56 led to the claiming of more basic civil rights, so has the right to get on the bus birthed other work for more complete civil rights for people with disabilities.

If this hunger to get the same consideration as others seems too whiney in this day and age, consider the statistics: one out of three Americans has daily contact with a person they care about who has a disability. We save money by keeping people in their communities. People with disabilities are actually being placed in nursing homes now because they can't get on a bus to do their own food shopping. It would be far cheaper to force public bus companies to treat shoppers with disabilities more fairly.

If you live long enough, you will age into disability. Access to public transportation then will allow you to stay active in your community longer.

What's not to like about letting people with disabilities use public buses like everyone else? Why aren't religious/liberal groups, who hated segregation based on race back then, agitating over morally wrong public transportation segregation based on disability now? After all, anyone has a 50/50 chance of being disabled enough to need adaptive equipment by the end of their lives. So isn't joining forces to fight for fully inclusive public transportation in their own best interests?

— Rus Cooper-Dowda

SEVENTEEN

The voice of the Supremes

Clint Eastwood's Mission Ranch had indeed broken the law, said the jury at the end of the two-week celebrity trial in San Francisco. There was no ramp to the registration office. An "accessible" guest room wasn't. No signs pointed to the accessible public restroom. All were violations of the Americans with Disabilities Act and California law.

Eastwood, standing before the cameras outside the courtroom, declared victory. The lack of access was a mere technicality: those "improvements" were already in the works.

Doubting that Diane zumBrunnen had actually been planning to stay at the resort, and so had not technically been denied access, jurors did not award her the money that California's Unruh Civil Rights Act would have granted someone who had suffered as a result of access denial. It was the state law, not the Americans with Disabilities Act, that allowed for damages anyway.

He had won, Eastwood crowed to reporters. He did not have to pay damages. He made light of the fact that it was the lawsuit that had impelled him to finally provide the access. He also failed to say that in making his choice to fight the charges, rather than simply comply, he had paid out tens of thousand of dollars to his own attorneys (which, evidently, were not "unscrupulous" ones).

"If you're right, you've got to hold your ground," Eastwood told the *San Francisco Chronicle*. "I also fought for the businessmen and businesswomen who own small businesses who are trying to get by and they get worked over by those people."

"He could have avoided the cost of attorney fees by settling the case and put his money into hiring an architect," Wolinsky told reporters later. "It's ridiculous for him to say he didn't know what needed to be done to eliminate physical barriers. I can't think of an area more clear-cut."

The federal courtroom in which the Eastwood trial took place was not accessible, either. People in wheelchairs had to be brought in through an exit door. Neither the witness stand nor the jury box was accessible. "Court officials had to remove a bench to allow room for observers in wheelchairs," said the *Chronicle*.

In the years following the 10th anniversary of the ADA, the Supreme Court continued to hand down decisions on the Americans with Disabilities Act. And although among themselves disability rights advocates, scholars and attorneys bemoaned the court's inability to understand what they felt were the very simplest rudiments of disability rights theory, publicly, their voices were silent. Rarely interviewed by reporters covering the Court, they were mostly also absent from the nation's opinion journals and editorial pages, save for a letter to the editor or two.

Board of Trustees of the University of Alabama v. Patricia Garrett was the first of what disability court watchers suspected would be many cases brought before the Supreme Court in an effort to prove the Act unconstitutional.

Congress had superseded its authority in passing the Americans with Disabilities Act, attorney Jeffrey Sutton told the Court. Sutton, an Ohio attorney hired by the University, had successfully argued before the Court against the Age Discrimination Act the previous year. Now he was saying there was no history of discrimination by states against people with disabilities sufficient to warrant Congress passing a law that superseded a state's "sovereign immunity" protected by the Eleventh Amendment. States had no right to have "extra Constitutional duties" imposed on them unless Congress "could show that the States brought this loss of authority upon themselves first by engaging in a widespread pattern and practice of unconstitutional conduct and, second, by showing that the remedial legislation is proportionate and congruent in nature," Sutton told the Justices.

More than 100 legal scholars had submitted a detailed brief to the Court outlining the history of state-sanctioned discrimination against people with disabilities. They submitted the brief, they told the Court, "to ensure that the well-documented evidence of widespread state discrimination against persons with disabilities is not forgotten by this Court." The brief listed hundreds of "state statutes, session laws, and constitutional provisions that illustrate pervasive state-sponsored discrimination against persons with disabilities, dating from the late nineteenth century through the time of the ADA's enactment and (in some cases) to the present."

Justice Stephen Breyer was likely thinking of the facts contained in that brief when he asked Sutton, "Why isn't it a constitutional violation where Congress has lots and lots of instances of States that seem to discriminate against handicapped people under instances where, given the information in front of them, for some reason or other, these handicapped people have not been able successfully to avail themselves of State law?"

Because, Sutton replied, Congress would have to have made a second finding — that states were not enforcing the laws that they had on the books. In the '60s, said Sutton, there was proof that states weren't enforcing their own voting laws when it came to blacks. But, he insisted that there was no such proof when it came to disability rights laws.

Outside, a small group of disability activists rallied, pressing the case for disability rights. Those who advanced the case against disability rights had already done their protesting, for the last decade, in the nation's media and in the courts. Observing that only disability activists were present at the demonstration, though, *The New York Times's* David Rosenbaum wrote that "No one, of course, demonstrated on the other side because no one is organized specifically to work against the disabled."

Sutton's argument convinced five of the Justices. Antonin Scalia, Anthony M. Kennedy and Clarence Thomas agreed with Rehnquist, who ruled that there was no real history of discrimination by states against people with disabilities sufficient to warrant Congress passing a law that superseded a state's "sovereign immunity" protected by the Eleventh Amendment. Racial discrimination in this country that had led to the Voting Rights Act of 1965 was real and documented, wrote Rehnquist; but evidence of disability discrimination was only "anecdotal."

"States are not required by the 14th Amendment to make special accommodations for the disabled," he explained "so long as their actions toward such individuals are rational. They could quite hardheadedly — and perhaps hardheartedly — hold to job qualification requirements which do not make allowance for the disabled."

The term "rational discrimination" was a legal concept: discrimination could occur so long as it was not "irrational." Those who had been pressing the case against disability rights for the last decade had insisted that disability discrimination made sense; it was "rational." It would be "entirely rational and therefore constitutional for a state employer to conserve scarce financial resources by hiring employees who are able to use existing facilities," rather than making access modifications, he said.

Sandra Day O'Connor ruled with the majority, but wrote her own opinion:

> Prejudice, we are beginning to understand, rises not from malice or hostile animus alone. It may result as well from insensitivity caused by simple want of careful, rational reflection or from some instinctive mechanism to guard against people who appear to be different in some respects from ourselves. Quite apart from any historical documentation, knowledge of our own human instincts teaches that persons who find it difficult to perform routine functions by reason of some mental or physical impairment might at first seem unsettling to us, unless we are guided by the better angels of our nature.

Sandra Day O'Connor was herself a breast cancer survivor. She had counseled Ruth Bader Ginsburg, when her colon cancer was diagnosed, "to have chemotherapy treatments on Friday so that she could be strong enough to come to work on Monday."

When she was diagnosed with breast cancer, Patricia Garrett, the woman whose case O'Connor was deciding, had been director of ob-gyn neonatal services for the University of Alabama, Birmingham, Hospital. She had a lumpectomy and underwent radiation and chemotherapy, but, hewing to her philosophy to not be "consumed by" one's disease, kept working. To get her to "take it easy" — although she'd never expressed a desire to — her boss forced on her a demotion and a $13,000 cut in salary. That was why she had sued the state university under the ADA. But to O'Connor and the other Supreme Court justices, it seemed, Patricia Garrett's encounter with disability discrimination was of little interest. The Justices were interested in abstract judicial reasoning about Constitutional law; about whether Congress had overstepped its bounds. Whether Patricia Garrett had actually been discriminated against, it seemed, was beside the point.

"The failure of a State to revise policies now seen as incorrect under a new understanding of proper policy," O'Connor wrote, "does not always constitute the purposeful and intentional action required to make out a violation of the Equal Protection Clause.

"If the States had been transgressing the Fourteenth Amendment by their mistreatment or lack of concern for those with impairments, one would have expected to find in decisions of the courts of the States and also the courts of the United States extensive litigation and discussion of the constitutional violations....That there is a new awareness, a new consciousness, a new commitment to better treatment of those disadvantaged by mental or physical impairments does not establish that an absence of state statutory correctives was a constitutional violation...."

"When the ADA was debated a decade ago, nobody suggested that it might one day be used to force employers to accept disruptive and insubordinate workers or salespeople who curse the customers. Discussion focused on people with severe and mostly visible disabilities," the ever-loquacious John Leo wrote of the *Garrett* decision. "Almost no one thought that backers of the ADA would push to include neuroses, drug habits, bad backs, or high blood pressure."

Jeffrey Sutton so impressed President George Bush that Bush nominated him to the U.S. Court of Appeals for the Sixth Circuit. Sutton had also represented the state of Georgia before the Supreme Court in *Olmstead v. L.C.*, arguing that states had no duty under the ADA to let people like Lois Curtis and Elaine Wilson live in the community. Keeping people with disabilities in institutions was not a form of discrimination, he'd insisted. It was a view shared by U.S. District Judge Catherine C. Blake, who told a dozen people, most with brain injuries, who had filed a class-action suit in Maryland more than seven years earlier to be allowed to live on their own, that "neither the Constitution nor the sweeping ADA required the state to treat such individuals in the community — even when medical professionals considered that setting more appropriate." Much as the Court had reasoned in the *Garrett* decision, Blake wrote that while "the plaintiffs' pain and frustration was genuine and understandable" they had "not shown sufficient reason for the court to order the State of Maryland to do more" — for to do so would be "unmanageably expensive."

If the *Garrett* case interested the Justices only as a constitutional issue, golfer Casey Martin seemed to interest them personally. He was brave and courageous — just the kind of person the ADA ought to protect, they seemed to think — so it was a simple matter for them to read the law's wording that "[n]o individual shall be discriminated against on the basis of a disability in the full and equal enjoyment of the privileges of any place of public accommodation" and find "golf courses" actually spelled out in the law as one of the kinds of "place of public accommodation" where discrimination was prohibited.

To most public commentators, though, Martin's victory was a story "about inspiration, not litigation," as one put it. Martin was a "courageous young man," wrote *Orlando Sentinel* sports columnist Mike Bianchi. The Omaha *World-Herald's* Tom Shatel found him a "uniquely courageous competitor"; a "symbol of courage"; a "courageous man playing despite a disability" who "should be allowed to ride" because "he's not a fraud, and he's not hurting the game. He's honoring it with his courage." Those who cheered Martin's victory did so not because they felt he'd met with illegal discrimination so much as they felt he deserved sympathy. Others, though, warned that the ruling would mean that wheelchair basketball players would "sue the NBA for entry," "gimpy baseball players [would] ask for motorized carts to run the bases." *Orlando Sentinel* sports columnist David Whitely knew there were "other Martins out there" that until now had "just accepted their handicaps as part of the game," but who would now likely think they deserved more. Using the same logic, *The New York Times* thought the decision the right one, because "...[T]he PGA Tour is never going to be inundated with applications from afflicted walkers who possess professional swings because such skills are rare in the population at large." Their wording reveals how they understood the concept of disability discrimination — they saw the Justices not so much enforcing a federal antidiscrimination law as making "an exception for Casey Martin" — one that "will not hurt the sport" but would "make the PGA look wise and compassionate...."

The New York Times's Linda Greenhouse thought the *Martin* case showed that the ADA's essential concepts remained "surprisingly undefined." Yet the public consensus seemed to be that, to be worthy of legal protection, a disabled person must show courage in overcoming obstacles, and must be "truly disabled."

In January, a few weeks before the *Garrett* decision, a statue of Franklin Delano Roosevelt in a fully visible wheelchair had finally been installed at the FDR Memorial, ending what *The Washington Post* called a six-year "emotional campaign" by the National Organization on Disability and its director Alan Reich. Reich called the statue's unveiling "the removal of the shroud of shame that cloaks disability," but the statue had been fought by Memorial architect Lawrence Halprin, who argued that it did violence to the Roosevelt who had consciously concealed his wheelchair from the public.

Charles Krauthammer, a wheelchair user himself, would write in the *Post* that he could not "think of a more grotesque abuse" of FDR's disability:

> FDR would never have said or done anything remotely like this. He never talked about his disability with anyone — his family, his wife, even his mother — let alone did stunts for war counselors and generals. If anyone dared broach the subject with him, FDR would freeze him out....FDR would have been mortified at the mere suggestion of making a public show of misfortune.

A group of disability scholars had been asked to recommend a quotation for the inscription to accompany the statue.

"We sought a quotation as crisp, powerful, and unambiguous as the bold 'I hate war,'" wrote Howard University's Rosemarie Garland-Thomson. "FDR's strategy in the Depression had been to alter the environment to meet the needs of the people. That was parallel, we reasoned, to the idea that people with disabilities need a material situation that accommodates the differences of their bodies or minds." Wanting a quote that would "avoid the stereotypical narrative that disability is a tragic experience to be overcome," they settled on Franklin's "We know that equality of individual ability has never existed and never will, but we do insist that equality of opportunity still must be sought."

Their recommendation was ignored, though, in favor of one N.O.D. liked better, one from wife Eleanor: "Franklin's illness gave him strength and courage he had not had before. He had to think out the fundamentals of living and learn the greatest of all lessons — infinite patience and never-ending persistence."

The scholars were dismayed. Besides not having the disabled FDR even speak for himself, the quote "told the stereotypical, apolitical story of disability as an individual catastrophe, psychological adjustment, and moral chastening…a private problem that an individual must overcome, not a public problem of environmental and attitudinal barriers."

"Celebrating the paralytic's 'courage' is the psychological equivalent of calling an accomplished black person 'a credit to his race,'" Krauthammer huffed. "It is a patronizing act of distancing wrapped in the appearance of adulation."

But the point to the statue, Reich countered, was to "inspire everyone to overcome obstacles."

Just a few weeks before the Justices had handed down their *Martin* ruling, Jerry Lewis had let fly a few choice words for those disability activists who had been picketing his telethon for years and accusing him of using pity-mongering ploys to raise money at the expense of their dignity. "Pity?" he sneered. "You don't want to be pitied because you're a cripple in a wheelchair? Stay in your house!"

The comment, to reporter Martha Teichner on *CBS Sunday Morning*, drew little outrage outside the ranks of disability activists. Reporters learning of the anger mistakenly thought that it was Lewis's use of the word "cripple" that had upset them.

The Jerry Lewis Telethon, running since 1966, was part of mainstream American culture, and Lewis, despite his "boneheaded" remark, deserved credit for his time and effort in raising millions of dollars for cures for the Muscular Dystrophy Association, said the PR industry *O'Dwyer Newsletter*, which reported on what it saw only as a public-relations snafu. Both Jerry Lewis and the MDA had offered apologies, it reported.

Those who made excuses for Jerry Lewis didn't recognize disability bigotry when they saw it, insisted attorney Harriet Johnson, who had one of the diseases Jerry was curing. "When bigotry is part of mainstream culture, it feels like 'the way things are.'"

My grandfather's generation of white men in the South didn't recognize sexism. They thought women really were magnolia blossoms requiring protection. They didn't recognize racism either. They thought African Americans really were inherently inferior, suitable to menial work, and that the structures of segregation were for the good of both races. They'd say it wasn't prejudice, but the way things are. This is where we are with disability today. Lewis says he uses pity because, hey, we're pitiful. And people agree.

If you don't see the profound *animus* in Jerry Lewis's statement, try substituting the minority group. What if he said, "If you don't want to be bashed for being gay, stay in your house"? Or, "If you don't want to be groped for being a broad, stay in your house"? Or — if you believe the "charity" work excuses hate — consider this scenario. What if the United Negro College Fund hired a white comedian to raise money from white people, using bigotry. "Give because they're so stupid, so hopelessly ignorant, they need their own schools to keep them out of our schools."

Would the success of such a pitch justify it? Or would we recognize that the more it succeeds — the more people buy into it — the more harm it does? I think — I hope — we're at a point now where people would be up in arms if one of those other minority groups were treated with such profound disrespect, for decades, by a charity ostensibly dedicated to "helping" them.

But with disability, it's a lesson yet to be learned.

An article in the Naples, Fla. *News* reporting on a "litigious law firm filing hundreds of ADA lawsuits" signaled that Mark Foley had not let up on his campaign to amend the ADA. His bill had gotten nowhere so far, but Foley had not given up. He now had the backing of the National Restaurant Association, and he was shopping his case again in the media. A few months later, the *National Law Journal* reported both the "hundreds of lawsuits" story and that Rep. Foley was continuing to "push for his amendment to the ADA." In the Fort Lauderdale *Sun-Sentinel* and on Fox News's *The O'Reilly Factor* it was the same dog-and-pony show, Eastwood and Foley, protecting the disabled by making them wait another 90 days for compliance with a law that hadn't been obeyed for eleven years.

California was at least a decade away from ensuring that the public had unencumbered access to its programs and facilities. None of California's public agencies had come into full compliance with the ADA. The Employment Development Department, which administered unemployment benefits and disability insurance benefits, did not comply. None of the state institutions warehousing nearly 4,000 "developmentally disabled" Californians was fully accessible. Caltrans had yet to complete access plans due in 1993. The state's division of motor vehicles had identified 4,523 architectural barriers in its facilities, but state agencies were under the honor system to comply with the law; they faced no consequences when they ignored it.

Fresno, Calif. wheelchair user Elias Gutierrez had complained repeatedly about the lack of curb ramps on sidewalks in his neighborhood, forcing him into the streets. It wasn't safe, he said. A month after the *Garrett* decision, the 60-year-old activist was killed by a car as he drove in his power wheelchair in the street. Officials in this city that had been named one of America's 10 "most livable" by the National Civic League the year before made no move to add curb cuts, though. In June 2002, the Ninth Circuit Court of Appeals ruled that cities did have an obligation to make sidewalks accessible — at least in Sacramento. The ruling was "the first and only decision in the nation" on the matter, said Larry Paradis of Disability Rights Advocates, who had pressed the lawsuit. In New York City, wheelchair users still could not get up onto the sidewalk; half the city's 158,738 street corners still had no cuts for wheelchairs.

San Francisco State University settled a suit over access, insisting all the while that its facilities and programs were already accessible. Despite laws, despite lawsuits, despite "receiving millions of dollars through voter-approved bond measures for the required upgrades," San Francisco's public schools were still not accessible, either. Students who couldn't climb stairs still missed class because elevators didn't work or didn't exist, got knocked down by heavy school doors, couldn't use bathrooms because handrails hadn't been installed.

A federal judge had ruled that Philadelphia's transit system was violating the ADA's requirement that paratransit users be given service equivalent to what riders of its regular bus system got. A little later, officials announced they would make it more difficult to use paratransit: Too many people were using it; it cost too much money. Ten percent of the 6,000 people signed up for the service could take a regular city bus instead, they said. That would save the system nearly $7.5 million a year.

Only 41 of Chicago's 6,700 cabs were accessible to wheelchairs; those who called had to wait as long as three hours to get picked up — if they got rides at all. Drivers routinely refused to respond to calls from wheelchair users.

Discrimination against disabled air travelers had been outlawed by the 1986 Air Carrier Access Act, but air travel remained a "difficult and humiliating experience," sources told *The Wall Street Journal's* David Armstrong. Gate agents refused to allow people to board who they thought might "act up"; attendants insisted that passengers sit on towels for fear they'd soil themselves (no airplane toilet was yet accessible); skycaps routinely lost or damaged wheelchairs costing thousands of dollars. Few airlines feared lawsuits, though; they'd thwarted the move to amend the Air Carrier Access Act to give winning plaintiffs a right to legal fees, which was common in other civil-rights laws. "Until recently," Armstrong wrote, "fines for violations were lower than most first-class fares."

The District of Columbia Housing Authority, in two of whose inaccessible housing units Marcus Young and Jordan Cook lived, had never complied with the 1973 Rehabilitation Act's accessibility requirements, nor those of the Fair Housing Act. Fewer than 5 percent of its 10,460 apartments were accessible. In 2001, the District also bought voting equipment that neither blind voters nor those in wheelchairs could use. Most of the District's 140 polling sites remained inaccessible.

Sen. Tom Harkin's press conference, to announce that two thirds of the polling sites the GAO had surveyed on Election Day 2000 barred people in wheelchairs (and that none had voting equipment that would let blind voters cast their vote in secret), got little coverage. Several months later, Harkin was back before the cameras to praise George W. Bush's "New Freedom Initiative," which would put up to $33 million into technology "for the handicapped." "Disability policy, I've never known any partisan debate on it," he said. Among themselves, savvy disability observers noted that while money went to entrepreneurs and research programs to develop the technology, none was allocated for disabled people to buy it.

Costs for access continued to worry people. It would cost at least $85 million annually to comply with new Internet access rules taking effect that June, said some in government. Despite the new rules, many agencies still uploaded documents in the inaccessible PDF format, and programs like Blackboard, proliferating as ways to construct online college courses, were chock-full of graphics and coding that made them unusable to people with screen reader browsers. The American Council on Education's Sheldon E. Steinbach, though quick to preface his remarks with "I don't think there's anybody that would take a public posture that this is not an appropriate next step," said that making online courses accessible to people with speech readers was an additional cost "that ultimately has to be paid in some manner, which usually means an increase in tuition and fees."

Vermont Senator James M. Jeffords continued to try to get the Individuals with Disabilities Education Act the funding it had always needed and never had, but Bush and the Republican leadership fought him. The funding Jeffords was trying to free up was "more than special education should have," *New York Times* education columnist Richard Rothstein insisted; it left "big needs unmet for regular classes." The law was up for reauthorization. Despite its good intentions, it had had "unintended consequences," said those who opposed it, citing its "open-ended 'accommodation' philosophy" toward "populations better served with prevention or intervention strategies." Conservatives called the IDEA "the largest unfunded federal mandate in American education." Hopes for funding were dashed thoroughly when House Republicans ruled out increases of $2.5 billion a year for six years for IDEA, because the money, said critics, would come from a program aimed at helping nondisabled poor children. "Why would we want to pit poor children against disabled children?" said Ohio Republican Congressman John Boehner.

A House-Senate conference committee rejected a Senate bill that would have ensured that psychiatric disorders were covered by insurance on a par with physical disorders, despite Sen. Pete Domenici's insistence that it was "one of the most important social and civil rights issues in the United States." Domenici's daughter had schizophrenia. The party-line vote was 10 to 7, with House Republicans all voting "no."

E I G H T E E N
A strange silence

Longtime journalist Michael Kinsley, most recently editor of online magazine *Slate*, revealed that he'd had Parkinson's for nearly eight years.

> Even eight years along, I can still pass as healthy most of the time, or could until this week; but there has been a slight pang of disloyalty to the cause in doing so. A woman with multiple sclerosis once said to me, unknowingly, about disease activists in general: "We all pray for someone famous to get our disease."

The disability experience needed to be understood in terms larger than that of the individual, Rosemarie Garland-Thomson had written, and it seemed at though Kinsley was moving toward that understanding himself. Until the Freedom Summer of the civil rights movement, when the sons and daughters of the New York media had gone South, reporters trailing, and seen for themselves the horrors of the Jim Crow South that came from racial oppression, it had not become real to America. In much the same way, disability rights activists hoped that someday, someone of celebrity status like Christopher Reeve would begin to talk publicly about the disability experience as a political one, would begin to champion disability rights.

Some felt hopeful on reading Kinsley's confession:

> I was officially, publicly healthy. Now, with almost no objective medical change, I am officially, publicly sick. How will that change the actual effect of the disease? Without, I hope, distorting the experiment, I predict that this notion of disease as a function of attitudes about disease will turn out to be more valid than I would have suspected eight years ago.

> If you're normal, or people think you are, you can clear your throat or trip on a rug or complain of a headache without raising alarms or eyebrows. When people know it is partly performance, you can't.

> Anyone who develops a chronic disease in mid-career dreads being written off — being thought of prematurely in the past tense. Three years ago, I was offered the editorship of *The New*

Yorker. I told the owner I had Parkinson's and invited him to change his mind, but he generously said it didn't matter. A few hours later, though, he withdrew the offer with no explanation. I chose to believe him that the Parkinson's didn't matter. To withdraw the offer for that reason would be, among other things, probably illegal. But I also doubt that he would have made the offer in the first place had he known all along.

Charles Krauthammer's political leanings would likely never allow him to endorse disability rights as a social good, even though it might have been in his own best interest. He seemed to be the only public persona who recognized the damage Reeve had been doing.

Yet he muted his criticism. "I have long been reluctant to criticize Christopher Reeve," Krauthammer had written back when the actor had "walked" on the Super Bowl. "It is not easy attacking someone who suffered such a devastating injury and has carried on with spirit." His reluctance to attack Reeve — although he went on to do exactly that — offers an insight into why the case against disability rights is so one-sided. It springs from the same wellspring of sentiment that makes people say that no one is against the handicapped, even as they deny people access and refuse them accommodations. It was the point Garland-Thomson had made about the FDR statue. Disability belonged first and foremost to the private realm — it was seen as "a personal matter between doctor and patient," as Paul Longmore had put it. More recently, Ruth O'Brien had written that "societal acceptance" for a disabled person depended "on how well disabled people conformed to society." And we ignore, or resist, efforts to make it into a public issue, even though disability affects far more of us than other issues which had been argued vehemently and contentiously in our nation's media for years: race relations, abortion, gay rights.

Many of us might take exception to the preceding sentence, insisting that these issues were argued publicly because they affected all Americans, because they were public issues. The same was true about disability, though — more so, since disability was the one thing that would likely touch all of us sooner or later, and disability discrimination was thus a real possibility for any of us, just like Patricia Garrett had found in what she might have thought the most unlikely of places. And who argued *that* point? Almost no one, certainly not our nation's public talkers.

The belief that disability was not truly a public issue explained why Andy Rooney's racial slur caused an outrage but his disability bigotry caused nary a ripple; why media pundits and columnists would chew for weeks over a racial gaffe but fail to note disability slurs altogether.

Months before he had written that he did not want to pick on Reeve, Krauthammer had noticed that "with the PC police so outraged at the alleged racism of George Lucas's new *Star Wars*, it is rather odd that nothing has been said about the savage mockery of physical deformity in *Wild Wild West*." It *was* odd, but no one other than Krauthammer had seemed to notice. Jerry Lewis's "if you're a cripple in a wheelchair, stay in your house!" remark had caused little stir outside the disability community, either.

Almost everyone who experienced disability and who had been the subject of a feature story (and a vast percentage of people considered "truly disabled" had been profiled in their local newspapers or on their local TV news programs) had found reporters turning their accounts of bigotry, social ostracism, prejudice, discrimination into stories of inspiration and overcoming, either glossing over — or never noticing — aspects of the story that knit it into the larger fabric of nationwide disability discrimination. A story a wheelchair user told a reporter about being denied job after job ended up not as a piece on the issue of job discrimination but a feature on the pluckiness of the disabled jobseeker.

Some reporters, who did understand the reality of the national problem of disability discrimination, found that their editors did not; that the editors neither regarded "the disabled" as a real minority group nor stories about disability issues facing them as important ones. "When Missouri Gov. Mel Carnahan died, the newspaper planned a series of stories about his contingency groups," said the *St. Louis Post-Dispatch's* Jennifer LaFleur. "It took a lot to convince editors that disabled people made up a true contingency group. If we treated another minority group the same way, our newsroom would be up in arms."

Disability issues were considered not a beat but a side issue in most newsrooms. They weren't covered consistently. Newsrooms often didn't know what might constitute a major disability story. Print journalists "are much more likely to use people with disabilities as examples in their news stories than as sources," says Towson University journalism professor Beth Haller, who studied news coverage of disability issues. Among the most significant findings of Haller's study that was that, in story after story, "national disability organizations were largely missing"; those interviewed were usually healthcare providers or government officials, leaving the impression, says Haller, that "people with disabilities can't speak for themselves." Given a story about a clear disability rights issue, copy editors composed headlines showing they viewed "rights" as "help." A story about a court settlement calling for accessible voting machines was headlined "District to Aid Disabled Voters."

Like most people, reporters somewhat feared examining disability. Upon encountering someone who had one, they felt outright pity. They associated disability with tragedy or adversity. They felt that "disabled people are different from us more than they are like us," Haller wrote, "that their disabilities somehow set them apart from the rest of us." Their beliefs flowed into their stories.

The "coping with adversity" theme still won Pulitzers. Tom Hallman had won one for his series on Sam Lightner's facial deformities. A study of journalism award-winners found a preponderance focused on "coping" and on "illness or disability." And they were awash in inspiration. What was wrong with inspiration? To Haller, who'd conducted the study, the problem was that it ran hand in hand with tragedy; neither dealt with the reality of the disability experience. "No matter who you are, what you do, how you feel, to some people you'll always be a tragic figure," said a woman whose story had been given the inspirational gloss.

Language changes. Reporters know not to use "Negro" any more; the other "n" word is verboten. Many avoid "black" in favor of the preferred "African-American." A tremendous battle preceded *The New York Times*'s concession to using "Ms." For over a decade the *Associated Press Stylebook* has been telling reporters to avoid the term "afflicted"; to replace "wheelchair bound" with the more accurate and less emotional "wheelchair user." To little avail. "When I have my students learn to use the *AP Stylebook*," said Haller, "I give them a sentence that uses 'wheelchair-bound.' Few of them know to fix it. Most don't even suspect it's incorrect." A definition of "diversity" from the Society for Professional Journalists in August, 2002 still failed to include "disability."

In early 1993, reporters were drawn to a courtroom in the suburb of Glen Ridge, N.J. Four men in their early twenties were on trial for the rape, four years earlier, of a high school classmate who was labeled "mildly retarded." The rape had taken place in a basement where the boys had invited the girl. They were charged with penetrating her with a baseball bat and a broom handle, among other things. The court case hinged on whether the woman was mentally competent to consent to sex. Was she, asked the court, a "mental defective"?

Women's groups were outraged at the "boys will be boys" attitude of defense attorneys. Members of women's groups attended the trial daily, keeping tabs on the issue and making public statements.

Reporters covering the trial looked in vain for disability comment. The more enterprising reporters finally tracked down reluctant groups for interviews only to learn that area disability groups did not want to speak out. They did not want to draw media attention to the issue, they said. Some said they had no firm thoughts on the issue one way or the other; others said they had thoughts but they didn't want to make them public. Or they had conflicting thoughts best kept to themselves. *New York Times* reporter Catherine Manegold wrote on the eve of the verdict that the reaction of disability groups was "a strange silence."

In January 2002, the Supreme Court ruled unanimously that because former Toyota worker Ella Williams could still perform tasks "central to daily living" like brushing her teeth or cooking, she was not truly disabled and could therefore not use the Americans with Disabilities Act to sue Toyota, which refused to give her work that didn't involve exacerbating her injury. Sandra Day O'Connor, listening to Williams's attorney argue the case the previous fall, had interrupted to insist that the ADA was supposed to focus on the "wheelchair bound," not "carpal tunnel syndrome or bad backs!" Now she wrote in the opinion that "Merely having an impairment does not make one disabled for purposes of the ADA. Claimants also need to demonstrate that the impairment limits a major life activity…[and] that the limitation…is 'substantia[l].'"

Despite his New Freedom Initiative and the fact that there was never any partisan debate over disability, George W. Bush's administration had backed Toyota in the suit — as it was backing employers in almost every case now coming before the Court having to do with disabled people suing companies for disability discrimination.

Repetitive-motion injuries and strains continued to account for most of the time lost from work for the more than 1.7 million workplace injuries reported again in 2000, according to the Bureau of Labor Statistics. Now Williams and others with nontraditional disabilities who faced discrimination on the job because of these injuries would never even get a chance to make their case in court. "If Americans knew what they had lost, they would weep," the Center for an Accessible Society's Cyndi Jones said.

Still, many who were disturbed that workers had lost a means of redress still felt that "legally, the ruling made sense." The ADA was "not the right vehicle….not intended to start a deluge of ADA lawsuits against employers who understandably refuse to accommodate every impediment of every worker."

"Even though Ms. Williams couldn't perform a certain job, would most of us consider her disabled? Would we think she deserves special accommodations, a handicapped parking place? Probably not," said the *Philadelphia Inquirer*. People with "true disabilities" would "retain protections that are undiluted by a flood of cases brought by workers who should be compensated in other ways," said Louisville's *Courier-Journal*.

The federal enforcement agency for employment discrimination under the ADA — the EEOC — had caused much of the problem, fumed the National Council on Disability, which blamed the agency "for fostering and not challenging an atmosphere in which the definition of disability became viewed as a technical and restrictive ticket to an exclusive private club of persons entitled to ADA protection." Aggrieved employees who turned to the EEOC for help with disability discrimination usually got nowhere. Over 94 percent of ADA job discrimination cases in court were decided in favor of business as well.

The Orange County Register called O'Connor's ruling "a common-sense approach to disability that could limit the number of lawsuits with little or no merit brought under the ADA." The paper quoted the Cato Institute's Hudgins, who said the fact that most cases were decided in favor of employers was "a sign of a poorly written law subject to too many possible interpretations." Even so, tut-tutted the *Register*, each one required "money spent on lawyers." It was ridiculous, said the *Register*, that the law considered "being regarded as having an impairment" a reason for discrimination. "No wonder there have been cases like the 400-pound subway worker," it said.

Rep. Steny Hoyer, who had shepherded the ADA through the House, was seeing, like many disability advocates, that a law could not guarantee what a culture did not understand. Both advocates and the ADA's Congressional supporters, he wrote, "failed to anticipate what this court's views of our views would be." Congress had intended something far more expansive than Justice O'Connor understood, he wrote. "We intended the law to be broad rather than narrow.

"Until the ADA passed, the average guy thought of a disability as something that meant you couldn't walk or see or hear." O'Connor still believed that.

"Is this what we had in mind when we passed the ADA — that lawyers for businesses and individuals should spend time and money arguing about whether people can brush their teeth and take out the garbage?" Hoyer wrote. "Not at all.

"In matters of statutory interpretation, unlike constitutional matters, Congress has the last word," he continued. "We can decide whether the employment policy effectively put into place by the Supreme Court's interpretations of the ADA is a solid one. Or we can decide to rewrite the statute."

Rewriting the statute was precisely what those who pushed the case against disability rights wanted as well. The ADA was one of the "worst-drafted statutes in the U.S. Code," snarled the Center for Equal Opportunity's Roger Clegg. Congress should take up the ADA again, he said — to make it narrower.

That spring, following the *Toyota* ruling, the nine Justices ruled on two more ADA employment cases. Robert Barnett, they said, just because he wanted an accommodation, had no right to expect to supersede a company's own seniority system. Mario Echazabal, they said, might have his health endangered if he worked for Chevron, and it was within the right of a company to refuse to hire someone whose health or safety it felt might be endangered by the job.

All three — Williams, Barnett and Echazabal — had won their cases at the lower court level; it was the Supreme Court that decided the law had gone too far. Barnett, a former US Airways baggage handler from San Francisco who had injured his back on the job and been reassigned to the mail room, sued when a worker with more seniority bid on the mailroom job, and was given it. US Airways had illegally taken away his "reasonable accommodation," said Barnett. That wasn't illegal, said the Supremes; company seniority programs can take precedence over disability accommodation. Echazabal had Hepatitis C, and although Chevron was happy enough to let him work as a contractor at the refinery in El Segundo, California, when he actually applied to work for Chevron, and his employment physical revealed the chronic liver disease, they refused to hire him, claiming the job might imperil his own health. They were refusing to hire him in order to protect him, they said. Advocates were furious, insisting that the "plain language" of the ADA itself had said that employers could not discriminate against someone unless they posed a "risk to health and safety of others" — not themselves. The ruling was paternalistic, they fumed.

Perhaps these cases were what people in other movements referred to as "bad cases." People before Rosa Parks had been thrown off Montgomery's buses for refusing to stay in the Negro section. But the N.A.A.C.P., looking to press the cause of integration, would not touch them. High school student Claudette Colvin's foul mouth and feisty attitude kept hers from being a test case. Parks, on the other hand, had been involved with the N.A.A.C.P. "There were no extraneous charges [against her] to cloud the segregation issue"; she "would make a good impression on white judges...as a symbol for Montgomery's Negroes... humble...yet dignified...." Parks's arrest gave Montgomery's Negro leadership the case they'd been waiting for.

The closest the organized disabled had to a Rosa Parks in terms of public image was Casey Martin, but his case had not been shepherded by the movement, either. He'd just happened along, a pro golfer who "had something wrong with him" and who got angry about the discrimination. Martin was not part of the organized disabled. And his case had not been about employment.

Unlike the disability movement, which had little money to press any lawsuit to the Supreme Court (the U.S. Dept. of Health and Human Services's $2 million had gone to Christopher Reeve, not the cause of disability rights), the U.S. business community had deep pockets and was not loath to dig into them to keep that lid on litigation clamped down quite tightly.

Pundits paid little attention to stories of those who won their ADA cases, or whose cases were so strong that employers settled. Those who wrote about the Supreme Court rulings seemed to have little more inkling than the Court as to what the Americans with Disabilities Act was all about. Michael Kinsley it seemed had never made a connection between himself with his own Parkinson's, which he suspected as having been the reason for the withdrawal of a job offer, and those who tried to use the law for employment discrimination. He seemed stuck, along with most of society, in the mindset that "disability" must simply mean the opposite of "ability," as he'd written in "Must we pay to hear bad pianists," his piece for *Slate* in June, 2002 — and that, thus, the ADA was an "inherently self contradictory law."

"Discrimination based on ability does make sense," he wrote. "Racial prejudice is at its heart irrational whereas prejudice in favor of ability is not." He seemed to buy the argument that had been put forth for nearly a decade by the forces countering disability rights, that the ADA was about "forcing employers to hire less qualified candidates."

Yet, like Kinsley himself, one in five of us had some condition that under one or another circumstances someone would call a "disability" — perhaps to keep us from some program, some job. Disability advocates had for years been referring to that "one in five" as a sleeping giant, about to awaken. But was it?

"Can you imagine what this country would have been like if, years after the 1964 Civil Rights Act, we'd still had bathrooms marked 'whites only' and 'colored only'"? Steve Gold said. "When Congress passed a law in 1964 saying racial access must be equal — why, if restaurants and bus stations had continued to keep separate bathrooms and separate water fountains, there would have been a bloodbath in this country!"

Anyone who felt that the case against disability rights had lost some of its stridency in 2002 might have been right, though. After all, it seemed, those pressing that case have won most of their battle. They can relax their vigilance. The law would protect only the truly disabled now, believed to be few in number — and only if it didn't cost business.

Reeve wanted "disability" to just go away. Reeve wanted to be cured. "Some people are able to accept living with a severe disability. I am not one of them," he told a Congressional committee a month or so after the *Toyota* decision. His 50th birthday had come and gone, and although he'd fueled a minor media frenzy by announcing he'd regained feeling in parts of his body, he still could not walk — he blamed opposition to stem-cell research.

The Supremes wanted people like Ella Williams to simply shut up. Such people weren't who Congress meant when they wrote the law, they said — despite Congressman Steny Hoyer's or anyone else's assertions to the contrary.

For the nation's workers, it was a Catch-22: Congress's intent in passing the ADA, as Hoyer and other members of Congress had repeatedly said, was to keep people in the work force. The Court told businesses they could get rid of such workers, though. "Instead of bringing people with disabilities into the workforce, the Supreme Court has kept them out," wrote O'Brien.

Still, in America one could succeed, like John Stossel's Marc Simitian, by pulling oneself up by one's bootstraps, by having courage and determination, and not pressing for rights.

This had been the central argument of those who pushed the case against disability rights, and for every Hockenberry who saw through it, and every Kinsley who might eventually see through it, there were millions who did not. Most people who had "something wrong with them" (and that was an astonishingly large number of us) believed, just as Stossel said, that it was up to us and us alone to overcome the discrimination we ran into. Much of what we saw as discrimination occurring because we were "disabled" was likely not, said the case against disability rights. For, after all, no one was against the handicapped.

Neal Gabler writes that

> what Reaganism did — and this may have been its signal accomplishment — was convince the average American that equal opportunity already existed, and that anyone who didn't succeed had only himself to blame, not the inequities of the system. This was the grand psychological transformation, and though it played on Americans' predisposition both to credit and to reprove themselves for their own situation, it succeeded largely by steadily redirecting attention from the macro to the micro, from economics to anecdote....It remains a potent idea, because people want to believe it.

More than most, people who incurred disability were told to believe this. And most, it seemed, still did.

Gabler was writing about economic inequity and our curious inertia about it, yet he could have as easily been writing about our approach to disability rights. What conservatives did, he said, was to convince people that wealth — he could as easily have said equality — "is a function of brains and gumption, rather than of inheritance or influence."

To paraphrase Gabler: After 20 years of inspirational tales of good cripples who succeeded despite their disability (which although nobody said it, really meant despite prejudice, barriers and lack of accommodation), "and as many years of government bashing," most of us believed still that only those who did not press for rights were deserving of them; that if we became disabled, we had better not whine about wanting access or accommodation.

To think in terms of disability rights would be "to deny the ideal of individual responsibility that is the very basis of America." That, when applied to thinking about the rich, Gabler said, was why "the rich will keep getting richer, the middle class will keep losing ground, the poor will keep getting ignored, and no one will say a single word about it."

When it came to disability, this was equally true: it was why those who pushed the case against disability rights would continue to win in the courts, why individual disabled people would be praised for spunk and courage, why those who pressed for rights would be called whiners and malcontents, and why no one would say a single word about any of it.

In early 2002, the Board of Elections in Louisville finally decided to buy some voting machines that blind people like Sandra Williams could use independently. They would not be at neighborhood polling sites, though. They would be installed at a special site, for the blind.

T H E   E N D

N O T E S

INTRODUCTION

Bush, on the campaign trail (xi): Renee Loth, "New messages unfurled for Georgia voters," *Boston Globe* (Mar. 2, 1992), A6. *See also* Christopher Georges, "Is the President a plagiarist? Campaign klepto-mania," *Washington Monthly* (Apr. 1992), 9.

Christopher Reeve "temporary setback" (p. xii): Interview: Sam Maddox, "Christopher Reeve: Making Sense Out of Chaos," *New Mobility* (Aug. 1996).

Ella Williams quotes (p. xiv): Gaylord Shaw, "A Definition of 'Disabilities': Supreme Court to hear case that could affect millions," *Newsday* (Nov. 6, 2001).

O'Connor quotes (p. xv): Oral arguments; referenced in David G. Savage, "Justices Debate Applying Disability Law to Job Injury," *Los Angeles Times* (Nov. 8, 2001).

CHAPTER 1

Wall Street Journal (p. 1): Jim Vandehei, "Clint Eastwood Saddles Up For Disability-Act Showdown," *Wall Street Journal* (May 9, 2000).

Newsweek (p. 2): "Perspectives" (May 29, 2000).

"Did you really keep" (p. 2): "Crossfire," *CNN* (May 18, 2000).

Stossel (p. 4): John Stossel, "The Blame Game: Are We a Country of Victims?" *ABC News Special* (Oct. 26, 1994).

Cato Institute calling for amendments (p. 4): Robert P. O'Quinn, "The Americans With Disabilities Act: Time For Amendments," *Cato Institute, Policy Analysis No. 158* (Aug. 9, 1991).

Handicapping Freedom (p. 4): Edward L. Hudgins, "Handicapping Freedom: The Americans with Disabilities Act," *Regulation* (Vol. 18, No. 2).

Quarter-million people (p. 7): *An Introduction to Spinal Cord Injury*, Paralyzed Veterans of America, online at http://www.pva.org/NEWPVASITE/publications/pubs/IntroSCI.htm

Nearly half a million letters (p. 7): Dana Reeve, *Care Packages: Letters To Christopher Reeve from Strangers and Other Friends* (New York: Random House, 1999).

ADA mandates (p. 8): "Unintended results: ADA mandates costly to public, private sectors," *San Diego Union-Tribune* (June 5, 1995).

Art Blaser (p. 9): "What's next for Christopher Reeve?" *Orange County Register* (June 11, 1995).

Buoniconti (p. 10): Nancy McVicar, "Projecting hope: Inspired by a young man's tragedy, the Miami Project To Cure Paralysis finds early success on way to healing spinal injuries," *Sun-Sentinel* (June 11, 1995).

CHAPTER 2

Steve Holmes (p. 12): Conversation with author.

"Blind bus driver" (p. 14): Robert L. Burgdorf, Jr., interview with author.

"Qualified" (p. 14): Text of Title I of the Americans with Disabilities Act of 1990 (Pub. L. 101-336) can be found at www.eeoc.gov/laws/ada.html

CR Act of 1964 (p. 14): "absolutely prohibits employers from using cost (or any other rationale) to justify disparate treatment of employees on the basis of race," says Yale Law School's Ian Ayres.

Predatory lawsuits (p. 15): "Handicapping Freedom."

Orange County Register (p. 15): "Hampering the disabled" (Sept. 15, 1989).

Thornburgh had told bill's backers (p. 17): Ruth Colker, "ADA Title III: A Fragile Compromise," *Americans with Disabilities: Exploring Implications of the Law for Individuals and Institutions,* ed. Leslie Pickering Francis & Anita Silvers (New York: Routledge, 2000), 296.

Groups ranging from (p. 19): "Nursing homes, others want exemptions from ADA Access," *The Disability Rag* (July/Aug. 1991), 8.

Attorney Jeff Fort (p. 20): *Toledo Blade* (Apr. 12, 1992).

Bike Shop Man (p. 21): John Hockenberry, interview with author.

CHAPTER 3

JCDecaux/Kaplan Fund (p. 24): Mary Johnson, "The Toilets of New York City," *The Disability Rag* (Jul./Aug. 1991), 13.

That was too bad (p. 25): Editorial, "Public Restrooms, Within Reach," *New York Times* (May 28, 1991), A20.

Most likely to doom (p. 25): Celia W. Dugger, "In New York, Few Public Toilets and Many Rules," *New York Times* (May 21, 1991), A1.

"Rights cede control" (p. 26): Philip K. Howard, *The Death of Common Sense: How Law is Suffocating America* (New York: Random House, 1994), 118.

"When someone had the nerve" (p. 26): Philip K. Howard, 114.

"Going to incredible expense" (p. 27): Editorial, *New York Times* (Nov. 18, 1979).

"The first object" (p. 27): Editorial, "Moving the disabled," *New York Times* (Jan. 3, 1984).

Many found it absurd (p. 30): Leslie Francis and Anita Silvers, "Achieving the Right to Live in the World: Americans with Disabilities and the Civil Rights Tradition," in *Americans with Disabilities: Exploring Implications of the Law for Individuals and Institutions*, xv.

"Just the other day" (p. 31): Mary Johnson, "The Toilets of New York City," *The Disability Rag* (Jul./Aug. 1991), 13.

Time magazine's Richard Lacayo (P. 32): Richard Lacayo, "Anecdotes not antidotes: Philip K. Howard is everyone's favorite anti-regulatory guru, but his best-selling book is flawed," *Time* (Apr. 10, 1995) online at www.time.com/time/magazine/archive/1995/950410/950410.ideas.html

What we question (p. 34): Mary Johnson, "There's always a 'but,'" *The Disability Rag* (Mar./Apr. 1992), 11.

Andy Rooney (p. 34): "A dear old office has been forsaken," *Chicago Tribune* (July 2, 1985), C13.

Madison Square Garden (p. 34): *Ibid.*

"You can accomplish 90 percent" (p. 35): *Ibid.*

"Upward of $100,000" (p. 35): Philip K. Howard, 4.

Joliet, Ill. schools (p. 36): Ken O'Brien., "Joliet schools rehab costs put at $73.9 million," *Chicago Tribune Southwest Ed.* (Feb. 9, 2001), 1.

The Warwick, R. I. public school district (p. 36): William Celis 3d, "To Overcome Disabilities," *New York Times* (Jul. 28, 1993), A15.

Patched-up building (p. 38): author's interview with architect Ron Mace (Feb. 10, 1994).

Los Angeles access problems (p. 38): Charles Lindner, "The disableds' worst enemy — their protector," *Los Angeles Times* (May 8, 1994), M2.

Disability policy (p. 39): Ken Herman, "Shaky start for bipartisanship; Cooperation easier on some issues," *Atlanta Journal-Constitution* (Feb, 2, 2001).

Thornburgh predicted (p. 39): Ruth Colker, "ADA Title III: A Fragile Compromise."

Melrose Diner (p. 39): Laura M. Litvan, "The Disabilities Law: Avoid The Pitfalls," *Nation's Business* (U. S. Chamber of Commerce, Jan. 1994), 25.

Five percent concerned access (p. 39): Ruth Colker, "ADA Title III: A Fragile Compromise."

Sunnyvale Town Center (p. 39): Ruth Colker.

International House of Pancakes (p. 40): "A look into a typical access lawsuit," *The Disability Rag* (Nov./Dec. 1992), 19.

Denny's Restaurant (p. 41): Ruth Colker, "ADA Title III: A Fragile Compromise."

CHAPTER 4

Hypersensitivity to tobacco (p. 49): John Leo, "Let's lower the bar," *U.S. News & World Report* (Oct. 5, 1998), 19.

"King Sized Homer" (p. 49): *The Simpsons*, Fox television (Orig. air date: Nov. 5, 1995).

King of the Hill (p. 49): "Junkie Business," Episode KH219, Fox television (Orig. air date: Apr. 26, 1998).

Report to Civil Rights Commission (p. 52): *Accommodating the Spectrum of Individual Abilities* (U. S. Commission on Civil Rights, Sept. 1983).

A law first enacted (p. 53): *See* Richard K. Scotch, *From Good Will to Civil Rights: Transforming Federal Disability Policy (Second Edition)* (Philadelphia: Temple Univ. Press, 2001).

That definition (p. 54): *The Americans with Disabilities Act* , P. L. 101-336 (Jul. 26, 1990), 104 STAT. 327

A qualified individual with a disability (p. 55): *The Americans with Disabilities Act*, Title I, Employment, Sec. 101: Definitions (42 USC 12111).

That's what Andy Rooney figured (p. 57): Andy Rooney, "The Ins and Outs of Handicapped Parking," *60 Minutes* (CBS News, Nov. 26, 1995).

Jesse Ventura (p. 60): John Williams, "One-on-One with Jesse Ventura," *Business Week Online* (Jan. 24, 2001) www.businessweek.com/bwdaily/dnflash/jan2001 /nf20010124_822.htm

"We never thought of the President as handicapped" (p. 62): Hugh Gregory Gallagher, *FDR's Splendid Deception* (Arllington, Va., Vandamere Press, 1994), 210.

Great Britain's similar law (p. 63): www.hmso.gov.uk/acts/acts1995/ 1995050.htm

"Don't call me disabled," (p. 63): Gary Mihoces, "Amputations don't pin down wrestler," *USA Today* (Mar. 29, 2001), 4C.

An admiring obituary (p. 63): Alan Feuer, "Celestine Tate Harrington, 42, Quadriplegic Street Musician," *New York Times* (Mar. 7, 1998), A11.

Nana Graham (p. 63): Celia Sibley, "Not just survivors: Mother, daughter help 'humanize' the disabled," *Atlanta Journal -Constitution* (Aug. 14, 1996), 1J.

Tennis players (p. 63): Yung Kim, "Taking their seats at center court: For wheelchair tennis players, only difference is extra bounce," *Los Angeles Times* (May 22, 1998), 46.

Fat people (p. 64): Kara Swisher, "Overweight Workers Battle Bias on the Job; Looks Discrimination Called Common, but Hard to Prove," *Washington Post* (Jan 24, 1994), A1.

Bob Thomas (p. 64): Obituaries, *Dallas Morning News* (Feb. 26, 1996), 16A.

Dan Massie (p. 64): Matt Batcheldor, " 'Unsung hero' Daniel Frank Massie battled injustice to the end," *Courier-Journal* (Feb. 5, 2001), B5.

Justice Byron R. White wrote (p. 66): *City of Cleburne, Texas v. Cleburne Living Center, Inc.* No. 84-468 (July 1, 1985).

"Most reasonable people" (p. 67): Jacqueline Rolfs, "When is 'reasonable accommodation' unreasonable? EEOC ignores court rulings in work guidelines to help disabled," *Star-Tribune* (Aug. 8, 1999), 5D.

CHAPTER 5

$200 million...over $40 million (p. 68): Sally Covington, "Right Thinking, Big Grants, and Long-term Strategy," *Covert Action Quarterly No. 63* (Winter, 1997-1998).

"Few would disagree" (p. 69): Edward L. Hudgins, "Handicapping Freedom: The Americans with Disabilities Act," *Regulation* (Vol. 18, No. 2).

"A horrendous, atrocious" (p. 70): Hudgins interviewed by John Hockenberry on "A just cause: Americans with Disabilities Act has helped disabled people get fair treatment, despite rumors of frivolous lawsuits," *Dateline NBC* (Aug. 24, 1998).

"Insisting that disabled individuals" (p. 71): Richard A. Epstein, *Forbidden Grounds: The case against employment discrimination laws* (Cambridge: Harvard Univ. Press, 1992), 487.

"Having a disability is a source of" (pp. 71-72): *Forbidden Grounds*, 480-482.

CHAPTER 6

Burgdorf wrote in a law journal (p. 76): Robert L. Burgdorf, Jr., " 'Substantially limited' protection from disability discrimination: the special treatment model and misconstructions of the definition of disability," *Villanova Law Review* (Vol. 42, 1997), pp. 409-585.

Linda Krieger (p. 76): Interview with author.

Woman with breast cancer (p. 77): *Ellison v. Spectrum Software*.

Woman with multiple sclerosis (p. 78): *Hileman v. City of Dallas*.

Many cases were simply stopped (p. 78): See Ruth Colker, "The Americans with Disabilities Act: A Windfall for Defendants," *Harvard Civil Rights-Civil Liberties Law Review* (Winter. 1999).

It meant, one of them said (p. 79): Hudgins, "Handicapping

Freedom."

"Experts consulted" (p. 79): Trevor Armbrister, "A Good Law Gone Bad," *Readers Digest* (May 1998).

The Supreme Court took up three cases (p. 79): *Sutton v. United Air Lines*, Inc. 119 S. Ct. 2139 (1999); *Murphy v. United Parcel Service*, 119 S. Ct. 2133 (1999); *Albertsons, Inc. v. Kirkingburg*, 119 S. Ct. 2162 (1999).

"Thus, Murphy could be" (p. 81): Leslie Francis and Anita Silvers, "Achieving the Right to Live in the World: Americans with Disabilities and the Civil Rights Tradition," in *Americans with Disabilities: Exploring Implications of the Law for Individuals and Institutions*, xxiv.

Justice Stephen G. Breyer worried (p. 81): *Sutton v. United Air Lines, Inc.*, Breyer, J., dissenting.

"The ADA has a three-pronged definition (p. 82): Robert L. Burgdorf, Jr, "Response to the June 22 rulings by the Supreme Court on the meaning of 'disability' under the Americans with Disabilities Act," Center for An Accessible Society website (http://www.accessiblesociety.org).

CHAPTER 7

"Most of San Diego's (p. 85): "Unintended results: ADA mandates costly to public, private sectors," *San Diego Union-Tribune* (June 5, 1995).

On July 13 (p. 86): Douglas B. Feaver, "Service for Handicapped Poses Problem for Metro," *Washington Post* (Jul. 14, 1978), C1.

APTA said (p. 86): Douglas B. Feaver, "Equipping Transit Lines for Disabled Would Cost Billions, Group Testifies," *Washington Post* (Sep. 20, 1978), A6.

At 5:30 p.m. (p. 88): Mary Johnson and Barrett Shaw (eds.), *To Ride the Public's Buses: The Fight that Built a Movement* (Advocado Press, 2001), 34.

"After years of dirt" (p. 91): Editorial, "Mass Transit Includes the Mass," *New York Times* (June 17, 1983), A26.

EPVA Attorney James Weisman (p. 91): Ari L. Goldman, "Subway projects barred on access for the disabled," *New York Times* (Jan. 5, 1983), A1.

"It is possible to sympathize" (p. 92): Editorial, "Moving the handicapped. Vertically." *New York Times* (Jan. 8, 1983), A22.

An earlier story in the Times (p. 92): Ari L. Goldman, "M.T.A. asks exception from wheelchair law," *New York Times* (June 9, 1983), B3.

Access would end up costing (p. 93): Editorial, "The $2,000 subway token," *New York Times* (June 23, 1984), A22.

"Can society afford" (p. 95): Laurie Wilson, "Hard decisions: Can society afford to spend more on disabled children than it does on others?" *Dallas Morning News* (Mar. 14, 1995), 20A.

Anoka-Hennepin School District (p. 95): Rob Hotakainen and Mary Jane Smetanka, "Average kids are losing: Soaring special education costs squeeze Minnesota school budgets," *Star-Tribune* (Dec. 3, 1994), ME.

A hidden toll (p. 95): Laurie Wilson, "Hard decisions: Can society afford to spend more on disabled children than it does on others?" *Dallas Morning News* (Mar. 14, 1995), 20A.

Commentator John Leo (p. 97): "Mainstreaming's 'Jimmy problem,'" *U.S. News & World Report* (June 27, 1994), 22.

Before the 1975 law (p. 97): *Back to School on Civil Rights* (National Council on Disability, Jan. 25, 2000).

Quotes around 'segregates' (p. 97): Jerry Markon, "Quandary over special ed: New U.S. rules put NY aid in jeopardy," *Newsday* (Nassau-Suffolk edition, June 29, 1998), A5.

At Sam Houston High (p. 98): Jennifer Rankin, "Parents question district's inclusion policy," *Arlington Morning News* (Apr. 28, 1997), 1A.

New York had a larger percentage (p. 98): Michael Slackman, "Special ed on LI, a victim of its own neglect: Politics created the system but now is loath to change it," *Newsday* (Nassau-Suffolk edition, Nov. 19, 1997), A6.

Scripps-Howard News Service (p. 99): Mary Deibel, "Schools must pay for nurses for disabled: Supreme Court's interpretation of 1975 law is certain to burden the nation's school districts" (March 4, 1999).

Ohio schools (p. 99): Jonathan Riskind, "Special education ignored, officials say Ohio schools spend at least $1.6 billion per year on special education that helps about 230,000 handicapped and disabled students," *Columbus Dispatch* (Apr. 11, 1999), 6D.

Per-pupil expenditures (p. 100): Eric Siegel, "City schools must tackle special ed," *Baltimore Sun* (Feb. 9, 1997), 1B.

One child in Boston (p. 100): Beth Daley and Amy Sessler, "Alarm sounds on 766 costs," *Boston Globe* (North Weekly edition, Aug. 25, 1996), 1.

In San Diego (p. 100): Joe Cantlupe, "Special neglect: In San Diego's public schools, special education has not lived up to its name," *San Diego Union-Tribune* (Aug. 24, 1997), A1.

A group of special education students (p. 101): Lisa Fine, "More Students Avoiding Smaller 'Special' Buses," *Education Week* (Feb. 7, 2001).

At the time of the passage (p. 101): "Brief Of Morton Horwitz, Martha Field, Martha Minow And Over 100 Other Historians And Scholars, Amici Curiae In Support Of Respondents," *University of*

Alabama At Birmingham Board Of Trustees, v. Patricia Garrett (99-1240) (http://www.bazelon.org/scholarsbrief.html).

States required parents to waive custody (p. 101): David J. Rothman, *The Discovery of the Asylum: Social Order and Disorder in the New Republic* (Little, Brown & Co., 1971), 221.

Pennsylvania's Western Center (p. 102): Dave Reynolds, "Parents Sue Under ADA To Keep Institution Open," *Inclusion Daily Express* (Oct. 31, 2001).

The Department of Justice was charged (p. 103): *Promises to Keep: A Decade of Federal Enforcement of the Americans with Disabilities Act* (National Council on Disability, June 27, 2000).

The National Association of Homebuilders (p. 106): Josie Byzek, "Living in the Past,: *Ragged Edge magazine* (May/June, 1998).

Providing adequate space (p. 107): Robert P. O'Quinn.

Tricia Crane (p. 107): Maura Dolan, "Disabled pupils get their day in court," *Los Angeles Times* (Oct. 13, 1999), A1.

Mark Belyea (p. 108): Beth Daley and Amy Sessler, "Alarm sounds on 766 costs," *Boston Globe* (North Weekly edition, Aug. 25, 1996), 1.

David Klot (p. 110): "Wheelchair vouchers," Letter to the editor, *New York Times* (Sept. 24, 1983), A22.

When law professor (p. 112): Sherry F. Colb, "Redefining the Status Quo to Include the Disabled: Reflections On The *Martin* Case And ETS' Old Policy Of 'Flagging' Disabled Students' Exam Scores," *Findlaw* website (Feb. 14, 2001), http://writ.news.findlaw.com/colb/

Chapter 8

The week the ADA's access (p. 116): Doug Bandow, "Regulatory reach of disabilities act," *Washington Times* (Feb. 7, 1992).

But the anti-ADA piece (p. 117): Susan E. Greenwald, "Access for the Disabled — at What Price?" *Washington Post* (Mar. 17, 1992), A17.

Roosevelt had struck a kind of implicit bargain (p. 117): Mary Johnson, "The Bargain," *The Disability Rag* (Sept./Oct. 1989), 5.

"School officials hate" (p. 117): William Celis 3d, "Wheelchair Warrior Lays Siege to Schools," *New York Times* (Jul. 28, 1993), A15.

"I just can't tolerate" (p. 118): Mary Johnson, "The Power of One Person," *The Disability Rag* (Jan. 1992), 5.

Kornel Botosan (p. 120): Gordon Dillow, "Complaints of discrimination prove lucrative," *Orange County Register* (Nov. 9, 1997), B1.

Dr. Kenneth Lefebre (p. 121): Edward L. Hooper, "The Psychologist, The Philosopher and the Absurdity of Equality," *The Disability Rag* (July, 1985), 14.

The "whole man" theory (p. 122): Ruth O'Brien, *Crippled Justice: The History of Modern Disability Policy in the Workplace* (Univ. of Chicago Press, 2001), 27-28.

"Experts did not think" (p. 122): Ruth O'Brien, p. 8.

"Those of the handicapped constituency" (p. 122): Eileen Marie Gardner, *The Federal Role in Education* (draft), (Heritage Foundation, 1983).

Providing an accommodation (p. 123): Marianne M. Jennings, "Disabled should play hand dealt, not demand new rules," *Deseret News* (Feb. 19, 2001).

CHAPTER 9

"The greatest tragedy" (p. 127): Martin Luther, Jr., *Stride Toward Freedom: The Montgomery Story* (New York: Harper & Row, 1958).

"People say to me" (p. 128): Sam Maddox, "Christopher Reeve: Making Sense Out of Chaos," *New Mobility* (Aug. 1996).

"When they told me" (p. 128): Roger Rosenblatt, "New Hopes, New Dreams: Christopher Reeve Is Preparing To Walk Again," *Time* (Aug. 26, 1996).

"We were not meant" (p. 128): "The Road I Have Taken: Christopher Reeve and the Cure An Interview-Interaction between Christopher Reeve, Dr. Fred Fay and Chet Cooper," *Ability* magazine (1998).

"An enormous black curtain" (p. 131): John Hockenberry, interview with author.

When a group of pregnant women (p. 132): Nancy Press, "Assessing the Expressive Character of Prenatal Testing: The Choices Made or the Choices Made Available?" in Erik Parens and Adrienne Asch (eds.), *Prenatal Testing and Disability Rights* (Washington, D.C.: Georgetown Univ. Press, 2000), 226.

The idea that disability is normal (p. 133): Norah Vincent, "Enabling disabled scholarship: A budding intellectual movement asks scholars to redefine normal. But who are these postmodern theories really helping?" *Salon.com* (http://www.salon.com/books/it/1999/08/18/disability).

"In its salvo against" (p. 133): Jerry Adler, "Taking Offense," *Newsweek* (Dec. 24, 1990), 48.

"A spoof of itself" (p. 133): Joan Beck, "As PC takes hold, the list of 'isms' grows long and silly," *Chicago Tribune* (June 3, 1991), C15.

"One must grope (p. 135): John Leo, "Our hypersensitive minorities," *U.S. News & World Report* (Apr. 16, 1990), 17.

Andy Rooney had been suspended (p. 136): John Carmody, "CBS News Suspends Rooney; Three-Month Layoff Follows Alleged Racial Slur," *Washington Post* (Feb. 9, 1990), D1.

The organized disabled in Atlanta (p. 138): Mary Johnson, "Progressives and disability rights: They just don't 'get it,'" *Ragged Edge magazine* (Nov./Dec. 1997).

In the Oakland, Calif. offices (p. 138): Margaret House, "Why I work in the peace movement," *The Disability Rag* (Jul./Aug. 1987).

CHAPTER 10

It came from University of Chicago (p. 140): Thomas DeLeire, "The unintended consequences of the Americans with Disabilities Act," *Regulation* (Vol. 23, No. 1), 21-24.

Investor's Business Daily reporter (p. 141): Kevin Butler, "How Successful Is Disabilities Act? Unintended Results Are Showing Up," *Investor's Business Daily* (Aug. 24, 2000), A26.

The two Massachusetts (p. 142): *Ibid.*

The ADA forced employers (p. 142): Steve Chapman, "The Other Side of the Disabled-Rights Law," *Chicago Tribune* (Jul. 30, 2000).

Although the major complaint (p. 143): Bernadette Malone Connolly, "ADA abuse," *Union Leader* (Sept. 29, 2000).

CHAPTER 11

Over a dozen Subcommittee (p. 146): All quotes from the May 18 hearing come from the official transcript of the *2000 ADA Notification Act: Hearing Before The Subcommittee on the Constitution of the Committee on the Judiciary* (U.S. House of Representatives, May 18, 2000, Serial No. 136).

The celebrity was often (p. 146): Jamie Talan, "Can an injured spine be mended? A look at what science has found, and where it's headed," *Newsday* (Apr. 11, 2000), C6.

He'd told David Frost (p. 146): Transcript, *BBC Breakfast with Frost* (Jan. 23, 2000).

Reeve defended the ad (p. 147): Bill Hutchinson, "'Walking' Reeve ad on TV shakes up the disabled," *N.Y. Daily News* (Feb. 2, 2000).

Time magazine commentator (p. 147): Charles Krauthammer, "Restoration, Reality and Christopher Reeve," *Time* (Feb. 14, 2000).

Disability rights advocates had again trooped (p. 156): Transcript, *Oversight Hearing on The Applicability of the Americans with Disabilities Act (ADA) to Private Internet Sites* (U.S. House Committee on the Judiciary, Subcommittee on the Constitution, Feb. 9, 2000).

"In light of costs" (p. 156): Memo to Canady from Subcommittee counsel Paul B. Taylor, "Hearing Proposal Regarding the Application of the Americans With Disabilities Act's Accessibility Requirements to Private Internet Web Sites and Services," (Dec. 16, 1999), online at www.raggededgemagazine.com/drn/taylormemo121699.htm

The Batelaans had been quoted (p. 164): "Embarrassed wheelchair merchants sued for no handicapped parking," *Palm Beach Post* (Aug. 20, 1999), A1.

CHAPTER 12

James Raggio (p. 166): Ted Rohrlich, "Businesses inaccessible to handicapped kept on run by paraplegic," *Los Angeles Times* (May 11, 1998), A3.

To John Parry (p. 166): *Ibid.*

Disabled people were tired (p. 167): Letter to the editor, *Los Angeles Times* (May 17, 1998).

The fact that businesses (p. 168): Mark Fiedler, ""Disabilities law stops discrimination" (letter to the editor), *Washington Times* (Feb. 29, 1992), B2.

"It is difficult to decide" (p. 167): Hiltraud Reeder, Letter to the editor, *Times-Picayune* (July 16, 1995).

If King's kind of thinking (p. 168): Joe Tagert, Letter to the editor, *Times-Picayune* (July 10, 1995).

"I'm sorry I angered" (p. 168): Andy Rooney, "The walking wounded have their say," *Buffalo News* (Dec. 23, 1995), B3.

When John Hockenberry interviewed Hudgins (p. 169): John Hockenberry, *Dateline NBC* (Aug. 24, 1998).

Stories about Mother Teresa (p. 169): Mary Johnson, "Mother Teresa and the elevator," *The Disability Rag* (Jan./Feb. 1991), 29.

Phillip Howard got things wrong (p. 169): Richard Lacayo, "Anecdotes not antidotes: Philip K. Howard is everyone's favorite anti-regulatory guru, but his best-selling book is flawed," *Time* (Apr. 10, 1995).

The New York Times had gotten it wrong (p. 169): Vincent A. Marchiselli, "To let the handicapped get to the subways" (Letter to the editor), *New York Times* (June 27, 1983).

"When the escalator" (p. 171): Revella Levin, "Subway elevators not for the disabled alone" (Letter to the editor), *New York Times* (July 14, 1984), A22.

"Why do we speak" (p. 171): Jennifer Q. Smith, "For all non-walkers" (Letter to the editor), *New York Times* (Jan. 11, 1984), A22.

It wasn't a small number (p. 171): Alan Hevesi, "Accessible subways, accessible costs" (Letter to the editor), *New York Times* (Jan. 28, 1984), A22.

The truth was that access (p. 172): Mary Johnson, "There's always a 'but.'"

CHAPTER 13

People were taught in rehabilitation (p. 176): John Hockenberry, interview with author.

"When we got off the bus" (p. 177): Rus Cooper-Dowda, correspondence with author.

"I'm not free to sit"; "I have to keep a little map" (p 177): Individuals
interviewed on Lou Waters and Jim Hill, "ADA at 10: critics argue
law is vague, misguided," *CNN Today* (July 26, 2000).

Six steps up (p. 177): Theresa Camalo, correspondence with author.

Art Blaser's Bay Club hotel (p. 178): Correspondence with author.

Eli Clare (p. 177): Eli Clare, "Stolen Bodies, Reclaimed Bodies:
Disability and Queerness," *Public Culture* (Fall, 2001).

Todd Fernie (p. 177): Correspondence with author.

Austin Community College's Brenda Lightfoot (p. 177):
Correspondence with author.

Fat people (p. 180): Carey Goldberg, "Citing Intolerance, Obese
People Take Steps to Press Cause," *New York Times* (Nov 5, 2000).

Portland, Ore. gradeschooler Sam Lightner (p. 180): Tom Hallman, Jr.,
"The Boy Behind the Mask" (4-part series), *Oregonian* (Sept 30-Oct
4, 2000).

The Supreme Court of Wisconsin (p. 181): Americans with Disabilities
Act: Record of Senate Hearings (May/June, 1989).

"Well, dear, it's quite expensive (p. 181): Julie Washenberger, correspondence with author.

"Nobody is quite sure" (p. 183): John Leo, "Let's lower the bar," *U.S.
News & World Report* (Oct. 5, 1998), 19.

If fears about the ADA (p. 184): Patricia Illingworth and Wendy E.
Parmet, "Positively Disabled: The Relationship between the Definition
of Disability and Rights under the ADA," in Leslie Pickering Francis
and Anita Silvers (eds.), *Americans with Disabilities: Exploring
Implications of the Law for Individuals and Institutions* (New York:
Routledge, 2000), 13.

With a 4.0 grade average (p. 185): Correspondence with author.

A disabled veteran (p. 185): Correspondence with author.

We fixated on (p. 186): *See* Joseph L. Graves, *The Emperor's New
Clothes: Biological Theories of Race at the Millennium* (Rutgers Univ.
Press, 2001).

It was Christmas Eve (p. 187): Randy Ellis and Nolan Clay, "Care centers bear history of abuse," *Oklahoman* (Dec. 17, 2000).

When aides finally checked (p. 188): Dave Reynolds, "Pro-institution
mom sues over fire ant attack," *Inclusion Daily Express* (June 25,
2001).

Thomas Bayon had lived (p. 188): Roni Rabin, "Greenlawn man's long road home," *Newsday* (Dec. 28, 2000).

A worker tossed cookies (p. 189): Randy Ellis and Nolan Clay, "Care centers bear history of abuse," *Oklahoman* (Dec. 17, 2000).

At the Woodward Resource Center (p. 190): Dave Reynolds, "Man in Iowa institution killed by restraint," *Inclusion Daily Express* (July 11, 2001).

Illinois's Equip for Equality (p. 190): *The State of Restraint Utilization in the New Millennium: Practical Recommendations for Positive Intervention* (Equip for Equality, May, 2001).

A report released by the Democratic staff (p. 190): *Report on Poor Enforcement of Nursing Home Protections in New York* (U. S. House Committee on Government Reform - Minority Office, Feb. 21, 2001) www.house.gov/reform/min/inves_nursing/index.htm

A General Accounting Office report (p. 191): *Nursing Homes: More Can Be Done to Protect Residents from Abuse* (GAO-02-312, Mar. 1, 2002).

Violetta King (p. 191): Robert Pear, "Unreported Abuse Found at Nursing Homes," *New York Times* (Mar. 3, 2002).

In an effort by the nursing home industry (p. 191): Marsha Shuler, "Bill would shield nursing homes," *Baton Rouge Advocate* (May 18, 2001).

The body of Victoria (p. 192): Dave Reynolds, "Resident's body found in her room, six days after her death," *Inclusion Daily Express* (Jan. 7, 2000).

"When I turned 18" (p. 192): Correspondence with *Ragged Edge* magazine.

Registered voters had been turned away (p. 193): "Brief Of Morton Horwitz, Martha Field, Martha Minow And Over 100 Other Historians And Scholars, Amici Curiae In Support Of Respondents" (online at http://www.bazelon.org/scholarsbrief.html).

Another voter with a disability (p. 193): "Equal Access to Voting," *Hearings before the U.S. House of Representatives Task Force on Elections* (1984).

When Fred Shotz (p. 193): Email correspondence with *Ragged Edge* magazine.

Denise Sherer Jacobson (p. 194): Email correspondence with *Ragged Edge* magazine.

"It's illegal but no one cares" (p. 194): Peg Banak, email correspondence with *Ragged Edge* magazine.

Shea Hales, Lolly Lijewski, Ron Lucey (p. 195): Email correspondence with *Ragged Edge* magazine.

Not one of the polling places (p. 196): *Voters with Disabilities: Access to Polling Places and Alternative Voting Methods* (GAO-02-107, Nov. 2001).

Andy Warber, Sandra Williams (p. 196): Email correspondence with *Ragged Edge* magazine.

Disability rights were "trivialized" (p. 196): Interview with Steve Gold, *Mouth* magazine (March/April, 1998).

CHAPTER 14

"If I am talking with a person" (p. 198): David Pfeiffer, email correspondence with author.

Sociologist Irving Zola (p. 198): *Newsletter* (Brandeis University Department of Sociology, 1999).

Society still perceives (p. 200): Marta Russell, "The Political Economy of Disablement," *Dollars and Sense* (September, 2000).

Most of society simply paid no attention (p. 203): Taylor Branch, *Parting the Waters: America in the King Years 1954-62* (New York: Simon & Schuster, 1988), 13.

CHAPTER 15

While the civil rights model (p. 205): Linda Krieger, interview with author.

In fact, the ADA presents (p. 205): Matthew Diller, interview with author.

Law professor with a paralyzed left hand (p. 205): *Redlich v. The Albany Law School of Union University*, 899 F.Supp. 100 (N.D.N.Y. 1995).

An employee with AIDS (p. 205): *McNemar v. Disney Stores, Inc.*, 91 F.3d 610, 619 (3d Cir. 1996), cert. denied, 117 S. Ct. 958 (1997).

"It is an absurd" (p. 205): Chai Feldblum, interview with author.

Disability discrimination "cannot be eliminated" (p. 207): *Accommodating the Spectrum of Individual Abilities* (U. S. Commission on Civil Rights, Sept. 1983).

Developed at the cost (p. 210): John Heilemann, "Reinventing the wheel," *Time* (Dec. 2, 2001).

For decades, a toothbrush (p. 213): Linda Matchan, "Today's Toothbrushes Are All Frills, All Fuss," *Boston Globe* (Jan. 10, 2002).

"Mighty Coca-Cola" (p. 213): Seth Stevenson, "I'd Like to Buy the World a Shelf-Stable Children's Lactic Drink," *New York Times Magazine* (Mar.10, 2002).

At the start of 2002 (p. 215): Press release from MobileAria.

A few weeks later, Cybernet (p. 215): www.cybernet.com/index2.html

"It wasn't long after sidewalks" (p. 216): Steve Jacobs, "Section 255 of the Telecommunications Act of 1996: Fueling the Creation of New Electronic Curbcuts," online at www.accessiblesociety.org/topics/technology/ eleccurbcut.htm

Although one would think (p. 219): Richard A. Epstein, *Forbidden Grounds: The case against employment discrimination laws* (Cambridge: Harvard Univ. Press, 1992), 487.

"Ultimately, the enforcement of IDEA's" (p. 219): *Back to School on Civil Rights* (National Council on Disability, Jan. 25, 2000).

There were not two problems (p. 220): Eric Siegel, "City schools must tackle special ed," *Baltimore Sun* (Feb. 9, 1997).

"Every kid has a quirk" (p. 220): Beth Daley and Amy Sessler, "Special Education Out Of Balance?" *Boston Globe North Weekly* (Aug. 25, 1996).

"If there were more opportunities" (p. 220): John Hildebrand, "Special Ed on Long Island: Troubled Search for Solutions," *Newsday* (Nov. 20, 1997).

If money earmarked (p. 220): Jordana Hart, "Mass. tells how it wants to fix failings in special-ed program," *Boston Globe* (June 29, 1995).

"For a long time" (p. 221): Kate Zernike, "Special Education Debate Shifts From Money to New Ideas," *New York Times* (May 13, 2001).

Sherman Oaks lawyer (p. 221): Maura Dolan, "Disabled Pupils Get Their Day in Court," *Los Angeles Times* (Oct. 13, 1999).

The preschool at Zeh Elementary (p. 221): Peter Schworm, "First lessons in integration: Preschool combines special-needs, other pupils in classroom," *Boston Globe* (Dec. 23, 2001).

CHAPTER 16

Critics accuse (p. 223): *Helping Employers Comply with the ADA: An Assessment of How the United States Equal Employment Opportunity Commission Is Enforcing Title I of the Americans with Disabilities Act* (U. S. Commission on Civil Rights, Sept. 1998).

It is true that accommodation (p. 234): Cal Montgomery, email correspondence with author.

These "special buses" (p. 237): Editorial, "The $2,000 subway token," *New York Times* (June 23, 1984), A22.

In 2001, Philadelphia's (p. 237): Jere Downs, "SEPTA to disabled riders: Prove it," *Philadelphia Inquirer* (Apr. 20, 2001).

The *Willamette Week* (p. 227): Nigel Jaquiss, "The Crushing Cost of Special Education," *Willamette Week* (Mar. 13, 2002).

Diapers in nursing homes (p. 233): James A. Kopf, "Testimony on Medicare Fraud," *Senate Governmental Affairs Permanent*

Subcommittee on Investigations (Federal Document Clearing House, Dec. 9, 1998).

A General Accounting Office study (p. 233): *Medicare - tighter rules needed to curtail overcharges for therapy in nursing homes* (GAO Report Apr.20, 1995).

"Typically, facilities charge" (p. 233): "Who pays for nursing homes?" *Consumer Reports* (Sept., 1995).

CHAPTER 17

"If you're right (p. 242): Maria Alicia Gaura and Alan Gathright, "Eastwood Wins Suit, But Jury Says Resort Needs Improvements," *San Francisco Chronicle* (Sept. 30, 2000).

More than 100 legal scholars (p. 243): "Brief Of Morton Horwitz, Martha Field, Martha Minow And Over 100 Other Historians And Scholars, Amici Curiae In Support Of Respondents" (www.bazelon.org/scholarsbrief.html).

Congress had superseded its authority (p. 243): *Board of Trustees of University of Alabama, Et Al., Petitioners V. Patricia Garrett, Et Al.*, No. 99-1240 Supreme Court Of The United States 2000 U.S. Trans Lexis 50 (Washington, D.C., Oct. 11, 2000).

Outside, a small group of (p. 244): David E. Rosenbaum, "Ruling on Disability Rights Is a Blow, Advocates Say," *New York Times* (Feb. 22, 2001), A8.

Sandra Day O'Connor was herself (p. 245): Jeffrey Rosen, "The O'Connor Court: America's Most Powerful Jurist," *New York Times Magazine* (June 3, 2001).

"When the ADA was debated (p. 246): John Leo, "Drop your water pistol! When perfectly reasonable principles are carried too far," *U. S. News & World Report* (Feb. 26, 2001).

U.S. District Judge Catherine (p. 247): Susan Levine, "Challenge to Confinement by Md. Rejected," *Washington Post* (Sept. 8, 2001), B5.

The New York Times thought the decision (p. 248): Editorial, "A Smart Cart for the PGA," *New York Times* (Jan. 18, 1998).

Charles Krauthammer (p. 248): "The Campaign to Undo FDR," *Washington Post* (June 15, 2001), A33.

"We sought a quotation (p. 249): Rosemarie Garland-Thomson, "The FDR Memorial: Who Speaks From the Wheelchair?" *Chronicle of Higher Education*, (Jan. 26, 2001), B11.

Just a few weeks before (p. 249): Martha Teichner, "King of Comedy: Comedian Jerry Lewis," *CBS Sunday Morning* (May 20, 2001).

My grandfather's generation (p. 250): Harriet Johnson, posting to email listserv.

An article in the Naples, Fla. *News* (p. 251): John Henderson,

"Litigious law firm branches into Naples," *Naples News* (Mar. 19, 2001).

A few months later (p. 251): Bob Van Voris, "South Florida's ADA industry," *National Law Journal* (July 16, 2001), A1.

In the Fort Lauderdale (p. 251): Shannon O'Boye, Sally Kestin and Bob LaMendola, "Lawsuits push enforcement of ADA, but some call them legal rip-offs," *Sun-Sentinel* (Aug. 26, 2001). *See also* Shannon O'Boye, Sally Kestin and Bob LaMendola, "Hotelier Clint Eastwood gets in on the act," *Sun-Sentinel* (Aug. 26, 2001); "Clint Eastwood Goes to Washington" Guests: Mark Foley, Clint Eastwood," *The O'Reilly Factor* (Fox News Network, Sept. 6, 2001).

California was at least a decade (p. 251): Emily Bazar, "Calif. agencies not fully ADA compliant," *Sacramento Bee* (June 18, 2001).

Fresno, Calif. wheelchair user (p. 251): "Fresno activist killed in street; city has failed to install curb cuts," *Ragged Edge* online (Apr. 28, 2001),
www.raggededgemagazine.com/extra/curbcutdeath042701.htm

In June, 2002, the Ninth Circuit (p. 251): "Sidewalks Must Be Accessible, Says 9th Circuit," *Ragged Edge* online (June 15, 2002), www.raggededgemagazine.com/drn/06_02.shtml#414.

In New York City (p. 252): Dave Reynolds, "Vets Win NYC Curb Cuts," *Inclusion Daily Express* (Sept. 13, 2002).

San Francisco State University (p. 252): Rebecca Trounson, "San Francisco State Settles Disability Suit," *Los Angeles Times* (June 14, 2001).

A federal judge had ruled (p. 252): Jere Downs, "SEPTA to disabled riders: Prove it," *Philadelphia Inquirer* (Apr. 20, 2001).

Only 41 of Chicago's (p. 252): Gary Washburn, "City sting finds cabs shun the disabled; Service pledges tied to fare hike," *Chicago Tribune* (May 14, 2001).

Discrimination against disabled air travelers (p. 252): David Armstrong, "Discrimination by Airlines Remains A Problem for Disabled Travelers," *Wall Street Journal* (May 9, 2001), A1.

"Disability policy, I've never known" (p. 253): Ken Herman, "Shaky start for bipartisanship: Cooperation easier on some issues," *Atlanta Journal-Constitution* (Feb. 2, 2001).

Costs for access (p. 253): Keith Perine, "Sites for the Blind," *Industry Standard* (June 14, 2001).

The American Council on Education (p. 253): Andrea L. Foster, "Making Web Sites Work for People With Disabilities," *Chronicle of Higher Education* (Feb. 2, 2001).

The funding Jeffords was trying (p. 254): Charles Ornstein, "Special-education funding obstacles frustrated senator: GOP has thwarted his efforts to increase budget for programs," *Dallas Morning News* (May 25, 2001).

Despite its good intentions (p. 254): Chester E. Finn, Jr., Andrew J. Rotherham & Charles R. Hokanson, Jr. (eds.), *Rethinking Special Education For A New Century* (Progressive Policy Institute & The Thomas B. Fordham Foundation, May, 2001).

Conservatives called (p. 254): Clint Bolick, "A Bad IDEA Is Disabling Public Schools," *Education Week* (Sept. 5, 2001).

CHAPTER 18

"Even eight years along" (p. 255): Michael Kinsley, "In Defense Of Denial," *Time* (Dec. 17, 2001), 72.

Yet he muted his criticism (p. 256): Charles Krauthammer, "Restoration, Reality and Christopher Reeve," *Time* (Feb. 14, 2000).

The previous summer he had written (p. 257): Charles Krauthammer, "Neither Ennobling nor Degrading," *Washington Post* (July 9, 1999).

"When Missouri Gov. Mel (p. 257): Reporter Jennifer LaFleur of the *St. Louis Post-Dispatch*, conversation with author.

Print journalists "are much more" (p. 258): Beth A. Haller, Ph.D., *News Coverage of Disability Issues: Final Report for The Center for an Accessible Society* (July, 1999), (http://www.accessiblesociety.org/topics/coverage/0799haller.htm).

They associate disability with tragedy (p. 258): Beth A. Haller, "Reporters need to explore why it is so difficult for society to see the human being underneath a disfigurement or disability," *Baltimore Sun* (Apr. 29, 2001).

"When I have my students learn" (p. 259): Beth A. Haller, conversation with author.

A definition of "diversity" (p. 259): *Diversity Tips and Tools, Vol. 1* (Society of Professional Journalists, August, 2002).

Or they had conflicting thoughts (p. 259): Catherine S. Manegold, "A Rape Case Worries Advocates for the Retarded," *New York Times* (Mar. 14, 1993).

Sandra Day O'Connor...had interrupted (p. 260): David G. Savage, "Justices Debate Applying Disability Law to Job Injury," *Los Angeles Times* (Nov. 8, 2001).

Repetitive-motion injuries (p. 260): *Lost-Worktime Injuries and Illnesses: Characteristics and Resulting Time Away From Work* (2000, U. S. Dept. of Labor Bureau of Labor Statistics, Apr. 2002).

Still, many who were disturbed (p. 260): Editorial, "Rights of disabled," *Philadelphia Inquirer* (Jan. 11, 2002).

People with "true disabilities" (p. 261): Editorial, "Disability unanimity," *Courier-Journal* (Jan. 10, 2002).

The federal enforcement agency (p. 261): *Promises to Keep: A Decade of Federal Enforcement of the Americans with Disabilities Act* (National Council on Disability, June 27, 2000).

Aggrieved employees (p. 261): David Williamson, "Funding for Americans with Disabilities Act enforcement inadequate to do job, study shows," *UNC News Service* (Dec. 14, 2001).

Orange County Register (p. 261): Editorial, "Limiting disability," *Orange County Register* (Jan, 11, 2002).

Rep. Steny Hoyer (p. 261): Steny H. Hoyer, "Not Exactly What We Intended, Justice O'Connor," *Washington Post* (Jan. 20, 2001), B1.

Rewriting the statute (p. 262): Roger Clegg, "Disability at Work: Who Is Covered by the Law?" (Letter to the editor), *Washington Post* (Jan. 30, 2002), A22.

Two more ADA employment cases (p. 262): *US Airways, Inc. v. Barnett* (00-1250); *Chevron USA Inc. v.. Echazabal* (00-1406).

People before Rosa Parks (p. 263): Taylor Branch, *Parting the Waters: America in the King Years 1954-62* (New York: Simon & Schuster, 1988), 130.

Unlike the disability movement (p. 263): "Millions Impacted by Paralysis to Gain Vital New Resource," *U.S. Newswire* (Oct. 5, 2001).

In his piece for *Slate* (p. 264): http://slate.msn.com/?id=2067457

"Some people are able to accept" (p. 264): Transcript, *Hearing on Cloning* (Senate Committee on Education, Labor and Pensions, Subcommittee on Health, Mar. 5, 2002).

For the nation's workers (p. 265): Ruth O'Brien, "The Supreme Court's Catch-22," *Ragged Edge* online (www.raggededgemagazine.com/extra/obrienwilliams012802.htm)

Neal Gabler writes (p. 265): Neal Gabler, "Class Dismissed: Whatever happened to the politics of pitting the haves against the have-nots?" *Los Angeles Times* (Jan. 27, 2002).

In early 2002 (p. 266): Sheldon Shafer, "New system allows the visually impaired to vote," *Courier-Journal* (Jan. 18, 2002), B1.

I N D E X

Medicaid 76, 102, 104, 105, 130, 190, 191

'medical model' of disability 27, 29, 44, 61, 71, 118, 133, 174, 212, 231, 237, 238

Metropolitan Transit Authority (NYC), MTA 90, 91, 92, 170

Miami Project to Cure Paralysis 10

Mikulski, Sen. Barbara 106

Minneapolis Star 67, 95

Minow, Martha 101

Miss Iowa 123

Mission Ranch 1, 22, 116, 149, 150, 153, 242

Montgomery Bus Boycott 239, 263

Montgomery, Cal 223, 224-226, 238

Mother Jones 127

Mother Teresa 35, 169, 172, 226

Mr. Magoo 123, 135

Murphy, Vaughn 80, 81

N

N.A.A.C.P. 23, 137, 263

Nary, Dot 19

National Association of Homebuilders 106, 156, 211

National Association of Protection & Advocacy Systems, NAPAS 5

National Council on Disability 83, 220, 261

National Federation of Independent Business 5, 20

National Federation of the Blind 134, 156, 158

National Journal, The 2, 5, 73

National Law Journal 251

National Organization on Disability 196, 248

National Restaurant Association 5, 251

National Review, The 148

Nebraska Law Review 103

New Freedom Initiative 253

New Hampshire Weekly 221

New Orleans Times-Picayune 45, 168

New York State Bar exam 112-114

New York Times, The 12, 13, 15, 25, 26, 27, 31, 33, 35, 36, 44, 50, 63, 90, 91, 92, 111, 118, 127, 128, 134, 135, 137, 165, 169, 170, 191, 196, 248, 259

New Yorker, The 256

Newman, Paul 10

Newsday 97, 146, 220

NewsHour with Jim Lehrer 166-168

Newsweek 133, 134, 175, 202

'no one is against the handicapped' 2, 3, 24, 41, 43, 46, 69, 114, 144, 187, 237, 256

Novak, Robert 2

National Public Radio, NPR 131

nursing homes 19, 36, 102, 187, 202
  'Nursing Home Compare' website 190
  abuse in 188, 191
  costs 36, 191, 233
  inspections 190
  want ADA exemption 19, 20

Nuzzi, Ellen 90-91

O

O'Brien, Ruth 122, 256, 265

O'Connor, Justice Sandra Day 65, 82, 184, 245, 260-262

S

Waters, Rep. Maxine 146, 155,
    162, 165
Watt, Rep. Mel 146, 147, 149,
    151, 154
web access *See also* Internet access
    156-162
Webster's College Dictionary 135
Weicker, Sen. Lowell 13, 14
Weisman, James 91-93
Weitbrecht, Robert 217
Western Center 102
'wheelchair-bound' 29, 30, 57, 92,
    110, 143, 183, 259, 260
Wild, Wild West 257
Willamette Week 227-228, 230
Williams, Ella xiv, xv, 47, 234,
    260, 262, 265
Williams, Sandra 196, 197, 266
Willis, Clyde 7
Wilma's Patio Restaurant 120
Wilson, Elaine 104, 246
Wilson, Laurie 95, 96
Wolinsky, Sid 166, 242
Woodward Resource Center, 190,
    191
Wunder, Gary 158-162

Y

Yale Law Review 103
Young, Marcus 178, 253

Z

Zames, Frieda 31, 172, 211
Zeh Elementary School 221-222
Zola, Irving 198
zumBrunnen, Diane 29, 153, 242